THE GREATEST SINCE MY TIME

by the same author
Wickets, catches, and the odd run
A history of cricket
Sir Gary
The greatest of my time
Championship cricket
Playing to win
Trevor Bailey's cricket book
Improve your cricket
Cricket
Cricketers in the making

with Fred Trueman
The spinner's web
Larwood to Lillee

Trevor Bailey

THE GREATEST SINCE MY TIME

The best cricketers of the last twenty years and the major changes in the game

Hodder & Stoughton

LONDON SYDNEY AUCKLAND TORONTO

British Library Cataloguing in Publication Data

Bailey, Trevor, *1923–*
The greatest since my time: the best
cricketers of the last twenty years and the
major changes in the game
1. Cricketers 1968–1988
I. Title
796.35′8′0922

ISBN 0-340-49091-8

First published in Great Britain 1989

Published by Hodder and Stoughton,
a division of Hodder and Stoughton Limited,
Mill Road, Dunton Green, Sevenoaks, Kent TN13 2YE.
Editorial Office: 47 Bedford Square, London WC1B 3DP.

Photoset by Rowland Phototypesetting Limited,
Bury St Edmunds, Suffolk.

Printed in Great Britain by St Edmundsbury Press Limited,
Bury St Edmunds, Suffolk.

CONTENTS

Illustrations

The photographs, all by Patrick Eagar, appear between pages 96 and 97

TO GRETA

for a very long partnership,

in gratitude

1

INTRODUCTION

1

INTRODUCTION

It was twenty years ago in 1968, though it does not seem that long, that I wrote *The Greatest of my time*. That book, which coincided with my retirement from playing first-class cricket, portrayed the cricketers of the 1940s, 1950s and 1960s whom I considered, from batting and bowling with and against them, to be the finest in the world.

The obvious title for this sequel, therefore, seemed to be 'Twenty Years After', echoing Alexandre Dumas' follow-up story of 'The Three Musketeers', my childhood romantic heroes. But Dumas seems to be little read now (even though he has often been filmed), and *Twenty Years After* is half-forgotten. So I acceded to my publisher's suggestion that the title of my earlier book should be reflected in the title of the new one, *The Greatest since my time*.

During the summer of 1988 I had noticed that there were only a few county cricketers left with whom I had played: Derek Underwood and Geoff Boycott had just retired while Keith Fletcher, Jack Simmons and Norman Gifford were all nearing the end of their long careers. The time seemed apt, therefore, to attempt a sequel to include those players whom I regard as the greatest of the 1970s and 1980s. Some of them I have played against, but all of them I have seen, studied and enjoyed on numerous occasions, either as a cricket writer, or as a member of the BBC's *Test Match Special* team. In addition, this has given me the opportunity of discussing the major changes which have occurred in cricket during the last twenty years.

One difficulty I found was the tendency of every former player, myself very much included, to believe that his era was the finest and his sport was not as good as it once had been. In athletics, for example, it is easy to point out how times are constantly being improved and records broken, though without, perhaps, taking sufficiently into account that a specially trained professional athlete will obviously run faster on an Olympic track designed for speed than an amateur on a cinder track; or the big improvements in the present golf clubs and courses which have assisted the present-day golfer. However my contention has always been that a great athlete would have been outstanding in any period, and would have adapted to new techniques and equipment. In cricket the length of a player's career and statistics makes comparisons between the past and the present even more difficult. There is nothing new about the tendency of cricketers to believe that the game is not nearly so good as it was when they were in their prime, and to distrust, and ridicule, those who claim differently. That will never change. The post-war players were very sceptical about the standard of county cricket played between the wars in the 1920s and 1930s, particularly with regard to the naivety in some of the field placings and the quality of the fielding, but there could be no denying the batsmanship of that period, with Hobbs, Hammond and Bradman plus a younger generation, Hutton, Compton, Edrich and Hardstaff all living examples. Has England ever produced four finer young batsmen of the same vintage, and how many more runs would they have scored if the war had not intervened? In some respects, when first-class cricket was resumed in 1946, I was even more impressed by the batting skills and techniques of several older, and less famous players, in particular Arthur Fagg of Kent, Les Berry of Leicestershire, Harold Gimblett of Somerset, R. E. S. 'Bob' Wyatt who had captained England in 1934 and 1935, and, most of all, Leslie Ames, while all the best wrist-spinners were of pre-war vintage. The missing years had inevitably robbed the quick bowlers of much of their menace. The control and the actions of Nobby (E.W.) Clark, Bill Bowes, Reg Perks, Alf Gover and Bill Copson remained, but the pace had gone.

The most accomplished players of today are just as convinced, as their many predecessors have been, that we are now looking back through rose-coloured spectacles, and that we do not understand the problems they have to face and how the changes have made scoring runs and taking wickets far more difficult. I also suspect, though I could be wrong, that today's stars are more sensitive to criticism and more worried by it, with the result that their rapport with the media is poor. It must, however, be added that this is not all their own fault, as they are exposed to more unpleasant attacks and revelations, though again to some extent this is due to the way they drop their guard and leave themselves wide open in an age when partnering Joan Collins can turn a person into a celebrity. There have been few Tests in the past decade when that prince of scorers, Bill Frindall, has not eagerly announced that another statistical record has been broken. The reason is the large increase in the number of Test matches being played, and usually it does not have much real significance, like the MCC claiming that the receipts for a Lord's Test were a record. This does not mean that the attendance was larger, but merely that the money taken was higher, ignoring that the worth of the money is far less. £1,000,000 today equals about the same as £100,000 in the early 1950s.

It follows that the more Test matches one plays in, the more runs and wickets one has the opportunity to make and to take. The two leading Test wicket-takers for England are Ian Botham and Bob Willis, so it comes as no surprise to learn that they both played in over 90 Tests, considerably more than their nearest challengers, while the same applies to our two leading run-makers, Geoff Boycott and Colin Cowdrey, who both have over 100 caps; yet by no stretch of the imagination could this distinguished quartet be considered as the two greatest bowlers and batsmen the country has produced. Their records will also be passed in time, if the number of Tests played per year continues to increase.

As a Test regular for ten years in the 1950s, I made 61 appearances for England. If I had been playing in the 1920s and 1930s this number would have been reduced to about half, say 30; while before the First World War it would have been under 20 Tests. In contrast, in the 1980s I could have expected to play in excess of 100 Tests, which ought to have about doubled my quota of wickets and runs.

On numerous occasions when England were being beaten by India, Pakistan and the West Indies, people have come up to me and said 'it was very different in your time' because England then had so many high-class batsmen and bowlers. Les Jackson of Derbyshire, for example, would have walked into any England XI over the past decade; but he only made two Test appearances. But it is not that simple, or uncomplicated, if one examines the past. It can, in fact, be very misleading because, automatically it seems, one remembers the cricketers of the past when they were at their peak!

I bowled against the following great English batsmen: Hammond, Ames, Hardstaff, Washbrook, Bill Edrich, Compton, Graveney, May, Cowdrey, John Edrich, Dexter and Boycott. I also batted against, and in some respects this is an even more impressive list, because it is the bowlers who are usually the key to international success: Bowes, Perks, Wright, Hollies, Bedser, Laker, Lock, Wardle, Jackson, Titmus, Trueman, Statham, Appleyard, Illingworth, Tyson, Snow and Underwood. Of course, if those batsmen and bowlers had all been at their peak, then that would indisputably have been a Golden Age of English cricket, but, of course, they were not; some were starting their careers, some were finishing. Illustrating this point, and showing England's batting was not all that strong, must be the number of times that I, although lacking the ability, was called upon to open the innings. Peter Richardson of Worcestershire and Kent, who played in 34 Tests, has won numerous drinks by challenging people to name who had been his most frequent opening partner for England. Not surprisingly, very few came up with my name, because I was no more than a willing, sacrificial lamb, a poor man's Chris Tavaré, and that is unfair on Tavaré, for whom I have considerably more regard than, apparently, the English selectors or the Kent Committee.

For five years (1953 to 1957) my international career coincided with England being able to claim to be the unofficial champions of the world. This was because we possessed the balance required to be effective on *all types of pitches and in all types of conditions*. We usually included five batsmen like Hutton, Edrich, Compton, May and Graveney, who were capable of scoring centuries against high-class opposition, and did; four bowlers – Trueman, Statham, Laker, Lock – who were able to produce a match-winning performance with the ball, and did; and in Godfrey Evans a superb wicket-keeper to all types of bowling while I filled in as the all-rounder. In contrast, the great West Indian teams of the past decade have struggled on a crumbling pitch, which is why in all conditions I would rate Sir Frank Worrell's team of the early 1960s superior. Many of the most accomplished of today's batsmen would have problems on a 'sticky wicket', because they never have encountered one just as, in the same way, the present England side would be far more effective in limited-overs cricket than an England side of the mid-1950s who never played such matches.

When Test cricket was resumed after the 1939–45 war, there were four major sides – England, Australia, South Africa and, though it was not realised until 1947–48, the West Indies – and two minnows, New Zealand and India. A visit from India was regarded as a minor tour. Abroad, New Zealand used to be granted a couple of Tests after the serious business of the fight for the Ashes had been decided; while we sent what was ostensibly our Second XI to India. It is entirely different today. New Zealand, India, and Pakistan (who played their first Tests in 1954) have won their last series against England, South Africa is no longer allowed to play Test cricket for political reasons, and the West Indies is currently the best side in the world, with Pakistan probably the number two. England and Australia, who for a hundred years had ruled almost supreme, have been struggling to hold their own with the newcomers, and have fielded several sides sadly short of batsmen and bowlers of international calibre. The outcome is that, apart from the West Indies at the top and Sri Lanka at the bottom (partly from limited opportunities), there is not much to choose between the relative abilities of the other teams, and a series between any of the five countries could go either way. Whether this indicates a levelling-up or a levelling-down is a matter of opinion, though I am inclined towards the latter, as too many sides depend for their success on one truly outstanding player, and are short of high-quality back-up. New Zealand without Richard Hadlee have been unimpressive; Imran Khan has been *the* dominant figure for Pakistan; England has been unable to fill the gaping void left by Botham; and one dreads to contemplate the Australian batting over the last five years without Allan Border.

It is often asked why there are so many official tours, and the players frequently complain, with justification, that they are playing too many Tests. The reason is essentially financial. The various Boards of Control want more money, and so do the players. The Boards of Control are also worried, having experienced the threat of World Series Cricket, that if they do not provide an abundance of overseas tours, their players will go on unofficial ones. For, though our finest cricketers may complain of having to play too much, they are keen to make additional trips, providing the rewards are attractive enough, like those highly remunerative visits to Sharjar. Also, if there was no England tour, how many of the players would fancy a friendly and financially rewarding visit to South Africa, which could probably lead to a fascinating restraint of trade case in the High Court, despite the threatened ban?

If the price is right, then official tours will continue, with the emphasis on shorter visits with the usual number of Tests, and a steady increase in the number of one-day internationals which are now producing bigger crowds, and, even more vital, have greater appeal for commercial sponsors and television. Cricket is easy to market, and is well marketed. The worry is that the money so produced is not always in the long-term interests of the game.

Like all past players I am frequently accused, often quite fairly, of being too critical. There is always a danger of this and there always will be, because it is far easier to play in the commentary box than out in the middle. We commentators, though, make our share of gaffes. In 1988, when attempting to describe Gus Logie's brave attacking innings at Lord's, I said, 'Logie has chanced his arm, and it has come off!'. However, I have always been intolerant of bad cricket, such as when I see a fast-medium bowler in a Test Match unable to maintain the line and length that should be automatic at that level, or the bowler in a limited-overs game who constantly over-steps the crease and is no-balled. Both these instances are as unprofessional as an actor forgetting his lines. I sometimes wonder, too, in a county match when both teams have known each other's strengths and weaknesses for several seasons, why a lengthy mid-over conference is required. A particular example of bad cricket occurred once when I was playing in the Caribbean. Our young opener had done extremely well to be still there for the last over before lunch, having effectively seen off three very fast international bowlers. He was then bowled by a ball from a slow left-armer which did not deviate and which he attempted to on-drive. If he had holed out off a full toss or a long-hop, that would have been understandable for such deliveries deserve punishment whenever they arrive, but that he should be bowled by a straight ball at that juncture, having done all the hard work, seemed to me to show a lack of crust. It offended my soul.

My soul has also been offended by the following: England's batting against the West Indies in the last three series; the large number of English batsmen and bowlers with obvious potential, who could have made so many more runs, or taken so many more wickets, if only they had been shown how to correct some quite minor faults in their technique or basic action. This does suggest that the standard of coaching among the counties is either very low, or that the players themselves are not prepared to listen, which baffles me. With videos available one should not even have to tell players, and the intelligent ones should be able to see for themselves.

However, the good moments in the last twenty years have far outweighed the bad. These are just a few of my favourite sights: Lillee and Thomson on the rampage together, directed by Ian Chappell, and supported by Rodney Marsh and the Australian close fielders; Vivian Richards' assault on Bob Willis at Old Trafford; Bishan Bedi posing those timeless questions to batsmen; Imran Khan's large, late in-swinger; Graeme Pollock driving off his front foot on the up along the ground; Holding flowing into bowl; Botham's batting bonanzas at Headingley and Old Trafford in 1981; an exquisite on-drive by Greg Chappell; Derek Randall bringing pace, excitement and humour to the covers; batsmen bamboozled by Abdul Qadir's googly; the pure perfection of the batting techniques of Barry Richards and Sunil Gavaskar; a leg-stump yorker from Andy Roberts immediately following his well-directed bouncer which had made its impression on an apprehensive batsman; a fine first day of a Lord's Test; a whole series of nail-biting finishes in limited-overs cricket, including Lamb's final over in which he achieved the near-impossibility of inventing 18 runs against Australia; and last, but by no means least, Graeme Hick's batting for Worcestershire which might almost be said to have brought a new dimension to the county scene.

Amidst all this joy, I retain one pet hate: umpires who surreptitiously glance at their light meters prior to coming off for bad light in front of a capacity crowd on an easy pitch against an attack incapable of injuring anybody unless it is pitch black!

2

BATSMEN

GRAEME POLLOCK

The South African Shark

In 1969 a powerful team from Barbados – it is hard to imagine one which was not – made a short tour of England. The side, containing six international players though not, unfortunately, Gary Sobers, played the International Cavaliers at Scarborough. The Cavaliers won a splendid match by 11 runs in the penultimate over, in which the highlight was unquestionably the batting of Graeme Pollock. In the first innings he enchanted everyone with a glittering 101 which contained nineteen 4s and a 6 off only 67 deliveries in 52 minutes, and he followed it up with 61 further exhilarating runs in the second innings. After his century I went into the Barbados team dressing-room to ask them their opinion of what, in terms of power and stroke production, was one of the best ten innings I have seen. It was summed up by one of their team who simply said that Gary, the uncrowned king of the island, could not have batted better, and there were no dissenters. It would be hard to imagine a greater compliment.

A year later, in 1970, English cricket followers had the opportunity of seeing the two finest left-handers playing together in the same side, when the British government virtually ordered the TCCB to cancel the visit of South Africa, and a Test series was arranged against the Rest of the World, for which full England caps were awarded. Although these five matches were eventually termed unofficial Tests, the quality of the cricket was considerably higher than is witnessed in the majority of Test series. England, well led by Ray Illingworth, lost the series by four matches to one. Sir Gary Sobers captained the Rest of the World, which included five South Africans – Graeme Pollock, Barry Richards, Eddie Barlow,

Mike Procter and Peter Pollock – as at the time South Africa probably possessed the strongest international eleven.

Along with most cricket lovers, I had been hoping to savour a number of Pollock/Sobers partnerships, which would also contrast their very different styles; but, sadly, though happily for the England bowlers, there were few opportunities, as Graeme experienced, what has happened to many great players at different times – a disappointing series. For the Rest of the World the two outstanding performers were Gary Sobers and Eddie Barlow. The former had the added incentive of being captain, and the latter has always had a desire, almost an obsession, to make runs and to take wickets in every game, while the fact that most of the matches were played on pitches which favoured the seamer, rather than the genuine paceman, helped to account for the success enjoyed with the ball by both these splendid all-rounders. However, in the final Test at The Oval we were at last privileged to see the Sobers/Pollock double-act, when they put on 135 delectable runs in the last session of the second day, even though the ball was 'moving about' and mere mortal players would have had to concentrate more on survival than on making runs. Graeme and Gary mixed counter-attack with defence, a policy which produced the required runs and also paid off, as neither lasted long on the Saturday morning, much to the regret of the large crowd who had come more to see them bat than England bowl, both being clean bowled by Peter Lever. I never saw Lever, before or after this occasion, quite so menacing.

During his all-too-brief international career, Graeme Pollock scored 2356 runs, including seven centuries and an average of 60.97 in only 23 Tests spread over five series. These are exceptional figures, but he will always be better remembered for the way these runs were acquired, some of them on difficult pitches.

He had the pedigree one expects from a cricketing genius. At thirteen he was selected for his school first eleven; he scored a century in the Currie Cup at sixteen; was nominated as the Cricketer of the Year at seventeen; and established himself as a Test player in the grand manner at nineteen during the 1963–64 South African series in Australia. On this tour, which was drawn, he hit his maiden Test century at Sydney and in the fourth Test he took part in a record-breaking stand of 341 with Eddie Barlow in under five hours. After Australia he was fit to play in only one Test against New Zealand, which could well account for this series also being drawn, though at this stage in his career 'the South African shark', who had devoured Australian bowlers so voraciously, still had one weakness, which the England spinners exploited when they toured South Africa under Mike Smith in 1964–65. They discovered that his Achilles Heel was against quality off-break bowling at the start of his innings. In fourteen innings, including the five Tests, he was dismissed by Fred Titmus and David Allen for under 32 on eight occasions. It was also strange that he twice, when in the seventies, fell victim to Geoff Boycott, perhaps because he could not resist the challenge of those gentle medium-pace outswingers and believed they should be dispatched all over the park. As with Ted Dexter and Vivian Richards, there was an arrogant streak in Pollock's batting, stemming from his knowledge that, at his best, he was capable of destroying an international attack, so why should he worry about mundane bowling when sailing towards what should have been another century?

Sadly for English cricket lovers, Graeme Pollock was able to make only one tour to this country, and that was only a three-Test series in 1965 when he was twenty-one; but he did more than enough then to show what they have missed since. His most memorable innings was at Trent Bridge in the second Test, which South Africa not only won, but the win also decided the outcome of the series. When Graeme went in to bat on the first morning the score was 16 for 2 and Tom Cartwright was moving the ball disconcertingly. Not surprisingly, Graeme started carefully and at lunch, when the total was 76 for 4, he had 34 runs to his credit. After the interval he simply cut loose, making 91 out of 102 in 75 magic minutes.

Later on, at Canterbury, he sent the older Kent supporters

home talking about Frank Woolley after he had struck an undefeated double-century punctuated by numerous extravagant, effortless fours and sixes.

Several years ago I sat down with Richie Benaud, Colin Cowdrey and Jim Laker to pick the fifty greatest post-war cricketers for a book being published by the Lord's Taverners, cricket's largest charity. The first thirty names were almost automatically chosen in five minutes. It was the next twenty, especially the last five, which occupied all the time. Graeme Pollock, along with Sir Donald Bradman, Sir Len Hutton, Sir Gary Sobers, Sunil Gavaskar and Viv Richards, was among the first twenty-five. Richie Benaud's comment at the bottom of the text was 'A tragedy his genius has been confined to his own country'. My comment was on what I found the most fascinating feature about his batting: 'Drives good-length seam bowling on the up along the ground off his front foot more violently than anybody, so that deep extra-cover becomes a more dangerous position than silly mid-off is when a mere mortal is batting'.

Graeme Pollock's height – 6ft 4 in. – enabled him to play forward comfortably to deliveries which shorter batsmen could not have controlled, but what made bowling against him so unrewarding was that he had the ability to hit a delivery which was just short of a length with a straight bat off his right (front) leg. Against him, the obvious counter of a short extra-cover was not sufficient because of the exceptional power of his driving and because he was also a master of the square drive. He was not only powerfully built, but he was also one of the first of the 'heavy-bat brigade'. This helped him when he failed to time the ball perfectly in the heart of the blade, for it still travelled to the boundary.

Graeme capitalised upon his height and reach, but though he was primarily a front-foot player, this did not mean he could not play off his back foot as any bowler foolish enough to bowl him a long-hop discovered, because he was a quite devastating puller. However, the most impressive example of his power and ability off his back foot probably occurred during the Australian tour to South Africa in 1966–67. In the first Test at Johannesburg he had helped speed his team to a fine victory with a dazzling innings of 90 in just over an hour. A few days later, in the second Test at Newlands, with South Africa 12 for 2, Graeme limped out to bat with a runner because of a pulled thigh muscle, which committed him to playing mainly on his back foot. Although it was a good batting pitch, Australia was in a commanding position having amassed 542 and Graham McKenzie was bowling very well. On the following morning three more wickets fell and at 81 for 5 all seemed irreparably lost until Graeme launched a spectacular counter-attack. His first hundred came off 139 balls with a high percentage of his runs made off his left foot and he went on, 'with a little help from his friends' in the middle order and tail, to make 209 out of 353.

The last time I saw him at the crease was for South Africa in Johannesburg in 1984 during the third unofficial Test against a formidable West Indian XI. How did it compare with official Tests? It was certainly, because of the racial undertones, just as fiercely competitive; in fact, I felt that the umpires permitted far too many bouncers from both sides. The rebel West Indian team was not nearly so powerful as their official side in recent years, but Rowe, Kallicharran, King, Lynch, D. A. Murray and Sylvester Clarke plus three handy seamers in Moseley, Alleyn and Stephenson would have challenged for a place in most Test teams. The standard of play was about the same, therefore, as seen in a high percentage of current official Test matches, and higher than that provided by Australia and Pakistan when World Series Cricket took away their most accomplished players. This also applies to a number of other series: for example, both South Africa and the West Indies would have fancied their chances of beating either England or the Kiwis who played in the 1988 New Zealand tour.

They would certainly have produced more attractive cricket as the South African team included such strokemakers as Peter Kirsten, Kenny McEwan, and Clive Rice, while Graeme

Pollock – although then in his forties – was still a finer batsman than anybody in the England or the New Zealand side, other than Martin Crowe and possibly Mike Gatting. The Wanderers pitch gave the quicker bowlers considerable encouragement. In these conditions, Clarke, Moseley, Alleyn and Stephenson, with King in reserve, formed a useful attack. Graeme, however, made 41 out of a total of 160 in the first innings, and 61 out of 236 in the second. In the process he was able to maintain the languid elegance which has always been a hallmark of his batting, and still show himself at least one class better than anybody else in the match. Also, in the previous encounter at Newlands, he had been even more brilliant, though on a pitch which gave the bowlers less assistance, with a dazzling century.

What superb batsmanship cricket and cricket-lovers have missed since South Africa was banned from the international arena.

GEOFF BOYCOTT

The Prince of Accumulators

Good batsmen can be divided into two broad, overlapping categories, stroke-makers and run-accumulators. Both have an important role to play, because together they provide that essential balance which a cricket team requires. There can never be a hard-and-fast rule, as it must depend upon the talent available, but a well-balanced batting line-up for a Test match would consist of two contrasting openers: one whose primary objective would be to blunt the opposing attack and, ideally, still be there at close of play, while his partner, though he too would like to remain undefeated, would have adopted a more adventurous approach – for example Geoff Boycott and Gordon Greenidge. Because a wicket is always likely to fall early, a strong case can be made for a grafter at no. 3, a value perfectly illustrated by Larry Gomes in the early 1980s for the West Indies, but I would prefer at no. 3 and no. 4 two great stroke-makers, such as Graeme Pollock and Vivian Richards to avoid the likelihood of two grafters batting together and possibly losing the initiative. In all forms of cricket it usually pays to give the finest performers the opportunity to arrive at the crease early in the proceedings. In these circumstances, my no. 5 would be a dependable rock, a batsman in the Ken Barrington mould. The second half of the order ought to contain a similar mix with several dashing stroke-makers, like Ian Botham and Kapil Dev, plus a couple of dependable 'stickers' such as Ravi Shastri and Alan Knott, although both were more than capable of adopting a positive role if required.

Except in limited-overs cricket, where the prime consideration is containment, I personally used to prefer bowling against a stroke-maker rather than a grafter, because the former was more likely to make a mistake. The latter would keep within his limitations, working on the principle that, if he stayed there, the runs would eventually accrue and that these could not be made in the pavilion. Conversely, bowlers are more likely to become unsettled if they are constantly being attacked. This, once again, stresses the importance of balance, whether it be in the batting line-up, or the bowling attack. The flashers and dashers, such as Bob Barber, Graeme Fowler, John Carr, or Simon Hinks, complement the nudgers and stickers and pushers, like Chris Tavaré, Peter Willey or David Steele. Not that a defensive batsman is incapable of scoring runs quickly; Chris Tavaré, at his best, thrives in limited-overs cricket where he has produced many match-winning, fast-scoring innings.

A great, as distinct from a good, batsman should always be able to fill either role. He should possess the ability to take an international attack apart, not by hitting bad balls to the boundary, because a class international attack should not send down such deliveries, but by hitting the good balls to the boundary, and using safe, straight-bat strokes off both front and back foot. In addition, his defence must be well organised, while, because he sees the ball earlier than an ordinary player, he is able to take the appropriate action later. However, if one assesses great batsmen in this fashion, it is difficult to include either David Gower, whom I love to watch but whose footwork, or lack of it, makes it unlikely that he could complete a six-hour hundred on a difficult pitch; or Geoffrey Boycott, whom I did not always enjoy but would want in my side, especially if the pitch was indifferent and the game needed to be saved. If one excludes that Gillette Cup Final in 1965 – when he made 146 with three sixes and fifteen fours against Surrey – Geoff did not dominate opposing attacks by the brilliance of his stroke-play, he simply wore them down.

A particularly good example of this occurred at Headingley in 1967, when Geoff opened the innings with John Edrich against India, whose attack was weakened by the breakdown on the first afternoon of two of their main bowlers, Surti and Bedi. After the early departure of Edrich, Boycott and Barrington ground their way towards the foundation of a big score and, at stumps, Geoff was undefeated for 106 out of a total of 281 for 3. The general feeling (shared by the England captain and Chairman of Selectors) was that, against such a depleted attack, more runs should have come from Geoff in the final session. On the following day, he took his score to 246 not out before the declaration at 550 for 4, and England went on to win by six wickets. The outcome of Geoff's first-day crawl, however, was that he was left out of the next Test. I have always felt that he was unlucky to be disciplined in this fashion, and I am sure he will never lose the improbable record of being dropped after making a not-out double-century in a Test which was eventually won by a considerable margin.

There was an automaton quality about Geoffrey Boycott's batting which, although it produced the runs, seemed lacking in soul. It reminded me of a professional dancer whose footwork and timing are perfect, but whose body does not have the excitement of inborn rhythm; or of a figure-skater, faultless in the compulsory figure sequences, but whose free expression lacks flair. He did not possess the grace of his Yorkshire predecessor, Sir Len Hutton, who could make a forward defensive stroke an object of beauty and whose off-drive created a moment to cherish. Although I greatly admired Geoff's technique, especially when runs were difficult to make, and the vast number he harvested with such determination, his batting lacked the easy flowing style of most great players; indeed on occasions against extreme pace his movements became jerky, almost puppet-like. His problem with the ultra-fast lifting ball stemmed from the fact that, having committed himself to a certain course of action, he could not at the last moment simply sway out of harm's way, like Sir Gary Sobers, or Barry Richards, and watch the ball fly past. He lacked the elasticity of movement.

He was not a beautiful player yet, despite his lack of charisma, he became one of the best known, most liked, most disliked, and most talked about cricketers in the world. To understand just how and why this was the case, it is essential to know something about the Yorkshire attitude towards cricket, which is summed up by the title of Don Mosey's book *We don't play cricket for fun*, the advice which Sir Len Hutton is reputed to have given Peter May when he was starting his international career.

For over a hundred years Yorkshire was the most important and powerful cricket county. Although there were occasional accidents, when clubs like Lancashire, Middlesex, Nottinghamshire, Surrey or even Glamorgan, snatched the Championship, Yorkshire would always be near the top, playing hard, efficient cricket. It was unthinkable in those days to select an England team which did not include several Yorkshiremen.

Cricket in Yorkshire became a virtual religion, with God, plainly a Yorkshireman, expecting his batsmen to score runs prolifically by obeying such commandments as 'Never cut until the end of May', his bowlers to take wickets and 'give now't away', and his fielders to hold catches, as 'catches win matches'. It was a plain, practical faith, more Old than New Testament in approach, stern but simple, in which frivolity was a sin, charity began at home and the laughter came after the game had been won with the enemy beaten, preferably routed. God entrusted the running of the club to his archangels, the Yorkshire Committee, who, because of the excellent results, could afford to treat their players in a way which, though perfectly acceptable in Edwardian England, did not take into account the social revolution that occurred during and after the second world war. The outcome was that the county lost some great cricketers, including Johnny Wardle, Willie Watson, Ray Illingworth and Brian Close, but a vast reservoir of home-grown talent was still there to fill the gaps, and maintain standards.

In 1968 Yorkshire, captained by Brian Close, won the Championship, the same year that the archangels, under the divine guidance of Brian Sellars, who had autocratically, and with great success, skippered the club in the 1930s and immediately after the war, refused to grant the highly talented Ray Illingworth a three-year contract. Ray left, joined Leicestershire, and became one of the best, probably the most astute, of the post-war England captains. Three years later Brian Close, not a great diplomat but a proven leader with a fine record, was sacked. I first read about this on my way to cover a football international at Wembley, and encountered Brian in the press bar after the match. I naturally expressed my condolences and asked him when he had first known. Although I was well acquainted with some of the 'strange happenings' in Yorkshire, I was still shocked when Brian told me that he had been given the option of resigning or being sacked, that morning, with an hour to make up his mind. As he had just had a Testimonial, he could hardly resign, because in doing so he would have insulted the many who had given their support. He was replaced by Geoff Boycott, who heard the news in Australia where he was touring under Ray Illingworth's captaincy. This was indeed ironic, as Ray would surely have been appointed if the Yorkshire Committee had not refused to give him that three-year contract. Incidentally, Brian Close was in favour of Geoff Boycott being his successor, but not for several years yet.

Boycott's first year as captain was described in the annual report as the worst in the club's history 'from a playing and a financial point of view', but Geoff himself made over 2000 runs with an average of over 100. This marked the commencement of the Boycott controversy and the formation of the Action Group which was to cost the club so much money, cause so much bitterness and do so much harm. Some Yorkshire supporters believed that here was a fine captain, who was also providing most of the runs, who had simply been let down by the rest of the team and the Committee. Others, especially those with a practical experience of first-class cricket, felt that a captain who was less run-conscious and self-centred would have achieved better results. It is impossible to believe for example, that, if Brian Close had been in charge, the club would, despite scoring well over 300 runs in their first innings on nine occasions, have managed only one victory, or that only two counties secured fewer batting bonus points.

Whichever of these two judgements is the more correct, there is no doubt that Boycott, during his eight years at the helm, must accept some of the blame for failing to maximise on the talent at his disposal. He did not succeed in arousing either the full support, or the confidence, of many of the players under his command. (Indeed, if you want to know what went wrong, what Boycott was like as a leader and have a few hours to spare, listening to those who served under him is most revealing.)

It should also not be forgotten that the side he inherited from Brian Close contained accomplished cricketers with international experience apart from himself – John Hampshire, Richard Hutton, Don Wilson, Phil Sharpe, and Doug Padgett – while Chris Old and David Bairstow would gain caps later and Tony Nicholson was chosen for that South African tour which never materialised. It is easy to understand the dissatisfaction of the Action Group, as with that nucleus of players they had a right to expect better performances and results.

The majority of the capped players who were Boycott's contemporaries did not enjoy his regime and quickly left the club while still good cricketers. The break-up of what should have been a reasonable team was in no small way attributable to him. By 1978 even the long-suffering John Hampshire had had enough, and the Yorkshire Committee relieved Boycott of the captaincy. 'It is not what you have done, but for what you are,' were the blunt words of the Chairman, Arthur Connell.

During the Boycott reign, the newcomers, especially the batsmen, never seemed to maintain their early promise, unless, like Bill Athey, they moved to another county. However there was one reason for the decline of Yorkshire during this period, over which Boycott had no control. This was the big improvement by clubs which, in their prime, Yorkshire frequently disposed of in two days, and it was the result of the large influx of overseas cricketers which changed the face of English domestic cricket. Although it raised the overall standard, it unquestionably helped to weaken our international XI by reducing the number of qualified players available, and also assisted our opponents by providing so many of their players with the opportunity to improve their cricket, absorb the problems of English conditions, and make money. The surprising feature is that it took the cricket establishment so long to realise the damage which was patently obvious at the time. Worcestershire fielded a team of which half the members had been capped by other counties, or had learned their cricket overseas. Yorkshire, to their eternal credit, adhered to their principles of only considering cricketers born in the county. It did, though, help to account for their lack of success. Put Rice and Hadlee, Richards and Garner, or Kanhai, Kallicharran, Gibbs and D. L. Murray into a number of Yorkshire elevens and they would certainly have carried off one of the four competitions.

My own first encounter with Geoff Boycott was on a deliciously green pitch at Clacton in 1963, when I had the satisfaction of having him caught behind off his outside edge early on; but I did notice that he played very straight and I had longer to study his admirably correct technique during the Scarborough Festival, where he made a solid 70.

Although Geoff was selected for Yorkshire Second XI at the age of eighteen, he took longer to establish himself in the First XI than it should have done for a player of his ability, possibly because his batting has always looked more impressive in the record books than out in the middle. Maybe his failure to gain instant recognition fired his obsession with runs and records. However, once he had secured a regular place in the team in 1963 he made sure of it being permanent by heading the averages, a position which he was to occupy for seventeen of his twenty seasons (in the other three he missed some matches and had to settle for second place) to underline that he was a master accumulator of runs, though not of batting bonus points. His batting was based on a superb defence and great concentration, and he relied on safe, straight-bat strokes off his back foot played fairly square on either side of the wicket for a goodly portion of his runs, while his patience was infinite. As captain of Yorkshire, his conviction that, if he failed, his side would not score sufficient runs, which indeed did have some justification, only served to increase his caution and determination not to lose his wicket, even on those occasions when a more positive approach would have been wiser policy. It was his inability to recognise these problems, despite his knowledge of the game, which prevented him from becoming an outstanding tactical skipper.

There were several ways in which Geoff was a model to any young aspiring batsmen. First, he looked a cricketer, because his clothes and gear were always immaculate. Second, he was always prepared to practise. He took nets very seriously and spent far more time there than most batsmen, while by sheer hard work, because he was not a natural athlete, he turned himself from an ordinary fielder into a highly competent performer. Third, he was dedicated to his profession. Fourth, he was seldom bowled, because he not only made few mistakes, but he also moved into line so that his pads automatically provided a second line of defence.

A weakness in his batting was his running between the wickets, and over the years he did manage to run out rather more than his fair share of partners. Although his judgement of what constituted a safe run for himself was invariably accurate, this did not always apply to his partner.

I once had a long discussion with an England captain who had had Geoff in his team overseas. He admired his batting, respected his knowledge of the game, and was particularly impressed by his assessment of pitches and how they were likely to play. His one complaint was that to gain his advice it was necessary to go down on both knees. One knee was not enough! Off the field Geoff remained essentially a loner, so that he had little to offer a touring party, which was why, when he returned early from one tour, his colleagues celebrated. There is also something unusual about a player who decides not to play for England, because he does not approve of the chosen captain, and later returns to the international scene with a century. His outlook and temperament were better suited to golf than to a team game like cricket.

The internecine rows which were to disfigure Yorkshire cricket for the final years of Boycott's career were both sad and costly. Although there is no doubt that the large pro-Boycott lobby was entirely genuine and sincere, I sometimes asked myself why their group did not contain first-class cricketers, past or present. Their defence was that all players were jealous of the master who produced runs in the quantities which Yorkshiremen expected from their heroes. This view raises one question: How can one be jealous of a man who has had the good fortune to have spent more than twenty years playing in a beautiful game with great distinction and for which he has been very well rewarded, yet has so few friends among the players? Personally, I have always felt sorry for Geoff because, far from being as self-sufficient as he has so often appeared, he is extremely sensitive. Money may ensure a large funeral, but it does not provide the tears.

CLIVE LLOYD

The Disciplined Calypso

I have always liked and admired Clive Lloyd, not merely for his explosive batting, or for being the longest serving, and most successful, Test captain in recent times, or for (in his younger days) his superbly agile fielding, but, far more important, for himself. Like Jack Nicklaus in golf, Tom Finney in soccer, Rod Laver in tennis, he has demonstrated that it is possible to reach the peak of his sport and yet retain a sense of proportion and behave in a civilised fashion. If I was picking my 'nice guy' cricket team, Clive would be one of my first choices as an outstanding player and also as a good companion with a generosity of spirit and a relaxed sense of humour.

I met Clive Lloyd for the first time in the mid-1960s, and ever since I have been fascinated why, when wearing casual clothes, he looks so unlike a high-powered athlete. His thick spectacles, his stoop, and his gangling walk suggest a character in a situation comedy, as a disaster plumber in the Cosby programme, say, rather than an international cricketer with exceptional agility, pace and lightning reflexes. Although he will be best remembered as a batsman and captain, in his early days, before he had knee trouble, he was so brilliant in the covers that Jim Laker said of him: 'Doesn't waste an inch of his physique, especially in the field. The modern West Indian answer to Learie Constantine'. His pace over the ground and ability to throw accurately on the move made him into one of the five great post-war cover-points.

His speed also meant that he was able to take a quick single which most batsmen would not even have considered. I was batting with him once in a Rothman's Cavaliers match when he called me for a run. Despite my backing up, I failed to make it to the other end in time. Although the years had slowed me, it was the only occasion I have been run out, while my partner had not merely reached home, but had turned and was off on his second run!

Later, after his knee trouble, Clive became an outstanding slip or gulley, where his long reach and large, safe hands took some magnificent catches off his battery of pacemen.

Like another tall and outstandingly gifted left-hander, Graeme Pollock, Clive Lloyd used a heavy bat with which he belaboured the ball with similar ferocity, especially off the right foot. Both would use their long reach to good effect and few, if any, have driven the ball consistently harder or further. Like all the best batsmen, both had been given that extra talent which enabled them to establish themselves at an early age in first-class, and then Test, cricket. Graeme came through younger, largely, I suspect, because his early coaching and the facilities available to him were better than in Guyana. This probably explains too why Graeme had the sounder technique.

Clive first appeared in Guyana in 1963–64 and, despite strong competition from the many Caribbean batsmen at that time, was chosen to tour India in 1966–67, where he proved an immediate success, coming into the team for the injured Seymour Nurse and celebrating with 82 and 78 not out. His partnership with his captain, Gary Sobers, on a pitch which gave the Indian spinners some encouragement won the game for the West Indies and underlined yet again that left-handers usually play leg-break and googly bowlers better than right-handers. Until their stand Chandrasekhar was threatening to win the game for India. From that moment, until his retirement, Clive became an essential part of the West Indian team.

Clive succeeded Rohan Kanhai as captain for the 1974–75 series when he took the West Indies on tour to India, Sri Lanka and Pakistan. Although it was not an outstanding team by West Indian standards, they beat India by three Tests to two in possibly the most exciting series ever staged there, and it would be hard to imagine a much more impressive debut as skipper. In addition to returning with the rubber, Clive was at the height of his powers as a batsman, hitting 636 runs and averaging 79.50. However, it was not merely the number, but the quality of his batting which served as an inspiration to his side, and left a lasting impression among Indian cricket lovers. In late 1987 I kept running into Clive Lloyd throughout the period of the Reliance World Cup, and we did several television programmes together. Everyone still spoke with reverence of his 163 in the first Test at Bangalore, when he reached three figures off only 85 balls. Apart from a brief period following his resignation after the Bridgetown Test against Australia in 1977–78 over World Series Cricket, he remained in command until the end of the 1984–85 tour to Australia. Since becoming captain he has led the West Indies in 74 Tests with the following remarkable record: won 36, drawn 26, lost 12. In addition, there have been numerous one-day internationals – one is tempted to add far too many – while he was in charge in the first two World Cup finals which both ended with him holding the trophy aloft.

Clive arrived as captain of the West Indies at an ideal time. The great West Indian team which, under Sir Frank Worrell, had been the finest in the world, had begun to disintegrate at the end of the 1960s and in the early 1970s, but it was still outstanding and his captain, Gary Sobers, remained the best cricketer in the world. The decline, however, was inevitable because replacements for bowlers of the calibre of Hall and Griffith, and batsmen of the quality of Nurse, Butcher and Hunte, were not easy to find, while Sobers himself was handicapped by injury. The outcome was that Clive experienced one of the most disastrous sequences in the history of Caribbean cricket, twenty Tests without a victory. It taught him how West Indian players reacted under stress and under the heavy criticism from their own supporters, who can be very intolerant – useful knowledge for a future skipper. This disastrous sequence ended at The Oval in 1973, in no small way due to Clive's 132 on the first day, which was made despite conditions which assisted seam bowling. I would rate this as one of the best, most valuable and disciplined innings which I saw him play. The West Indies went on to win the short series without being an exceptional side, but it marked the start of their renaissance.

When Clive was appointed to the captaincy in 1974–75, he was the logical choice. Like the majority of his team, he was of African, as distinct from Indian, extraction, popular with his colleagues as well as being more responsible, and the most accomplished batsman who, like Gary Sobers, was especially good in a crisis. He possessed by then considerable experience, not only in Test Cricket, but he had also played first-class cricket for Lancashire, whom he had joined back in 1968. Results more than justified his appointment, his only setback being when West Indies toured Australia in 1975–76 for the unofficial championship of the world, and came back badly beaten, despite Clive himself batting extremely well.

In 1978–79 a substandard Australia, because most of their best players had been left out for defecting to World Series Cricket, toured the West Indies and were predictably overwhelmed in the first two Tests. However Clive resigned the captaincy for the third Test as a protest against his own selectors, who had decided to omit several players who, like himself, were under contract to WSC. He was reinstated in time for the 1979 World Cup in England which the West Indies won, and from then until his retirement led what was easily the strongest team in the world. The culmination was the 5–0 massacres or 'blackwashes' of England. On his fourth tour he made his opponents do, what Tony Greig had once unwisely said he himself would make the West Indies do, 'grovel'. Their almost total domination of international cricket was mainly due to their fast attack, supported by brilliant fielding and sufficient batting, and the new tactics it produced. Although other Test teams had used four fast bowlers, the formula had never before proved so effective. There were five reasons why it did so now in the 1970s and 1980s – the quality of the bowlers, the pitches on which the matches were played, the lack of protection given to batsmen by the umpires, the new lbw Law, and the fact that Clive Lloyd was able to maintain a persistent pace barrage all the time. Rather sadly, it also meant that, for the first time, spinners were no longer an essential ingredient in a five-day Test.

Each member of Lloyd's first quartet of fast bowlers – Roberts, Holding, Garner and Croft – was an international-class bowler, but despite all being right-armers, they were very different in method, and provided variety. The devastation they achieved, combined with the money and the fame they acquired, served as an inspiration to numerous young Caribbean imitators, who saw pace bowling as providing an escape from comparative poverty and a fast gateway to riches. The outcome was that well-built West Indians with the gift of being able to project a ball at great speed, of which there were many, were soon fighting to climb aboard a rich gravy-train and were eagerly snapped up by English counties – who appreciated the value of having at least one genuinely quick bowler on their staff and were prepared to pay – or by the League Clubs.

The second reason for the success of the fast attack lay in the pitches and in the lush outfields, which assisted pace bowling far more than they used to do in the past. Today, a quick bowler is able to obtain movement, both in the air and off the wicket throughout the day because the ball does not become so worn, indeed it is not unusual to find the ball still swinging when the second new ball has become due.

Third, there is always an element of danger batting against very fast bowling, especially when the bowlers are permitted to send down a great many bouncers and consistently bowl short of a length. There is no doubt that over the years the West Indian pacemen have been allowed by the umpires to contravene Law 42:8; a classic case of this was at Old Trafford in 1976, when Brian Close and John Edrich were subjected to a barrage of bumpers in poor light.

Fourth, the new lbw Law forces batsmen to play at deliveries pitching outside the off stump, when previously they would have moved across, covered up and left them alone. The outcome now is they often have to play at the ball which rises sharply outside the off stump, and a big in-swing bowler will employ slips rather than leg-slips.

Fifth, the practical and tactical advantage of having *four* fast bowlers was that Clive always had two fresh bowlers at his disposal. In addition, as none of them was expected to bowl more than twenty overs in a day, they were still able to go flat out if the opposition was still batting on the second day. An over rate of 13 overs per hour or even less not only allows fast bowlers to retain their vigour, but greatly reduces the number of runs that the batting side can reasonably hope to score in a day. The non-stop blitzkrieg by the West Indian quickies softened up the opposition in a way which was not unreminiscent of 'bodyline' and, judging by the number of casualties – despite far more protective clothing, including helmets – far more dangerous. In fact it has not been too much fun batting against the West Indies in recent years, but I would not criticise Clive Lloyd for his tactics. However, I do believe that umpires should have taken firmer action, yet I also sympathise with them. Why should they stick their necks out when surely the authorities should know what is fair, and what is unfair? Umpires were blamed for not calling the throwers in the early 1960s, but the real blame lay with the officials who picked them in the first place.

The one time that Clive Lloyd's captaincy came badly unstuck was in New Zealand in 1980. Having won the series in Australia for the first time, he did not expect to have much difficulty beating New Zealand thereafter. But it did not work out that way, as he lost and, worse, the behaviour of his team was bad. It included umpire charging, kicking down the stumps, and refusing to take the field after tea on the third day of the first Test, unless the umpire was removed. I could not help feeling then that Clive Lloyd was perhaps too much the 'nice guy' to discipline his cricketers as they should have been disciplined.

BARRY RICHARDS

Batting Perfection

It is more than a decade ago that I wrote that Barry Richards was technically the most perfect batsman I had ever seen, and that still applies. In all respects he was straight out of the best coaching manual, a model for every young player. The same could be said of Sunil Gavaskar, but the Indian maestro did not possess as much grace because his build was short and squat.

No batsman during the past twenty years has committed himself to a stroke as late as Barry Richards. Vivian Richards and Graeme Pollock would be moving on to their front foot, and Geoff Boycott and Zaheer Abbas going back and across, before Barry Richards had decided to play back, forward or half-cock. It was his ability to read the length of the ball so early which enabled him to do this with the result that he always appeared to have so much time, and was equally proficient in both attack and defence, off his front and off his back foot. His feet would be in the correct position, and this meant that he was so well balanced and positioned he automatically played the right shot. The reason that he made batting look so easy and that his style was so perfect was due to his footwork, which stemmed from excellent early coaching. It is impossible to become a great player without exceptional natural ability, but it is sometimes forgotten that batting is not a natural art. It has to be learned.

To the aesthete in me Barry Richards has always been special. From the moment I first played against him for the Rothman International Cavaliers I have been a fan. His stance, high backlift and the unhurried strokes off front and back foot, all possessed beauty. He did not generate as much excitement as did the brutal strokeplay of his namesake Vivian, but his strokes had the elegance and discipline of a Keats sonnet, exemplified for me by a magical moment in a one-day limited-overs match between Hampshire and Yorkshire. Ray Illingworth was, as usual, bowling very accurately to an on-side field and Barry solved the problem he posed with a classic piece of improvisation. He simply moved outside his leg stump, from where he caressed the ball over short extra-cover with a text-book lofted off-drive. Subsequently, I have seen numerous imitations, for eventually this became a common ploy in this form of cricket, but none has been performed so exquisitely.

The sad feature of Barry's career, of course, has been that a player with so much talent should have been denied the opportunity of displaying it at the highest level. Like Graeme Pollock, and Mike Procter, he was a victim of South Africa's exclusion from the international scene, apart from one four-Test series against Australia in 1969–70. Although he was only twenty-four, he did more than enough to emphasise his quality by scoring 508 runs in seven innings in the four Tests and with an average of 72.57. His first Test century was made the more remarkable in that it was completed only four deliveries after lunch, which underlines the fact that, in addition to a well-organised defence, he possessed all the attacking strokes, which he executed so well that he was able to score off good-length bowling. One of the biggest differences between a very accomplished, and a great player, is that the former will be content to keep out a good ball, whereas the great player can, in the right circumstances, hit it to the boundary without undue risk. This explains both why Barry so nearly managed a century before lunch in a Test match, and why he was so difficult to bowl against.

Although we shall never know how many runs Barry would have acquired in a full Test career, or how he would have coped with a barrage of bouncers, I have no doubt he would have been highly successful because, as I say, he bore the hallmark of class; indeed the experience would almost certainly have made him an even finer performer. As it was, he missed the challenge of Test cricket. There were occasions in the county game when he was able to harvest so many easy runs that, with some of the bowlers lacking the ability to test him seriously, he became bored with the proceedings. He then might indulge himself, attempting the extravagant or the foolhardy, or simply allow his concentration to waver, weaknesses which would never have occurred if he had been driven by the extra incentive of batting for South Africa with the outcome of a rubber at stake. He was never a seeker of records like, for example, Geoff Boycott, for whom another century meant providing him with a further stepping-stone towards yet another statistical record which meant so much to him. In Barry's case it was this lack of incentive which made me feel sometimes that, although he liked batting, he did not possess that consuming passion for the game which prevents boredom coming to the surface in a county match between two middle-of-the-table sides in front of five hundred spectators. Great batsmen, like great actors, are at their best before a large audience and thrive on the big occasion. Through the timing of his birth, Barry Richards did not enjoy enough major occasions. He had to settle for rep in the provinces, without the chance to star in the West End or on Broadway.

Barry therefore became a cricketing itinerant who sold his batting talents to an employer. In England this happened to be Hampshire, but it could have been any club, with the result that playing for Hampshire meant less to him than to somebody who had been born in the county, or who lived there permanently. He probably would have done even better for his adopted county if they had been regular candidates for honours, as this would have kept both the runs and the adrenalin flowing. He needed another incentive, and this seems to be substantiated by his remarkable performances for South Australia in 1970–71, when he was sponsored for a dollar per run. His response was 1538 runs, with an average of 109.85, including a double-century and 146 against the MCC, who were touring. How many more runs might he have made for Hampshire if he had been on a similar arrangement? The snag is, of course, that he would not have been able to stay ten years with them, as he surely would have driven and stroked them to bankruptcy long before!

In the decade Barry spent with Hampshire, he made over 15,500 runs; more remarkable, he had an average of over 50. Only exceptional players average more than 50 for a long period of time, especially somebody who is not record-conscious. He would have done even better if he had retained the enthusiasm of his first season with the county in 1968 when, as a replacement for Clive Lloyd, he was the leading run-getter in the country with more than 2,000 runs. A couple of summers later, he was joined by Gordon Greenidge, who, though brought up in England, later decided to play for the West Indies. The West Indian was entirely different in technique and temperament, but he learned much from the presence of Barry at the other end, while he must also have made batting much easier for Barry too. Together they were easily the best, and most effective, opening pair on the circuit – hardly surprising, as both were world-class players, and would have formed the finest pair in international cricket, had they been able to play together at that level.

There are disadvantages about opening the innings – always facing the new ball, having to bat immediately after a long period in the field, and being asked to negotiate those thankless thirty minutes before stumps – but these are more than outweighed by the many advantages. The opener has first chance to cash in against a mediocre attack on a good pitch, while on a bad one he has the opportunity to settle before the effects of the roller have worn off. Although at the beginning of an innings the field setting will normally be at its most attacking, and increases the chances of a batsman losing his wicket, conversely, runs are more easily obtainable. However, the greatest bonus an opener enjoys is that he is allowed more time to play himself in and out to adjust to the conditions than in any other position in the order. This is especially valuable in limited-overs cricket. In the one-day game, it is not only the best position, it is frequently the key position, as was borne out by the Reliance World Cup in 1987, when the 'Man of the Match' in the majority of the games was an opening batsman.

Inevitably, Barry, with his ability to score quickly, using technically correct strokes, as he demonstrated so eloquently when making 325 for South Australia in one day against Western Australia, flourished in the one-day atmosphere. The crowds which turned up to watch him open for Hampshire in limited-overs cricket were far larger than those for normal county first-class matches, and provided him with an additional stimulus.

He also thrived in his two seasons of World Series Cricket in Australia 1978–79 and 1979–80, where the standard was higher than in most Tests and one-day internationals. There was certainly no shortage of bouncers in the five-day matches and the atmosphere between the teams was often distinctly frigid. At Gloucester Park, in 1978, Barry savaged Australia with a remarkable 369 out of a total of 625 for 1, but far more impressive were his two knocks in a low-scoring match at Sydney for the Rest of the World against Australia. Australia made 174 in their first innings on a difficult pitch to which the Rest of the World replied with 168, including 28 magic runs from Barry. Australia's second innings total of 214 looked sufficient, and it surely would have been if the South African had not steered the Foreign Legion home with a superb, undefeated, century.

GLENN TURNER

The Professional Kiwi

My first sight of Glenn Turner was in 1969 batting for New Zealand at Lord's in the first Test, which England won by the not inconsiderable margin of 230 runs. However I was impressed by his performance in the second innings in which he carried his bat for 43 out of a total of 131 on a difficult pitch that was taking spin. Underwood – who enjoyed a remarkable series against the tourists with 30 wickets at 10.70 in three matches – exploited it to the full, and took 7 for 31 in 32 overs. At 73 for 8, it had appeared that the Kiwis would be out for under 100, but Glenn Turner received some unexpected assistance from the 'tail' which prolonged the proceedings, and if this had been forthcoming earlier in the innings it could have saved the match, as it rained heavily throughout the final day. At this point in his career Glenn was twenty-two years old.

Nobody can hope to become an opening batsman at the highest level unless he possesses a solid defence and the exclusive attention required to remain at the crease for long periods. On the evidence of this performance, it was obvious that Glenn Turner possessed both these qualities, because he batted for four and a quarter hours without giving a chance, or having too many problems, while the wickets were tumbling around him. His innings underlined a fine technique and exceptional powers of concentration, which owed much to the experience he had gained during his previous summer with Worcester, plus the fact that they had promoted him from the middle order, where he had struggled, to open the innings where he could afford to take his time. Unquestionably, New Zealand had discovered a batsman who would make an ideal sheet-anchor, but some people questioned whether he had the strokes or the strength to develop into a great batsman. I had no such doubts, because if you can stay at the wicket long enough, the runs will surely come, especially if you batted at Worcester at that time when the pitches, unlike the more recent ones, favoured batsmen.

Glenn Turner was also opening the Worcester batting in limited-overs cricket, which was growing in both importance and in the number of matches being played. Here it was essential to score quickly and an opener has the best opportunity. Just how effective he was in one-day matches is reflected by his figures for New Zealand and for Worcestershire. He averaged 47 for his country in 41 matches, even though admittedly he was helped by being able to cash in on a really big scale against East Africa and Sri Lanka. His average for his county in this form of cricket was 38.02, for whom he amassed almost 7000 runs in 195 innings, including 8 centuries and 47 fifties.

However, the most important reason why Glenn was destined for greatness lay in his approach, which was single-minded and dedicated. This had started to pay a handsome dividend by the following summer, 1970, when he was the first batsman in the country to reach 2000 runs and when he set up a new county record with ten centuries. He used the arc of the V with straight-bat strokes for a large number of his runs, his placement being very sure and his off-drive probably his most attractive feature.

To churn out figures on the scale of Glenn Turner – he is, for example, the only New Zealander to score a hundred centuries – requires a singleness of purpose which can blind one to the possibility of there being another approach, or a different answer. Perhaps for this reason, too, controversy, though from different causes, also surrounded two other world-class openers of this era, Geoff Boycott and Sunil Gavaskar. Glenn's frequent disagreements with the New Zealand administration, various managers and the distinctly conservative media, numerous Australians and even Worcestershire at the end of his career, do suggest that he cannot always have been blameless. Rather like Boycott, he was a master of saying the wrong thing at the wrong time, for diplomacy did not exist in his calendar. Unlike Boycott's controversy with the Yorkshire committee, however, Glenn's rows with the New Zealand Board of Control stemmed from a difference of opinion on how cricket should be played and rewarded rather than from a clash of personalities. To understand the situation, it is necessary to know the first-class cricket scene in New Zealand, and why the outlook of Glenn Turner, who became the first professional captain of New Zealand, was essentially more English than Kiwi.

I played my first Test match series against the admirable New Zealand team of 1949. They were all amateurs. Although one or two of them may have obtained their job through their ability as players, cricket for them remained essentially a game, not their livelihood. Their outlook was closer to that of English club cricketers rather than county cricketers, which is why over the years the New Zealand touring teams, though among the weakest, have been the most popular. Even when county cricket had become an entirely professional game and commercial sponsorship, limited-overs cricket and television had begun to increase the players' rewards, the views of the Kiwi administrators did not really alter. As a result they inevitably had doubts from the outset about a person who had signed for Worcestershire in 1967 when he was only twenty and before he had established himself in their Test team. This is why they took so long to appreciate that Glenn Turner had blossomed from the competent, if limited, batsman who had begun to play for Otago in 1964, into one of their finest players. Unknowingly, perhaps, they rather resented that his advance owed more to his adopted county than to his country.

Also, it is never easy for a national team to accept a player who plays most of his cricket in another country. Even such an outstanding batsman as Martin Crowe who, sad to say, broke down in the 1988 season, did not appear to be accepted as eagerly by his colleagues during the 1987 World Cup as I expected, even though his brother Jeff was captain. Possibly subconscious jealousy, combined with the feeling that he is not really one of them, is inevitable.

With Worcestershire Glenn Turner was not merely an outstanding performer but he thought about the game more seriously than most of his contemporaries. He quickly learned that the views of Walter Hadlee, the President of the New Zealand Cricket Council, differed from his own views, especially in the matter of money for players. Glenn was prepared to put these forward strongly, as he was convinced he was correct.

Glenn's second tour to England in 1973 not only saw a much improved performance by New Zealand under Bevan Congdon, but was the season when Glenn achieved the rare feat of making 1000 runs before the end of May. Unfortunately, though not surprisingly perhaps, this was followed by relatively few runs in the Test series. If Glenn had been able to retain his early summer form, the Kiwis would surely have won their first Test in England. It was also true that Glenn dominated the scene to such an extent that he, rather than the tourists, scooped most of the early headlines. It was not until the Tests that the general public realised the strength of the tourists' batting line-up as a whole.

By 1975 Glenn Turner looked to have become the most important influence in the present and future of New Zealand cricket. He had established himself as a world-class batsman, was his country's best player, and had toured England, Australia, the West Indies, Pakistan and India. He was twenty-eight years old and had been elected the first full professional captain of New Zealand. However, his long stay with Worcestershire meant that his outlook was bound to differ from his colleagues', let alone those of the Kiwi Cricket Council. He was not only professional but money-conscious. He expected to be paid far more as skipper than any of his predecessors. The amateur establishment found him rather too concerned about finance for their taste, rather in the same way as an Edwardian gentleman would never allow himself to be personally involved in trade, but was only too happy to own the shares.

Everything started to go sour for Glenn at the end of the first season of the Shell-sponsored domestic tournament, which had replaced the Plunket Shield competition, and included a final between the two top sides. In his book *Opening Up* Glenn attempted to justify his actions in that match as captain, which, though I can fully understand them, I consider were a bad mistake. The situation was that his side, Otago, having been sent into bat, was dismissed for 262 and Canterbury replied with 452. The rules of the competition decreed that, in the event of a draw, the first innings would determine the result. Glenn decided that, as Congdon's side had both a lead of 190 and a good, tight attack there was no way in which Otago could win. As a result he dropped himself down the order and saw his batsmen fail again, although they could hardly have been encouraged when their most accomplished performer did not bat in his normal position. Glenn was eventually joined at the crease by Peter Petherick, his no. 11. He then declared, on the grounds that Peter might have been hit by a bouncer from Richard Hadlee who, earlier, had almost felled his no. 10, likewise a real non-batsman. Glenn's surrender by declaration was not appreciated by the New Zealand Cricket Council, hardly surprisingly, for they had arranged the Shell sponsorship.

There was further disagreement after Glenn had flown to South Africa to play for a multi-racial team, and the Council, who had agreed to pay his air fare home, would not transfer his air ticket to his wife, Suki. When he arrived back in Worcester after his short visit to South Africa, he received one of those condescending, pompous letters which cricket boards have been writing to their employees for over a hundred years. To make matters worse, as captain of New Zealand, Glenn was seeking increased money for overseas tours, which was not quite as straightforward a matter as it would have been in England, because some of the New Zealand team would be on full pay from their civil jobs, though not Glenn himself. It was then that Glenn had the misfortune to captain a New Zealand team on what can only be described as a disastrous tour to Pakistan and India. The Kiwis were not only outplayed in both series, but Glenn himself failed to supply his usual high quota of runs. It is never easy to lead a side in these circumstances, and it must be far worse for a captain whose views and approach differed from some of his party.

From then on the events were all too foreseeable. On one side there was the amateur, slightly Edwardian establishment, trying to raise the standard of New Zealand cricket, save money, and struggling to comprehend the social and financial revolution which was taking place at international level, yet convinced it was doing the right things. On the other, there was Glenn Turner, keen to raise the standard of New Zealand cricket, a sensitive, anglicised Kiwi professional, demanding more money from his Board for himself and his players, and equally convinced he was in the right. The establishment trotted out several sacred nostrums, including that the game is more important than the player, team spirit, patriotism, and maintaining standards, but forgetting how much attitudes, behaviour and dress had changed all over the world, often for the worse, since the first world war. Glenn had joined Worcestershire in which half the staff had not learned its trade in England, let alone in the county. He quickly realised that good run-hungry batsmen and wicket-hungry bowlers produced more success than 'team spirit' or that born leader whom England selectors have been seeking ever since F. S. Jackson. New Zealand is a small, underpopulated country and, like with so many of his countrymen, Glenn's outlook was inclined to be insular. The outcome of the continuous clash between the establishment and their finest cricketer was that Glenn only appeared intermittently for his country after 1976, even though he was at the height of his powers which included making a triple century, 311 not out for Worcestershire v. Warwickshire in 1982. His self-imposed absence brought him a bad New Zealand press, which accused him of putting money before country, and then tended to ignore the part played by the New Zealand Council and, especially, Walter Hadlee in a long, protracted disagreement.

I discovered early in life that one can make an error in mistaking a New Zealander for an Australian, for there is no great love lost between these two very different nations. Australia ignored New Zealand cricket until after the second world war, so that even today the average Kiwi hopes England will beat Australia; and fewer Test matches have been played by New Zealand against Australia than against any other country. In these circumstances, it was hardly surprising that Glenn Turner, with his long 'Pom' association, ability with the bat and quiet, restrained self-assurance, went down in Australia about as well as a Calvinist at a Roman Catholic festival. He abhorred the Australians' constant sledging, their language, and the personal abuse they continually hurled at him. It offended his professionalism, his views of how cricket should be played and his own code of behaviour.

The sad feature about Glenn's career with New Zealand was that the inability to find a compromise led to its being so curtailed. But it is good to see now that the differences, though they will never be forgotten, nor forgiven in certain quarters, are at least being ignored. He was appointed cricket manager, termed 'coach' in Australia, for the 1986 England tour by the New Zealanders, when he had the satisfaction of seeing England lose a series to New Zealand for the first time at home. Although this was mainly due to the efforts of Richard Hadlee and Martin Crowe, assisted by the inability of our selectors to make up their minds as to what England's most effective side might be against either them or India, Glenn Turner's knowledge of, and advice on, conditions in England greatly assisted his players; and when Bob Vann was taken ill and forced to return home early Glenn took over complete responsibility as full Manager.

GREG CHAPPELL

The Craftsman

The Australian team which toured England under Greg Chappell's captaincy in 1977 performed well below its capability, and was heavily beaten. Although the forceful leadership of Greg's elder brother, Ian Chappell, as well as the runs he provided, were sorely missed, the main cause for the failure was that half the side had contracted to join the Kerry Packer 'pirates' the following winter. This destroyed the team spirit which, over the years, has played an important part in the success of Australian cricket. It also, not surprisingly in the circumstances, turned out to be one of Greg's own least successful tours with the bat. Nevertheless, my abiding memory of that unhappy series, apart from the arrival of Ian Botham on the international scene and the wonderful support given to the England seamers by the close catchers, was watching Greg Chappell at the crease.

When he was in full flow Greg reminded me of a schoolmaster who was a first-class cricketer batting with schoolboys. Admittedly, a batting line-up of McCosker, Davis, Serjeant, Walters and Hookes had to appeal to, and be welcomed by any respectable seamer in England; but it is rare for a batsman to look not one, but two classes better than anybody else in his team. Indeed, during his remarkable century on a pitch taking spin at Old Trafford, three classes better would be a more accurate estimate. Of all the outstanding batsmen I have seen since the war, few appealed to me as much as Greg Chappell, not for the runs, though they were plentiful enough, but for the style. There was an elegant panache about his batsmanship which made him special and reminded me of Sir Frank Worrell. Although, as a bowler, I always fancied my chances more against Frank than against Everton Weekes or Clyde Walcott, I found Frank's style the most aesthetically satisfying of the three.

Despite the mechanism of the on-drive being practically the same as that for the off-drive, most batsmen find it a far more difficult stroke to execute. The reason lies in the stance, when both feet are pointing to the off side, so that, if a batsman decided to walk without turning, he would automatically move to the off, as that is the natural direction. It follows therefore that to advance the front foot towards mid-on is both an unnatural and a rather awkward movement. The on-drive is practically the only stroke where the left leg moves to the on-side without the right foot moving towards point or gulley first. The adjustment of both feet and shoulders needed for perfect balance is not easy to acquire; but Greg Chappell not only succeeded, he executed this stroke with more grace than any other batsman. In fact, he played it so well that opposing captains sometimes used an extra fieldsman in an attempt to block the shot, even though that meant leaving another gap elsewhere.

Like most great, as distinct from good, batsmen, Greg had the knack of making runs when they were especially vital, and he thrived on the incentive of a capacity crowd. This underlines how, in addition to ability, he possessed that other vital ingredient, a fine temperament. On his debut in first-class cricket, always one of the big moments in a player's life, the eighteen-year-old Greg made 53 and 62 for South Australia against Victoria in 1966–67. His first Test against England in 1970–71 provided an even more impressive example as, after five unimpressive scores for his state, he was picked on potential and certainly not on current form. This was a typical example of the difference in approach between Australian and English selectors. It is very rare in England for a young batsman to be chosen more for his promise than for runs in the book; Colin Cowdrey, in 1954–55, was one of the few exceptions. English selectors tend to rely too much on figures and not nearly enough on flair. To some extent this is due to the fact that our batsmen have many more opportunities to make runs, and there are more candidates from whom the selectors can choose. It would be true to say that Greg Chappell, whose highest score in his five previous innings in 1970–71 had been 25, would never have been picked for England in that situation. However, there can never be any substitute for real class, which Greg demonstrated by arriving at the crease with England well on top and Australia struggling at 107 for 5, and rescuing the situation with a masterly 108 and sharing a stand of 219 with Ian Redpath (171).

One of the main reasons why Greg Chappell became such a prolific run-maker, with twenty-four Test centuries to his credit, was the expert coaching he received in his formative years, while he also had the advantage of having an ideal pedigree, weaned on the game from an early age with Vic Richardson his grandfather, and two brothers who played state cricket and represented Australia. As a result, he was technically one of the most correct players Australia has produced. He also benefited from the two years, 1968 and 1969, he spent with Somerset, where he learned to tighten up his defence against the ball that moved off the seam and which helped him, at twenty-two, to enjoy such a memorable first tour to England in 1972, including centuries at Lord's and The Oval. Australia won both matches, again emphasising how he has so often risen to the big challenge when runs really counted, unlike those high scores made on an easy pitch, when both teams have become convinced that a run-festival draw will be the outcome.

Even outstanding batsmen are liable to experience a bad patch, however; for example, Denis Compton in Australia in 1950–51, Peter May in South Africa in 1955–56, and Graham Gooch in England in 1986. Greg Chappell was no exception, though it is especially rare for anybody whose basic technique was so sound and correct. In his third period as captain, 1981–82, he followed a glorious double-century against Pakistan with ducks on no fewer than seven occasions.

Although Greg had gone to Somerset as a batsman who had

shown promise also as a leg-spinner, he soon discovered that there was no room for leg-break bowling on the English county circuit, and he returned home as a useful medium-pacer. He was essentially a change bowler, able to swing the ball and cut it back into the right-hander. His great value in Test cricket was that, in addition to picking up the occasional wicket, he could be used to rest the strike bowlers, while in limited-overs cricket he was often employed as a fifth bowler who normally proved economical.

Greg was not in the same class as a captain as his elder brother, Ian; but he did a workmanlike job for both Australia and Queensland, while nobody could have enjoyed a better start than when he took over from Ian against the West Indies in 1975–76. Once again he displayed his ability to turn in a major batting performance when it most mattered: he recorded two centuries, which contributed a major part in Australia's eight-wicket victory in his first Test as skipper. He went on to take the series 5–1. Greg was lucky in three respects. First, and most important, he had four front-line pace bowlers – Lillee, Thomson, Walker and Gilmour – plus the defensive off-spin of Mallett. Second, he batted superbly on a number of occasions. Third, the West Indies, who had started as favourites, wilted under the pressure, particularly of the pace bowlers. Finally, he always had Ian on hand to provide advice and plenty of runs.

His leadership, however, lacked the poise, personality and inspiration which were such features of his batting, but he was a shrewd tactician: he could be relied upon to produce runs, which not infrequently proved decisive; he quickly recognised the strengths and the weaknesses of the opposition; and he was ruthless without appearing to be aggressive. Like his brother, he believed that the end justified the means, and was not too concerned about how it was obtained. Rather sadly, his captaincy will most be remembered for the occasion when he forgot that cricket was a game, and instructed his other brother, Trevor, to bowl the last ball of the day along the ground, thus making sure that the six runs which New Zealand required to win after what, until that moment, had been a wonderful day's entertainment, was impossible to obtain. His action, simply too mean to forgive, brought down universal condemnation, and resulted in a change in the one-day cricket rules to prevent a recurrence of such 'unfair play'.

SUNIL GAVASKAR

The Little Master

The events of 1987 and the winter of 1988 contained much which cricket lovers will want to forget. Amidst the general gloom, however, there was the Reliance World Cup, and three innings I was fortunate enough to witness by Sunil Gavaskar.

Against all predictions the Reliance World Cup was a splendid tournament for, though played hard, it still contained moments of chivalry and honesty for which cricket was once rightly famed. Sunil's three innings, all entirely different, convinced me that 'the little Master' was not just a great player, but a cricket immortal.

The first of those innings graced the MCC Bicentenary Match at Lord's in August 1987, where Sunil conjured up 188 for the Rest of the World, demonstrating his perfect defensive technique, concentration, and a wealth of stylish and memorable scoring strokes. He marked his farewell to first-class cricket at the headquarters of the game with a classic exhibition of batsmanship which seemed almost god-like in its execution.

Halfway through the World Cup I met up with the main body of the English Press who had been in Pakistan and I was asked what to date had been the highlight of the Indian section of the tournament. I had seen some very good cricket, but the most memorable episode had been a Gavaskar cameo against Australia in Madras, which alone had been worth the journey to India. He had provided an interlude of magic, fit to put alongside Len Hutton's astonishing assault on Lindwall and Miller in the second innings of the second Test in 1946–47. It also produced only 37 runs but was equally unforgettable.

In Madras, not only did Sunil destroy the Australian opening attack, but when Taylor came on to bowl he went down the pitch and straight-drove a good-length first ball over mid-off for six. Until that innings I had not appreciated the ferocity he was capable of producing. I had been inclined to put him in the same category, though more elegant, as Hanif Mohammad or Geoffrey Boycott – able to provide a big Test innings, but unlikely to dominate to the extent that the bowlers did not know where to bowl to escape the slaughter. The best example was still to come, however.

At Chandigarh I watched Sunil hit his first one-day international century against New Zealand in 85 balls and, if it had been necessary, he would have reached it far quicker. The most fascinating feature of his tour de force was that it contained only three slogs, one in the opening over, otherwise all the runs came from high-calibre text-book strokes. Most surprising of all, perhaps, he never improvised, like moving outside the leg stump to drive through the off side. He simply obeyed the basic principles of batsmanship and, unlike with his swashbuckling partner, Srikkanth – who from time to time played and missed, or snicked the ball – I only counted two false strokes throughout, one of which came when he was nearly exhausted. The opening partnership of 136 came in 17 overs and despite the New Zealand bowling being below international standard, Gavaskar's batsmanship was still a perfect example of a breakneck charge executed in text-book style. As a result, for the third time in the year of his retirement from cricket, Gavaskar caused me to purr with pleasure, something which does not happen as frequently as I would like.

Great cricketers, I believe, with the exception perhaps of certain slow bowlers, should be successful at first-class level in their teens, and ready for international cricket by their early twenties. Sunil Gavaskar was no exception to this. He made his debut for India in the second Test in Trinidad, having missed the first through injury, in the 1970–71 series. He did well with 65 and an undefeated 67, but these two innings only provided the stepping-stones to what was to be one of the great batting feats in history, as in four Tests, at the age of twenty-one, he was to make 774 runs with an average of 154.80.

Although the West Indian attack was neither as hostile as it had been, nor as it was to become, it still contained Boyce, Sobers and Gibbs; perhaps even more important, the pitches were of high quality, but only a superb craftsman with a great temperament could return figures of that magnitude. The outcome was that Sunil Gavaskar arrived for his first tour to England in the following summer with a reputation comparable with that of the young Bradman of 1930, and I, in company with all cricket lovers, was looking forward eagerly to seeing the new 'little master', all 5ft 4½in. of him. Although it proved to be something of an anti-climax, the three-Test series did enough to confirm his ability, not so much by the number of runs, but rather by the manner in which they were acquired, while he also had the enormous satisfaction of being a member of the first Indian team to win both a series in the Caribbean and in England.

My first sight of Gavaskar batting was at Colchester, where the tourists experienced their only defeat of the tour on a pitch which gave some encouragement to the Essex seamers and took spin in the later stages. In the first innings he succumbed to the ball that all opening batsmen, especially those of small stature, dislike, caught behind by one that lifted a little and left him; but in the second innings he contributed a solid half-century before being stumped.

Any doubts about his being special were removed by the first Test at Lord's. In their second innings, the Indians required 183 runs to win in four hours and twenty minutes. Despite a poor start, Sunil, with active assistance from Farouk Engineer, struck 66 for the third wicket in 55 minutes in a flamboyant partnership which put the England pace bowlers to the sword. Until Ray Illingworth introduced his spinners, bad weather looked the only way to prevent an Indian victory. But when Norman Gifford had Gavaskar caught for an exquisite half-century, the innings disintegrated, so that eventually it was the visitors who were saved by rain. What impressed me most about Gavaskar's batting on that occasion were the number of runs he gathered off good-length bowling by hitting the ball on the up, but along the ground, with a straight bat. Sadly, the match will be most often remembered for the incident in which John Snow sent Sunil crashing to the ground, as he was attempting a quick single, and the bowler a run-out. Although in his autobiography Snow claims it to have been a pure accident, this was hardly my impression of the event. I wrote it off as just another unfortunate occurrence, however, it has to be said that Sunil himself has been involved in rather more than his share of incidents, although on this occasion he was the innocent party.

Why has such a likeable character as Sunil Gavaskar, with his marked sense of humour, become embroiled so often in disagreements? To turn out as many runs as he consistently does demands, in addition to outstanding ability, a singleness of purpose and absolute dedication. On occasions this can lead to a personal fixation which can cloud one's judgement and which may, though not always correctly, give the impression of selfishness. A classic example occurred at Lord's in the 1975 Prudential World Cup, when Sunil decided that England's total of 334 was unreachable. His answer was to occupy the crease for the whole of the allotted 60 overs, and finish with 36 not out, which exterminated all spectator enjoyment. Another incident took place in the third Test at Calcutta against England in 1985 which completely baffled me at the time, and still makes no sense in retrospect. The situation was that India, with the series level and led by Sunil who had won the toss, batted first, and were still batting after lunch on the fourth day. Admittedly, most of the second day was lost, but he made a mockery of cricket and eventually declared some twenty minutes after lunch on the fourth day, but even this belated gesture appeared to be due more to a demonstration by the frustrated crowd, three overs of bowling farce from David Gower, and the real threat of a riot, than to the game itself. Although the 'Maharajah of Bombay' has never been popular in Calcutta, on this occasion the local fans had every reason to be discontented. Would Gavaskar have acted the same way in Bombay?

Easier to understand are his numerous disagreements with Indian administrators whose record of handling players, especially captains, has been poor. A major reason for this is that India is a continent containing many different countries, rather than one country. This automatically makes selection far more difficult. Our football selectors have enough problems on the odd occasion when they have to choose a Great Britain XI, but that would be nothing compared to picking the best European side to play five matches against South America. In India the ideal would be for each state to be represented. But such compromises on this point have often weakened India, as indeed they have been known to weaken the West Indies.

Being the captain of India is a less secure, and more hazardous occupation than managing a League Football Club. However able the captain, nobody holds the job for long, unless he commands the strongest team in the world which performs accordingly. If there are a few poor results, the axe will assuredly fall. The big difference between an Indian skipper and a football manager is that the former is often given more than one opportunity because there are only a few feasible candidates, while the latter seeks new pastures with another club. The weakness of reappointing a discarded captain, of course, is that it destroys continuity and can easily lead to dissension, as happened with both Sunil and Kapil Dev. It is also liable to create disharmony within the ranks of the team, so that the man in charge will be constantly looking over his shoulder, wondering whether his most probable successor is giving him full support, or scheming his downfall via a dagger in the back, an oral injection of poison, or more subtle methods.

The vastness of India in both size and population, combined with the religious, language and cultural differences of the many states, have all combined to provide the Indian Board of Control with more problems than are experienced by any of the other national Boards. To make matters more difficult, their finest players in recent years are, with the exception of their equivalents in Pakistan, probably held in higher regard by the general public than in any other part of the world. Cricket there not only possesses a large following, but the advent of television has led to an enormous increase in adulation and financial rewards, without the players experiencing the same competition from outstanding performers in other sports as is the case in England, Australia and New Zealand. The administrators are naturally keen to avoid clashes with idolised stars and are prepared to allow them considerable latitude. At a practice session during the World Cup at Bombay I noticed that Sunil was absent and, on enquiring why, was informed by one of his colleagues with a broad smile that he was not feeling too well and was probably resting at home. I gained the impression that Sunil had simply decided, quite fairly, that he did not require a net on that occasion. Which does not mean that he dislikes practice, quite the reverse.

Tactically, Sunil was one of the best Indian skippers, astute though inclined towards caution. His conviction that his judgement was invariably correct, however, which assisted his batting, did mean that there were occasions when he was unable to think objectively. The most famous occurred in the third Test at Melbourne in 1980–81, when he was so incensed by a lbw decision against himself – rather odd when one remembers that he had toured Pakistan in 1978–79 – that he wanted to forfeit the match by ordering his partner, Chauhan, to leave the field with him. India in fact won that match, a close one, by 59 runs.

After the glories of the previous winter in the West Indies, Sunil's first tour of England in 1971 had come as something of a disappointment, even though he was the leading run-scorer. The reason was mainly that the ball did not come on to the bat as fast and moved more off the seam than it had done in the Caribbean, and the bounce was less dependable. Gavaskar also overdid the drive on the up in these conditions and paid the penalty. Like most small men, he was exceptionally good off his back foot, but discovered many pitches in

England where it paid to spend more time on the front foot. This was a major reason why he did not score as heavily in 1980 for Somerset as did Viv Richards for whom he was deputising. Richards had played far more cricket in England and had a pronounced initial movement on to his front foot.

The hallmark of great players – like Jack Hobbs, Wally Hammond, George Headley, Everton Weekes, Denis Compton and Len Hutton – is how well they played on bad wickets when the bowlers were on top. As a result of his perfect technique, allied to his skill, this also applied to Sunil Gavaskar, and I have selected three examples, two of which I witnessed, to illustrate his ability in this situation.

In 1974 England played India at Old Trafford in early June. The weather was cold and wet, ideal for Mike Denness who possessed a much stronger attack for these conditions. Sunil responded to the challenge with a masterful century, in which his hooking, later to be largely discarded from his repertoire, was one of the major features and, until run out, he was never in trouble. As a result of the rain which had fallen on the previous evening when the pitch had been uncovered, England declared before the commencement of play on the final day, hoping that Derek Underwood would secure victory. It did not work out that way, and it was again the English quickies who did the damage, although not before Sunil, for the second time, had demonstrated how to play seamers on a seamers' wicket. He scored so freely that as long as he remained at the crease an Indian win appeared feasible, but on 58 he received a brute of a delivery from Chris Old which lifted off a length, and the last seven wickets fell for 79 runs. England won by 113 runs, but Gavaskar had made 101 out of 246 in the first innings and 58 out of 182 in the second.

I did not see his historic innings against Pakistan at Bangalore in 1987, the final and decisive match of the series on a pitch which had been designed for spinners. As India looked to have both the better spinners and a stronger batting line-up, a victory for the home side seemed assured, especially after Pakistan was dismissed for 116 in the first innings, routed by

Maninder Singh. But that did not happen. Although the Indian first innings of 145 was less than expected, and more than a shade disappointing, it still represented a useful lead on that strip. The big surprise was that Pakistan was permitted to scramble to 249 in the second innings, the result of determined batting and the failure of the Indian bowlers to exploit the conditions as well as the comparatively inexperienced Iqbal Qasim and Tauseed Ahmed. The pitch was treacherous throughout the match, but by the time the Indians began their second innings it had become a dusty, unpredictable road to disaster. In addition to the amount of turn varying, the bounce was unreadable, with one ball shooting along the ground, the next behaving normally and another lifting sharply. Only a master craftsman with a superb technique could have played a major innings on it, which is exactly what Gavaskar produced. He steered India to within 16 runs of an impossible win, by remaining at the wicket for 323 minutes, in which time he also filched a remarkable 96 runs and deserved victory rather than defeat. In terms of technical perfection, it was surely the finest performance of his career, a view completely endorsed by the Pakistan players who, despite desperately trying to remove him throughout his stay at the crease, had been captivated.

I suppose that in England we remember above all Gavaskar's 221 in the final Test at The Oval in 1979. What impressed me about that masterpiece was his judgement of what was required and how best it might be achieved. When England declared at 334 for 8, India was set to score 438 runs in approximately 500 minutes, a massive task for any team batting last. The target probably should, and could, have been even higher, if Geoff Boycott's 125 had been gathered faster than at seventeen runs per hour, and if the English batsmen in their second innings had shown any interest in attempting to increase the tempo before the arrival of David Bairstow.

Sunil's objective was to bat out the remainder of the fourth day and be ready to return to the crease on the final day. His reasoned approach to his task was to take the runs as they came, to look for them but not to chase them. If he was still there at tea time on the fifth day, then the whole situation would be reviewed to see if there was any realistic chance of winning. By this time England had also realised for the first time that they could lose the game, for in Test cricket captains seldom intentionally make a declaration which will give any realistic chance to their opponents. As a result, they had begun to slow down the over rate to make sure that this did not occur, by deliberately reducing the number of balls delivered. Although this naturally made the task of Gavaskar and Vengsarkar more difficult, at 5pm, when the final 20 overs were left, India required 110 at an average of 5.5 runs per over, a tough but, with nine wickets in hand, a far from impossible target. It was not to be, with Ian Botham, who has always relished a challenge, yet again proving the catalyst by removing Gavaskar at 367. He then capitalised on the predictable panic which ensued, after Kapil Dev, promoted to no. 4, was out for a duck, so that eventually, in the last four overs, it was the visitors who found themselves holding out for a draw.

It always seems to me, however, that Gavaskar's massive effort, once again, deserved a better result for India.

GORDON GREENIDGE

The English West Indian

A large number of outstanding West Indies cricketers, including Vivian Richards, Keith Boyce and Joel Garner, owe much to what they learned on the English county circuit; but none to the same extent as Gordon Greenidge. The first three all arrived in this country having played first-class cricket in the Caribbean, whereas Gordon arrived from Barbados as a twelve-year-old in 1963, went to school in Reading, played for the England Schools Cricket Association, and so was qualified to represent either the West Indies or England. One outcome of his being brought up in England, rather than 'little England' (i.e. Barbados), is that Gordon lacks the ebullience of most West Indian players and is understandably more suspicious. He has always been inclined to be dissatisfied even after a good innings and, following a splendid 70, he will blame himself for failing to turn that into a hundred. Would he have been better off if he had opted to play for England rather than the West Indies?

Oddly, in view of future events, he initially stood a better chance of being picked by the West Indies than for England, and that may well have influenced his decision. However, for the long term, he made the wiser choice as, quite apart from spending more than a decade with the best team in the world, it is easier to retain one's place during a lean spell with the West Indies than it is with England.

He joined the Hampshire staff when he was seventeen, but did not make a big impression for the county until he was nineteen. If he had still been living in Barbados, I fancy he would have been thrown in at the deep end earlier. However the important point was that, once given the opportunity, he immediately showed that he had both the ability and the temperament to succeed. He was called upon to open the innings with Barry Richards – at the time probably the finest, unquestionably the most elegant, opener in the world – for the last seven matches of the 1970 summer, and consistently produced the figures, including a double-century first-wicket partnership. In those last seven matches of that season he established his right to become Barry's permanent partner. They soon were the most accomplished opening pair in county cricket, and for a period in the world – the graceful blond South African and the dark, and brooding, Bajan, a combination which had the additional incentive of competition.

Gordon learned much from batting alongside Barry Richards, indeed even an ordinary batsman would have benefited, but Gordon was a student of cricket hungry for success and prepared to work at improving every aspect of his game with more dedication than most English-born cricketers. In addition to being able to study a master at close quarters, Gordon methodically worked at the strokes which suited him most. When he played the forward and the back defensive, he made sure his feet were in the right position, his head was over the ball, as if he was smelling it, his bat perfectly straight and very dead, and his pads served as an additional line of defence. In complete contrast, when on the attack, he loved to blast the ball. His cutting and hooking were extremely vicious and though he revelled in full-blooded drives, he soon realised the benefits of also being able to push the ball on either side of the wicket sufficiently softly to provide a comfortable single. His improvement as a batsman was gradual, which tends to support my view that there have been several more naturally talented West Indian batsmen than Gordon Greenidge, but none have spent, or indeed been able to spend, as much time improving their technique. It certainly paid off and can be measured in the steady increase in runs scored each season until, in 1973, he was invited back to play for Barbados. This provided him with another formidable challenge.

Barbados has produced more great cricketers per square

mile than anywhere else, so it is not surprising that the Bajan is inclined to be arrogant about his cricket, rather like Yorkshiremen in the 1930s, 1940s and 1950s. When Greenidge, almost a foreigner in his home island and who had learned his cricket elsewhere, first came back to Barbados, there were many people who would have been only too pleased to see him fail, for that would underline the strength of their cricket and also save the cost of bringing him over from England. Although batting is in general easier in Barbados than in England, it often takes time, especially for a player brought up on English wickets, to adapt to the extra bounce, the heat, and the light; but there was extra pressure on Gordon, on trial as he was at the toughest and most demanding school in the world.

He did not fail and, although his batting did not captivate the islanders with its splendour, it was good enough to warrant an invitation to return when, typically, he increased his productivity. The result was that he was selected to tour India, Sri Lanka and Pakistan with the West Indies in 1974–75. He was, as expected, a success and the West Indies appeared to have found a high-quality opening batsman, which has often been something of a rarity in the Caribbean. West Indies cricket has produced an abundance of no. 3, no. 4 and no. 5 batsmen, but precious few openers, apart from Conrad Hunte, and now Desmond Haynes. It is true that Jeffrey Stollmeyer, a correct and elegant strokemaker, and Allan Rae, a solid left-hander proved a remarkably effective pair, particularly in 1950. In thirteen Tests they opened on 31 occasions with a highest stand of 239 against India and with an impressive average partnership of 72; but they did have the considerable advantage of making most of their runs against mundane seam attacks on very good wickets. I would certainly rate Greenidge and Fredericks as superior. However, without any question the finest West Indian opening pair of batsmen has been Greenidge and Desmond Haynes who, in the 1988 Madras Test, became the first duo to have opened in one hundred Test innings. Although this record yet again illustrates the enormous increase in the amount of international cricket played, it remains an astonishing feat. They are the most consistent pair in history. They have lasted for over a decade, in which time England has tried countless combinations with a conspicuous absence of success. Continuity does help.

My first encounter with Desmond Haynes was when he played for my side in Barbados, during the Fred Rumsey Festival, just prior to joining the West Indies on their 1979–80 Australian tour, when he teamed up with Gordon Greenidge. Desmond, who had learned his cricket on a minute, rough and uneven cricket ground perched precariously on Holders Hill, was clearly a well-organised batsman. I was not too worried when various Bajan cricketers informed me that 'He hook de ball too much in de air, man' – indeed, that was the way he perished in that particular game – because it is a fault which, except for the instinctive hooker, can be easily cured by self-discipline. From the outset what impressed me about Desmond was, in addition to his batting and a basically sound technique, his love for the game and his admirable attitude to life. He has remained unaffected by fame, and is universally popular. He is one of my favourite cricketers, and Barbados has good reason to be proud of him.

The profitability and longevity of the Greenidge–Haynes association stems from several qualities. First, both are outstanding players. I would place Greenidge among the 'great' and Haynes into the 'very good' category. Second, they complement each other. Despite an excellent defence Gordon is by inclination an attacking stroke-maker whom, over any series, one would expect to harvest his runs faster than his partner. Although Desmond has a wide range of strokes and a pleasing style, he is essentially an accumulator. Third, both are capable of, and have produced, big hundreds, a requisite in Test cricket. Fourth, over the years they have developed a fine understanding with the result that they are able to score fast without taking risks because, unlike Graham Gooch, for example, they pursue quick singles. This not only keeps the scoreboard moving, but distracts the bowlers, and, though valuable in all versions of the game, has been made even more so by the one-day internationals.

The objective of every opening pair is to see off the menace of the new ball and to provide their team with a stand of fifty or preferably a hundred. Their job is to lay the foundation for a big total. The loss of one of the pair should then provide his partner with an even greater incentive to make a century, possibly, though not necessarily, in a 'sheet anchor' role. In some respects the most intriguing feature of the Greenidge–Haynes partnership is that, although they have recorded some massive first-wicket stands, including 296 against India in 1982–83, they have not reached three figures together as often as one might have expected; yet the loss of one of them early has, time after time, resulted in the other playing a major innings.

Is there any reason why, apart from Greenidge and Haynes and Conrad Hunte, the West Indies have produced so few high-calibre openers?

In English county cricket the easiest place to make runs is as an opening batsman, and this has been made even more so by the amount of limited-overs cricket. In the West Indies this is different because of the extra bounce in the pitches at the start of an innings with the new ball. This especially applies in club matches, which are often two-innings affairs, but once the menace of the new ball has been overcome, runs are much easier to acquire, so the best number to bat in the Caribbean is normally at no. 3 or no. 4.

The hopes that in Gordon Greenidge the West Indies had discovered a great opening batsman were temporarily dashed when he toured Australia in 1975–76 and fell a victim to the pace, lift and swing of Lillee, Thomson, Walker and Gilmour. He was not only dropped from the team, but was not selected for the tour to India which followed. This setback stemmed from his failure to adjust from the slow English pitches to the faster, bouncier ones in Australia. It was one thing hooking and cutting Chris Old, Hendrick or Julien at Southampton, but a very different matter attempting the same shots against

Lillee or Thomson at Perth. But after his disasters in Australia, Gordon again displayed his dedication and determination to overcome obstacles. He tightened up his defence and, without reducing the power of his attacking strokes, which have always been a feature of his play, made them more disciplined. The outcome was that he regained his Test place and seems likely to remain an automatic choice for the West Indies side until he retires. Of all the West Indian openers, he is the greatest.

Although Gordon has made several successful return visits to Australia, which illustrate that he will make runs anywhere in the world, I still feel that he is at his best in England on the pitches which he knows so well, and on which he is able to make an adjustment so late. For me, he is the perfect all-round no. 1. He cuts and hooks better than Graham Gooch. Because he has had more experience of them, he has won more one-day matches than Sunil Gavaskar. He possesses more strokes than Geoff Boycott did, and greater physical strength than Glenn Turner. His cutting is so powerful that it is not unusual to see gulley placed in a position that would be more accurately described as short third man!

I have witnessed many of Gordon Greenidge's finest Test innings, but for the best I must go back more than ten years, to July 1976, when he scored three superb centuries. These were all the more fascinating for being so different in character. The most remarkable was his 134 on a pitch of uneven bounce, a seamer's delight, at Old Trafford, on which he scored his runs out of a total of 211, and where England were then rattled out for a miserable 71, despite a more promising start than the West Indies, who at once time had been 26 for 4, and who also had a long tail. If Tony Greig had been given a third seam bowler with real penetration, it might have been a different story. In the second innings this lack became even more noticeable as the West Indies batsmen cut loose and Greenidge hit his second hundred of the match.

In the next Test at Headingley, on a good wicket and against a much stronger fast attack of Willis, Snow and Ward, Greenidge and Fredericks provided their side with a 'dream start', being still together at lunch with 147 runs on the board. They both went on to complete delightful centuries, and at the close their side had made 437 for 9; in fact they gathered runs so quickly that it could have cost them the match if England had batted as well in their second innings as they did in their first. The fact that these three innings by Gordon Greenidge occurred before he had teamed up with Desmond Haynes, illustrates how long Gordon has been around without any reduction in his skill. The only difference these days is that he is more injury prone, but this seems to make no difference to the runs he scores; indeed it is often said, with good reason, that he is even more difficult to remove when he is 'on one leg'.

Gordon Greenidge has given far more to both the West Indies and Hampshire than vast quantities of runs in that, when he bats, he takes full account of the context of the match, and he is at his most valuable in situations when runs are at their most difficult to acquire. He is one of the least selfish of the great players, and he has been able to maintain both his hunger for runs and his deep love of cricket for much longer than most. In these circumstances, it was rather hard to understand why his contract was not renewed by Hampshire for 1989, but then no player should expect long-term loyalty from a county, even though that is what the counties preach. Expediency has always been their prime concern and, on this occasion, Hampshire wanted to retain Jefferies, largely on the evidence of the Benson and Hedges Final, as well as Malcolm Marshall. In addition, they had more good batsmen than most counties, so that if they had re-signed Greenidge one of them would have had to lose his place. This would have been especially hard on a local player, because two of the slots were already occupied by South Africans. There was also the extra cost involved. As a result, the Committee decided that there was no room for Gordon although he was still probably the best opener in the world. The sad feature is that, unlike with some of the overseas stars, Gordon Greenidge's loyalty to his club has been exceptional.

VIVIAN RICHARDS

The Tiger

During the 1983 season I was often asked my opinion about Nick Cook, the Leicestershire left-arm bowler, who had been brought into the England XI as a late replacement for Phil Edmonds. He did very well, taking 17 wickets in two matches and finishing second in the averages; but I was even more impressed by his bowling for Leicestershire against Somerset, when he found himself up against Vivian Richards on an ideal batting pitch with a fast outfield. This provided the perfect test for a young left-armer, having to bowl at a master batsman in form and indeed Viv went on to score a superb double-century; but Nick Cook made him work for his runs. If you want to judge a bowler's potential, see how he performs against an in-form Vivian Richards, who will go down as one of the truly great batsmen in cricket history.

No batsman since Bradman, Compton and Sobers has caught the imagination of the public to such an extent. It has not so much been the records Richards has broken for the West Indies and Somerset, but the manner in which he has batted that has established his genius. At his best the 'uncrowned king of Antigua' has looked at least one class better than any other member of some very strong West Indian batting sides. For a decade he has been the finest batsman, certainly the most feared, in the world, for he possesses that rare gift of being able to destroy opposing attacks in both Test and limited-overs cricket by a sustained, tigerish, assault, which combines brutality, bravado and beauty.

I have seen Viv bat on many occasions, and play a number of outstanding innings. From these I have selected the five which, for different reasons, underline his claim to be, or to have been, the best in the world. Two of them occurred in Tests, two in one-day internationals, and one in a Gillette Cup semi-final.

The semi-final between Somerset and Essex at Taunton in 1978 was among the five most satisfying limited-overs matches I have watched. The fact that my own county finished as the losers off the last ball of the day shows what a special match it was. There was a capacity crowd, 574 runs, lovely weather, a marvellous climax, and a century by Richards which, as so often in one-day cricket, eventually proved to be the decisive factor.

On winning the toss, Brian Rose of Somerset decided to bat, even though the pitch was slightly damp and initially gave some assistance to the bowlers. He was probably influenced by having earlier in the summer lost the Benson & Hedges semi-final after putting in the opposition, but he must have been worried when, with the ball moving around, the first wicket went down in the second over. This brought the great man to the crease, and characteristically he replied with an immediate counter-attack, picking up a respectable second ball from Norbert Phillips off his front foot and dismissing it to the mid-wicket boundary. Viv did have some problems in that first hour, and indeed he might have been caught when he was 22 off John Lever's left-arm swing which exploited the conditions well; but, while Rose hung on grimly, Richards continued to keep the score moving briskly along. He became more extravagant when he was joined by Peter Roebuck, who had all his work cut out trying to survive. Three strokes which I especially treasure because they contradict the idea that Richards is too dependent upon the leg side for his runs, were a front-foot drive high into the crowd over extra-cover and, later, two off-drives to the boundary, one with the weight on his back foot and the other off his front foot. The sufferer was Stuart Turner, who until then had dealt a succession of immaculate maidens.

In the 1979 Prudential World Cup final the West Indies beat England by 92 runs. This defeat was mainly due to four factors: first, England went into the match with only four main-line bowlers; second, although it is desirable to have an opening partnership which provides a solid platform for a late slog, it cannot afford to use up as many overs as Boycott and Brearley did on this occasion, because it places too much pressure on the later batsmen; third, Collis King struck a remarkable 86 in only 77 minutes, out of 139 he put on with Viv Richards; finally, and most vital, Richards himself made 138 not out which on almost every occasion would be sufficient by itself to secure victory in a one-day game. There were many fine strokes in Vivian's innings, but what I remember most was his treatment of Mike Hendrick in the final over. The way Viv struck the boundaries was contemptuous, and summed up by the last ball, which he summarily dismissed from outside his off stump with a straight bat into the crowd at square leg, for six!

The first Texaco match at Old Trafford in 1984 marked the start of what was to be possibly the most humiliating series that England has ever suffered. England lost this one-day match by the not inconsiderable margin of 104 runs, because our selectors were unable to read the pitch and included only one spinner (Miller), and Viv Richards made an undefeated 189 out of a total of 272 for 9 in 55 overs, despite his side at one time struggling at 100 for 7. Without in any way detracting from Viv's tour de force, it would never have occurred if another slow bowler had been included. Miller, by no means a big spinner, took 3 for 32 in 11 overs, while Willis, Botham, Foster and Pringle were being dispatched by a positively imperious Richards to all corners of the field, with five massive blows landing high in the stands. His domination on a slow pitch which took spin was such that he provided 93 of the runs in his stand of 106 with Mike Holding.

Great players thrive on big occasions. Viv Richards celebrated his first appearance in a Test match at Lord's in 1980 (he had missed the 1976 Lord's Test through injury) with a century in a game which England would almost certainly have lost if they had not been rescued by rain in the later stages.

On a good pitch England, batting first, were dismissed for 269, despite a splendid hundred by Graham Gooch. The West Indies replied with 518, and though Desmond Haynes contributed a fine 184, it was the 145 from Vivian Richards which enchanted everybody but the England bowlers. He dismantled their attack with ease and elegance, even though Ian Botham, who knew his ability better than anybody, attempted to block the on-side. What impressed me especially about this innings was that Viv attacked Derek Underwood more effectively than I have seen any other right-hander do in a Test match.

My final choice underlines the brutal, macho streak in Richards' approach to batting. If he had been a boxer, one can imagine him being prepared to swap punches with an opponent, because he was convinced that he could hit the harder. As a batsman, he tends to regard a bouncer as a challenge, though in Australia, when both Lillee and Thomson, especially the latter, were bowling, he learned quickly that the hook could prove fatal; but he had no such fears about Bob Willis at Old Trafford. In the third Test of 1980, his answer to three West Indies wickets tumbling quickly in the final session was to unleash a fusillade of strokes against Willis. He continued in the same fashion the following morning and reduced England's main strike bowler to employing a field more suitable for the final stages of a one-day game than the middle of a Test match. But it was all to no avail as the ball simply kept racing to the boundary. This astonishing onslaught was eventually ended by Ian Botham when Richards had made 65, but his destruction of Willis is reflected by Bob's final figures, 1 wicket for 99 in 14 overs out of a total of 260.

Like an increasing number of players in different sports, Viv has always been inclined to explode, displaying a petulance far removed from the relaxed, laid-back manner he presents so much of the time. The first major example occurred when he was a teenager playing for Antigua against their great rivals, St Kitts. He had already become a local hero, not merely because of the runs he was scoring, but even more for the excitement of his batting. His fans turned out to see the boy wonder destroy the opposition, and were shattered when he was adjudged caught and then knocked down his own wicket. His refusal to leave the crease and his argument with the umpire immediately before he eventually stalked off, provoked a pitch invasion by a large number of spectators, shouting 'No Viv, No Match'. The administrators, not surprisingly, were caught out by the demonstration, and made a decision of convenience, which was not in the Laws of Cricket. They persuaded Viv to resume his innings, despite a two-hour delay, in order to continue the match, and again he was dismissed without scoring. Later, the authorities banned Viv for two years for his behaviour. If this had not occurred, I believe he would have been capped earlier for the West Indies, and might well have never played for Somerset.

This was not the last occasion that Vivian showed reluctance to accept a bad decision gracefully; another occurred in the second Test at Delhi in 1983–84, when he was given out lbw to Kapil Dev. He not only strode from the field in obvious dudgeon, but caused some destruction in the dressing-room, while his comments on Indian umpires were nearly as tactless as those by Mike Gatting about Pakistan umpires. Despite an apology, it left behind an unpleasant taste and many people felt that, if he had then been captain of the West Indies, the tour would have ended early. It was this tendency to lose his temper, and inability to conceal his anger, which prevented his being invited to skipper the West Indies earlier, and why Clive Lloyd reigned as long as he did. When Richards eventually took over, his captaincy initially was neither so successful nor so impressive as expected. The lack of success was largely due to the West Indies being not as formidable a team as they had been, as so many of the finest bowlers and batsmen had either retired or were past their peak, while the newcomers, especially the batsmen, were not of the same calibre. This is why the West Indies were often forced to struggle in Pakistan, India and New Zealand. In addition, Richards' field placings sometimes seemed to lack imagination, and there were occasions when he appeared to lose interest. This might also account for the time he sometimes wasted between overs, when he seemed to forget that spectators are important, and ignored them by conducting the game at his own tempo, slow, slow, quick, quick, slow.

Viv joined Somerset in 1974. At that time they had more than their allowed quota of overseas players. He was a comparatively unknown West Indian batsman, and without the persistence and financial support of Len Creed, a wealthy committee man, it would never have taken place. In his twelve years with his adopted county, he provided them with thousands of runs. Once again, however, it was not the quantity but the quality of the runs which made them unforgettable. It was during his long association with Somerset which ended so acrimoniously, that he became the finest batsman in the world. Although he contributed much to the club, one cannot help feeling that any county which possesses three of the finest cricketers, not just in England, but in the world – Richards, Garner and Botham – should have been even more successful, especially as they had good support cricketers.

Viv provided Somerset with majestic runs, some magnificent moments in the field, and a few handy wickets with his off-spinners. Nevertheless it was not merely a one-sided arrangement, as he undoubtedly benefited from the association greatly. Playing regularly on pitches in England meant that he had to tighten up his defence, which made him a much more effective player, particularly in this country, New Zealand and, to some extent, in Australia, because he discovered that it was necessary to spend more time on the front foot. In the outcome he developed into the first truly great cricketer from the Caribbean who was a front-foot player, though this did not mean that he lost his ability to play off his back foot. In addition, he gained in confidence from playing so many innings in both first-class and limited-overs cricket. In particular, he quickly learned how to score runs off good-length balls on and sometimes even outside the off stump by punching them through mid-wicket with a straight, slightly angled bat with the weight on his leading leg. This was one of the reasons why he was so difficult to contain, and was often able to force captains to station an extra fieldsman or two in the mid-on area in an attempt to close off these highly profitable avenues.

In 1988, after the disappointment of not reaching the semi-finals in the Reliance World Cup and a very close and exciting series against Pakistan in the Caribbean, Viv took a young and comparatively inexperienced team to England. Although they started badly in the one-day internationals, they came back to thrash England almost as easily as they had done in 1980 and 1984, yet without the aid of the big innings he normally has produced for them. Although the superiority of the West Indians was partially due to the inability of England selectors to decide upon their best batsmen, attack, or even captain, the skill and enthusiasm of Vivian Richards as captain played a considerable part. This tour saw the very best of him, not so much as a brilliant batsman, but as a thoughtful skipper, who seldom missed a trick and provided just the right amount of advice, discipline, and encouragement that his young side required. And he did it with charm and courtesy, two ingredients which suggest that, when he eventually retires from the game, he could have a highly successful career in West Indian politics, because he also possesses personal magnetism and an inner toughness which is essential, although a cynic might suggest that his integrity could prove a handicap. The years he has had to spend in different parts of the world have served to increase his love for Antigua and it is hard to imagine him not eventually returning to that lovely island for good.

GRAHAM GOOCH

'Goochie'

After I retired as Secretary and Captain of Essex, I played cricket, when radio and journalistic activities permitted, for Westcliff Cricket Club. I enjoyed club cricket far more than charity or Wandering club cricket, where the result is basically immaterial, because I have always wanted to be part of a team where the primary interest was the outcome of the match, not personal performance. The only disappointing feature was the reluctance of clubs to risk losing a match in order to increase the chance of a win, which strangely was more frequent than in the first-class game, and it led to a high percentage of draws. The Leagues which have now been formed, where the result of every game has greater significance, would have suited me better.

On one Saturday I found myself playing against Ilford, a strong club not noted for its generosity when making declarations, at Valentine's Park. Although it was a good, firm pitch I found that around 'military medium', which was then my pace, I could achieve movement off the seam, and obtain some wickets. However, I did notice, with irritation tinged with admiration, that a teenage batsman, who was especially strong off his legs, would from time to time dispatch a reasonable away-swinger, that pitched about middle stump, to the on-side boundary; more important, he on-drove me off his back foot along the ground for four and scored about 70. It was easily the most impressive innings I saw played against Westcliff that summer, and was enough to show that the boy had the ability to become a better than average county cricketer. It was my first sight of Graham Gooch who, since the retirement of Geoff Boycott, has become the only opening batsman, from the army of players who have been entrusted with the job for England, of outstanding class.

Graham Gooch now has a career Test average in the high thirties and a first-class average in the early forties. That might seem to dispute my claim that he is a batsman of world class, until one examines against whom he has made his runs and the number of Tests against comparatively easy bowling on true pitches which for one reason or another he has missed. That, together with his outstanding record in limited-overs cricket, is why I believe he is a great international opening batsman, as distinct from a very fine one, like John Edrich, or Conrad Hunte, or Desmond Haynes.

Graham is a big man, six foot tall and weighing about thirteen stone, and for the past decade he has used a tree-trunk bat, which is held aloft before the ball is delivered. Despite this he is essentially a touch player, who has struggled more than most if his timing was fractionally out, and this explains why he has experienced several bad patches. The worst occurred in 1987 when, after celebrating the start of the new season with a big hundred, he followed it up with two successive 'pairs' at Chelmsford, struggled painfully for several weeks, and was not chosen for the Tests. It stemmed largely from his head being slightly out of alignment so that he was not bringing his bat down straight and it took him most of the summer to correct it. This fault was not dissimilar to that of a professional golfer who suddenly finds himself slicing every drive, but even more worrying because Graham at his best is not merely content to hit the ball hard and hope that it eludes a fielder, he *expects* to miss him. He is professional and good enough to be cross with himself when he fails to do this; and it is in fact the hallmark of the international class, as distinct from the good batsman. As his game is built around punching the ball hard to the boundary, the 'drop come one' shot has, unlike with Gordon Greenidge, never had a major role in his repertoire. When he cannot pierce the field, he struggles.

Since I have always advocated introducing young players with outstanding potential into international cricket at an early age – rather than established county cricketers in their late twenties who may be having a successful summer but are unlikely to improve – I was delighted when Graham was selected for the first Test against Australia at Edgbaston in 1975; but I was also worried because, after a splendid start that season, he had been struggling in the weeks immediately prior to his international debut. It was something which the selectors chose to ignore. The outcome was that Gooch did not score in his first innings and he completed a 'pair' in his second when he received a near-unplayable delivery from Jeff Thomson which lifted and left him. He failed to make much impression in the second Test, with the result that he was dropped and his confidence suffered a further blow as he failed to make many runs for Essex. It was to be three years before he was given another opportunity, but by that time he had established himself as an opener for his county, and in this position he proved successful against New Zealand and Pakistan in 1978. From that moment he became an automatic choice for his country, apart from his three years in purgatory following the rebel tour to South Africa in 1981–82, which he captained, and also when he declared himself unavailable for domestic reasons.

On the night before the Reliance World Cup semi-final between England and India in Bombay in 1987 I encountered Graham and other members of the England party at a quiet pre-match reception. He reckoned that, if the ball turned, as an initial inspection of the wicket had certainly suggested, he would attempt to counter-attack the left-arm bowlers Shastri and Maninder Singh by sweeping against the spin, a method which he had been practising assiduously in the nets earlier in the day. As Kapil Dev won the toss and followed the common practice of putting in the opposition, especially just after breakfast on a wicket which was likely to be at its most helpful in the early stages, Graham was soon able to put his theory into practice. It worked better than even he could have expected. Against anything well pitched up on, or outside the leg stump, he swept the ball square, or fine; against any ball pitching outside his off stump he lapped with a cross bat off his front foot to mid-wicket, his front leg outside, and forming a barrier against him missing, or against the arm-ball. His belief that his approach would be more successful than hitting with the spin using a straight bat proved correct, as he reached a memorable hundred out of a total of 157 for 2. It is true that he might have been caught when he was 88, and at 115 he eventually was, but by this time he had literally swept England into a commanding position which enabled his side to reach 254 for 6 in the allotted 50 overs. It was one of the most fascinating examples of a tactical innings it has been my pleasure to watch, carefully planned and perfectly executed.

What made it all the more unexpected was that, up until this match, Shastri and Maninder Singh had been both effective and economical. Kapil Dev took too long to realise the danger, because nobody had adopted Gooch's tactics even on much better batting pitches and, indeed, they had not been necessary. As a result the Indians were completely unprepared for his 'sweeping' assault, and understandably surprised, because none of their own batsmen would have attempted that form of attack in those circumstances. Nor would it have been found in any text-book on the game. Oddly, the next time I saw Graham at the crease was against Kent in the first-ever four-day county match on a slow, easy-paced Chelmsford pitch. He celebrated the opening of the first-class season with a double century in a very high-scoring match, but the surprising feature was that the only occasions when he appeared to be in any trouble against an insipid attack was when he was trying to sweep Richard Davis, a very tall, inexperienced slow left-arm bowler. Yet in India he had destroyed with this method two high-class left-handers on an untrustworthy surface.

Graham's method of batting is neither out of the coaching manual, nor stylish, but it is very effective and above all it suits him. His foot is often some distance from the ball when he plays his off-drive, but his bat will have come down very straight, while his push off his legs from over the crease with an angled perpendicular bat, possibly the most lucrative of all his shots, is frequently taken off the stumps. One of the reasons for his success has been his penchant for straight-bat strokes, which has been influenced by the heaviness of his bat and by his 'bat aloft' stance. Although his 'help-on' hook from the half-cock position has become a Gooch speciality, I did once see him pull Garner violently to the mid-wicket boundary three times in the same over, a rare and treasured sight. At times he has reminded me of an old-style heavyweight who stood up and swopped punches with his opponent without worrying over much about footwork.

This does not mean that he never uses his feet. Against genuinely fast bowling, he regularly moves right back on his stumps which is one reason why he has usually dealt with the West Indian pace attack better than most of the English players. He often gives spinners, whom he is inclined to treat with contempt, the charge, but against the majority of the bowling encountered in county cricket – seam, between medium and fast-medium – he stands nearly upright and bludgeons them away with a straight, often angled bat from over the crease.

Although there are occasions when it pays to choose horses for courses, outstanding batsmen and bowlers will be effective in all forms of cricket. The best place to bat in limited-overs cricket is as an opener, not least because he has the opportunity to bat more frequently and for longer than batsmen in other positions. Could this be why England, in the last twenty years, has capped so many opening batsmen who had done well for the counties, but who lacked the class to succeed at the highest level? Graham Gooch, however, who possesses that class, has naturally proved himself to be a match-winner in one-day cricket, both for England and Essex. He has long since forgotten the number of 'Man of the Match' awards he has collected. There are several reasons for the stream of awards, the most obvious being that he is a great batsman with the concentration needed to play a long innings. He also has the ability to take apart, not merely a county attack, but an international one, the most famous example probably being his undefeated 129 at Port-of-Spain against the West Indies during that ill-fated tour by England in 1985–86. His value, especially at county level, has been further increased by his useful medium-pace, away-swing bowling, and by his slip catching.

If Graham had not embarked on his South African adventure he would certainly have captained England long before he was given the job at The Oval in the last Test against the West Indies in 1988, and in all probability before Willis, Gower, Gatting, Emburey and Chris Cowdrey. This would have been due more to his ability as a batsman and his seniority as a player than for his being either a natural leader or a brilliant tactician. His brief spell as captain of Essex did not prove a success and he resigned because, not only did his county's fortunes slump, but he also suffered a disastrous spell with the bat. It is to be hoped there will be no repetition now that he has been reappointed.

Although Graham scored more runs than any batsman for that rebel England side he captained in South Africa in 1981–82, his leadership lacked the debonair drive, motivating self-confidence and positive panache required for those especially demanding circumstances. As a result his team failed to do as well as it should have done. He has never been sufficiently out-going to be ideal captaincy material, while the results obtained by Essex, an above-average county, when Graham took over from Keith Fletcher for several matches in 1988, were disappointing. Twice having made a sensibly challenging declaration and with an attack containing three current England bowlers, he allowed both Lancashire and Nottinghamshire to climb back into the game and win, which cast several doubts about his tactical perspicacity under pressure. One wonders whether it would be wiser to allow him to concentrate entirely on the job he does so well, making runs with dedicated professionalism.

Graham is a happy family man who does not enjoy cricket tours because they entail long periods away from his wife, Brenda, and the children. The money that is now available for the star performers, together with Gooch's own massive Benefit, have meant that, unlike cricketers in the past, he can afford to pick and choose. It is also easy to understand why he has preferred to spend winters in Cape Town, where he can have his family with him, there is not too much travelling and, though the cricket is serious, it is more of a holiday than an England tour would be. Therefore it came as no surprise when he intimated that he was not sure that he wanted to go to India with the England side in 1988–89. He changed his mind after sampling the honour and satisfaction of leading his country at The Oval, and, on 15 August 1988, he made a statement to the press and on the radio to the effect that he might be prepared to tour India as captain instead of going to South Africa. His initial reluctance to make the trip and his change of heart hardly suggested, however, that he was the ideal choice and it is difficult to understand how the selectors even considered someone who had been reluctant to make the tour. A skipper must be prepared to make instant decisions, a requirement which Graham did not display on this occasion, while the abysmal timing of his announcement indicated a lack of tact, while wearing a South African hat at the height of the controversy was needlessly provocative. Few people, other than our selectors, were surprised when the Indian government – not, it should be added, their Board of Control – cancelled the tour. I believe it would have gone ahead, if his South African connections had not been emblazoned around the cricket world.

Graham is a pleasant, frequently misunderstood man who is a keen supporter of the 'Hammers' and has become a car-phone fanatic, spending almost as much time on it as he does at the wicket. He is eagerly awaiting the time when it will be feasible to take a phone out with him to the middle and to ring home between overs! He has never enjoyed a good rapport with the media, whom, with some cause, he mistrusts. This means that he does not find it easy to deal with the many questions, some deliberately mischievous, which every England skipper has to answer. Like many other great batsmen, including Denis Compton and Geoff Boycott, the mantle of captaincy has never fitted naturally or easily upon his shoulders. That too made his appointment to lead England in India, quite apart from the other snags, incomprehensible.

JAVED MIANDAD

The Imp

Javed Miandad is a small, agile right-hander with a vast repertoire of attacking strokes. He has an insatiable hunger for runs and a sound defensive technique, with the ability to concentrate for long periods, and he is at his best in a crisis. Just as important, possibly more so in an era dominated by hostile fast bowling, he, unlike many dainty stroke-makers, is not afraid of pace, invariably moving into line and sometimes unleashing a violent hook. His hooking and brilliant cutting are assisted by his body being square-on at the moment of contact, and he uses plenty of bottom hand in both strokes. Although a brilliant batsman and a bonny fighter, there is, sadly, a danger that he will be remembered more for his many rows than for his ability as a batsman.

The first-class cricket world is small and rather narrow and, though incidents do occur, the atmosphere is usually convivial. At the time of writing, it could be said that a failure by Miandad invariably delights not only the opposition, but nearly every other cricketer, apart from those from Pakistan. He has managed to become the most universally disliked player on the international circuit, so it was predictable that he did not remain long with either Sussex or Glamorgan, and there were few regrets on his departure apart from the missing runs. Although he was certainly appointed captain of Pakistan too early, it was through a revolt among his players that he was deposed in 1981–82, indeed the only two surprises were why that did not occur sooner, and the stupidity of the Pakistan selectors for picking him as skipper at that stage in his career. His well publicised fracas with Dennis Lillee in 1982 provided yet another example of his unsuitability to lead his country at that time.

Javed Miandad is a classic case of how truly great players – as distinct from very good ones such as Chris Broad, Dennis Amiss or Derek Randall – are not just scoring runs in first-class cricket in their teens, and in Test cricket in their early twenties, but are putting together those major scores which require ability and application from the outset. Javed played an innings of over 300 when he was only seventeen, hit a double-century on his third appearance for Pakistan, and made six centuries for his country before he was twenty-one, the hallmark of real class. At this juncture, the world appeared to be at his feet.

Although he did not provide a massive innings against England on their tour to Pakistan in 1977–78, a batting average of 131 indicates that he was scarcely a batting bankrupt, but in the following summer in English conditions he experienced, like so many outstanding players from time to time, a lean patch. In a three-Test series he only averaged 17 for his five innings, much to the relief of the England bowlers whom he had ruthlessly plundered earlier in the year. His failure was partly due to the fact that Pakistan's five most accomplished players were missing, having joined the Packer Circus. The tourists became depressed, which was reflected by several abject performances in which they failed to realise their potential.

Bowlers who were hoping that Javed's run-drought would continue, were quickly disillusioned when, in a high-scoring series in Pakistan against India, the first meeting between the two countries for eighteen years, he averaged 119 and would certainly have made even more runs if he had batted higher in the order. As it was, Zaheer Abbas, at no. 3, aided by the regular failure of the opener Sadiq Mohammad, had the first chance of climbing aboard a galleon loaded with runs, and he made the utmost of the opportunity against an attack which never once was able to bowl out their opponents.

Zaheer Abbas, incidentally, had an outstanding record for Pakistan and Gloucestershire and was one of the most elegant and prolific batsmen of this period. He scored more than a hundred centuries, including several massive ones, while his remarkable feat on four occasions of making a double-century and a single century in the same match, is a testament to his powers of concentration. On good pitches he regularly destroyed attacks with graceful efficiency, but, perhaps because he needs glasses, he looked suspect against quality fast bowling in a rough battle. He reminded me of a fine West Indian batsman, who used to murder county attacks, yet against whom I always fancied my chances on a 'green wicket'.

The excuse for Javed's attitude and aggression on the field, which has been at times reminiscent of John McEnroe, has been given as a tough up-bringing in a district of Karachi where he was born in 1957 and where it was necessary to fight for everything – in cricket as well as life. He had to claw his way to the top of his profession, and in his determination to remain there he has never stopped fighting. His outstanding ability at a very early age was quickly realised by A. H. Kardar, President of the Board of Control for Cricket in Pakistan from 1972–77, who was convinced that here was the finest Pakistan player to appear since Imran Khan.

However, although his aggressive behaviour on the field has sometimes gone to excess, off the field he is a pleasant individual with considerable charm, which explains why he has become a great favourite with his present club, Bolton, in the Lancashire League.

When he came to England after the 1975 World Cup to play League cricket, he stayed with a good Pakistan cricketer, Qamar Ahmed, who has become one of his country's most respected writers on the game. Javed was then not only young, but very shy, with a passion for green chilis stuffed with spices, which he liked to fry in batter. The indications now are that he has begun to mature, and that one day he may possibly be able to lead Pakistan with grace and without any loss of determination, for, during his early years in England and his association with Sussex, he showed that he possessed what is perhaps best described as an 'impish' sense of humour. Although his bird imitations were fun they were not, however, always appreciated by the batsman who was about to play a stroke.

Javed was exceptionally fast between the wickets and soon realised the additional value of quick running in limited-overs cricket. It was also easier to pinch a quick single, if the fielding side has not been alerted by a call. In other words it is possible for two batsmen, who have complete faith in each other, to dispense with many calls and rely on a beckoning gesture, or even a look. However, his Sussex colleagues understandably did not have complete confidence in his calling which, like with so many players from the east, was apt to be unpredictable. However, in Paul Parker he found a colleague with whom he could harmonise. Having explained to Paul that he did not always call – a fact which only the deaf could not have realised – he suggested that if Paul watched his eyes, a wink would provide the signal for a single. This worked well, because Paul Parker was probably even faster between the wickets and his speed enabled him to rectify any misunderstanding.

DAVID GOWER

'Golden Boy'

In the 1970s and 1980s there have been better, more spectacular, and correcter batsmen than David Gower, yet I preferred to watch an innings by David more than anybody else, because he had so much to offer in terms of style as well as runs. In addition to being a cricketer, he looked the part, with the tall lean build, rather languid manner, handsome features, blue eyes and blond hair of a matinée idol of the 1920s, while his cavalier approach was reminiscent of the Golden Age. Whenever he strolls nonchalantly out to the crease, one knows that, if he remains, the runs must flow quickly and elegantly. He reminded me of another wonderful left-hander, Frank Woolley, the same relaxed stance, high backlift and follow-through with the full swing of the bat which will despatch fast and slow bowling to all parts of the ground. Although both men hit the ball very hard, they gave the impression that they were *caressing* boundaries. It was this ability to stroke fours and sixes, and to make batting look easy when clearly it was not, which so appealed to me.

David Gower was able to make scoring runs appear simple because he always appeared to have so much time; and he was also a beautifully balanced mover. These characteristics applied as well to another England left-hander, Willie Watson, about whom Sir Len Hutton once complained that it all came too easily to him, both his cricket and his football. Willie would glide over the ground very quickly without seeming to be in a hurry, and David has the same deceptive pace which makes him dangerous in the field and such a delight to bat with, as his judgement of what constitutes a run and his own pace between the wickets is excellent.

One of the many charms of David's batting is that it is largely instinctive. This can hardly be better illustrated than by the first ball he received in Test cricket. He was selected for the first Test in 1978 against Pakistan who, denuded of their five most accomplished players, casualties of World Series Cricket, were the weakest team that country had sent to England for twenty years. David arrived at the crease with England comfortably placed, 101 for 2 facing a total of 164 and Sarfraz Nawaz, the only class bowler in the Pakistan attack, injured. Liaquat Ali responded with what might be described as a friendly bouncer, which David contemptuously pulled to the mid-wicket boundary. He went on to provide the only batting of true international quality until the arrival of Ian Botham at no. 7. Although England did reach 452 for 8 declared, a batting line-up of Brearley 1, Wood 2, Radley 3, Roope 5, Miller 6, explains why this twenty-one-year-old left-hander lifted the tone, so immediately and dramatically.

When David Gower remains at the crease for any length of time, whatever the situation, he automatically accrues runs both sweetly and swiftly, because he is not only an instinctive stroke-maker; but his footwork is frequently at fault, and this enables him to hit the balls into areas which a more orthodox player would not. His square-drive off his front foot played with his bat a long way from his body and his two feet in a half-cock position provides a perfect example, indeed he scores many runs from over-the-crease positions, neither forward, nor back. His methods depend upon the keenness of his eye and one would not fancy his chances of still being able to churn out the runs like Geoff Boycott did in his forties. David's technique means that he is often giving opposing bowlers a chance, especially outside the off stump, because it is only a matter of time before he will attempt to drive a widish ball through the covers without moving his front foot outside his off stump, or to cut without his left foot moving towards the off side, with the bat brought down on the ball and the wrists rolled. As a result he is obviously more effective on true firm pitches where the bounce is true and he can hit through the line with confidence, so that David is usually more successful overseas than in England.

At the commencement of the 1988 summer, I saw him batting for Leicestershire on a heavily grassed, guaranteed-result pitch, where the bowlers were able to make the ball deviate and rise sharply off the seam. Although these conditions were well exploited by Leicester's four-man pace attack, they did not suit David's highly individual style. Wickets like these are better for batsmen like Peter Willey – who is prepared to wait, drop the rising ball dead by giving with the bat at moment of contact, and dab, nudge and push – or, the sound and solid Nigel Briers, than for a daring stroke-maker with the mercurial touch. The inevitable outcome was that David neither spent the time at the crease, nor acquired runs in the quantities one would expect from him on the standard Grace Road wickets of yesteryear; it also meant that he went into the Tests against the West Indies without the confidence which stems from making runs in the middle. The outcome was sad and predictable. The 'golden boy' of English cricket, who with 7000 runs in 100 Tests had proved his ability at the highest level, found himself struggling against a good West Indian attack on wickets which, in the main, were far less helpful to pace than they had been on England's last tour to the Caribbean. There he had headed the English averages by a not inconsiderable margin when the bowling was considerably more hostile. The outcome this time was that the selectors dispensed with his services for the final Test when, ironically, the Oval wicket would have suited him far more than any of the other four.

David Gower was a much more effective captain than many people have appreciated. He may not have been one of the game's outstanding leaders, but he was better than any of his immediate contemporaries. His biggest handicap was so often being in charge at the wrong time and with the wrong team; indeed the make-up of the side he was given to lead on his debut as captain of England never ceases to make me chuckle. It was against Pakistan at Lord's in 1982 when he took over from the injured Bob Willis and was given this attack: Ian Botham, Robin Jackman, Derek Pringle, Ian Greig and Eddie Hemmings, four right-arm medium to medium-fast seamers, and one flat off-spinner. This meant that, although he could change his bowlers, he could not change the bowling. Not surprisingly, Pakistan won by a margin of ten wickets.

David's most unenviable task, however, was to lead England against the West Indies in 1984 and again in 1985–86, when all ten Tests were lost and England was 'blackwashed' by the World Champions. Whoever had captained in England, when Peter May and his fellow selectors appeared to have no idea of what constituted our strongest side and used twenty-four players in the series, was destined to lose heavily. However, I believe David should have done better in the Caribbean, because there the England team played below its potential. David himself batted bravely and was the only player to average over 30, but his relaxed style of leadership, which had worked so well in India in 1984–85, was unsuited to this situation. He sorely missed his vice-captain, Mike Gatting, who had his nose broken by a ball from Malcolm Marshall before the Tests began and was out of action until the final Test, by which time the England party had become a bitter, beaten and bemused outfit. On the tour to India and Sri Lanka the Gower–Gatting combination had provided a nice balance, not unlike one often encountered in a platoon during the war, with Gower in the role of the rather aesthetic, intelligent lieutenant with a public school background and Gatting as the vital sergeant, who could be relied upon to supply a touch of down-to-earth realism in a crisis. When a team is winning, such matters as indifferently organised practice and voluntary nets go unnoticed and unmentioned, but not when the side is being thrashed and the media are looking for reasons other than the superiority of the opposition.

Those two horrendous 'blackwashes' which his team experienced against the West Indies tend to make people forget just how well David captained England in India in 1984–85 when he won the series 2–1 against formidable opposition with a

(Above) **Graeme Pollock.** The completion of a lofted off-drive, with the eyes following the flight of the ball, and with the leading right shoulder having been followed by the left in the powerful follow-through.

(Below) **Geoffrey Boycott.** Geoffrey Boycott's bread and butter shot — the square drive off the back foot played either side of the wicket, safe, sound, and productive. Here he is guiding the ball past cover — note the position of his right foot, parallel to the batting crease, the head still, the eyes following the flight, and the controlled follow-through.

Clive Lloyd. The conclusion of a perfectly executed straight drive. Note the stillness of the head, the position of the feet, and the full follow-through with the blade facing the leg side.

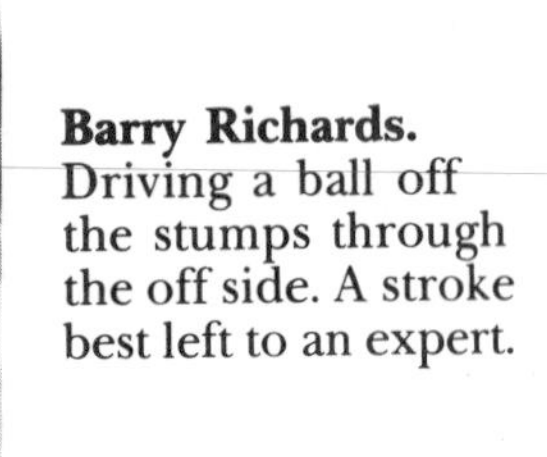

Barry Richards. Driving a ball off the stumps through the off side. A stroke best left to an expert.

(Left) **Greg Chappell.** The completion of an on-drive off the front foot, generally regarded as the most difficult of strokes because it is the only time that the front foot moves to the on-side for a straight-bat shot.

(Right) **Glenn Turner.** The dead-bat forward defensive shot, with the left leg well bent, right toe behind the batting crease, head over the ball at the moment of impact, and the locked left wrist.

(Below) **Sunil Gavaskar.** The follow-through of a straight drive off the back foot. The toe of the right foot, which was pointing towards cover at the moment of contact, has swivelled round with the power of the stroke and the body is now leaning forward.

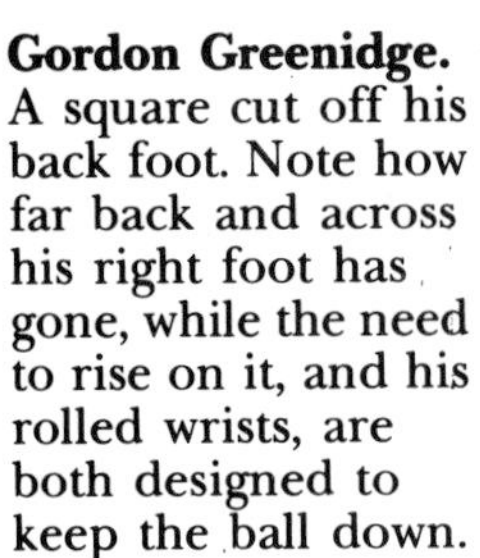

Gordon Greenidge. A square cut off his back foot. Note how far back and across his right foot has gone, while the need to rise on it, and his rolled wrists, are both designed to keep the ball down.

Vivian Richards completes another awesome lofted on-drive with both batsman and wicket-keeper following the flight of the ball before it disappears into the crowd.

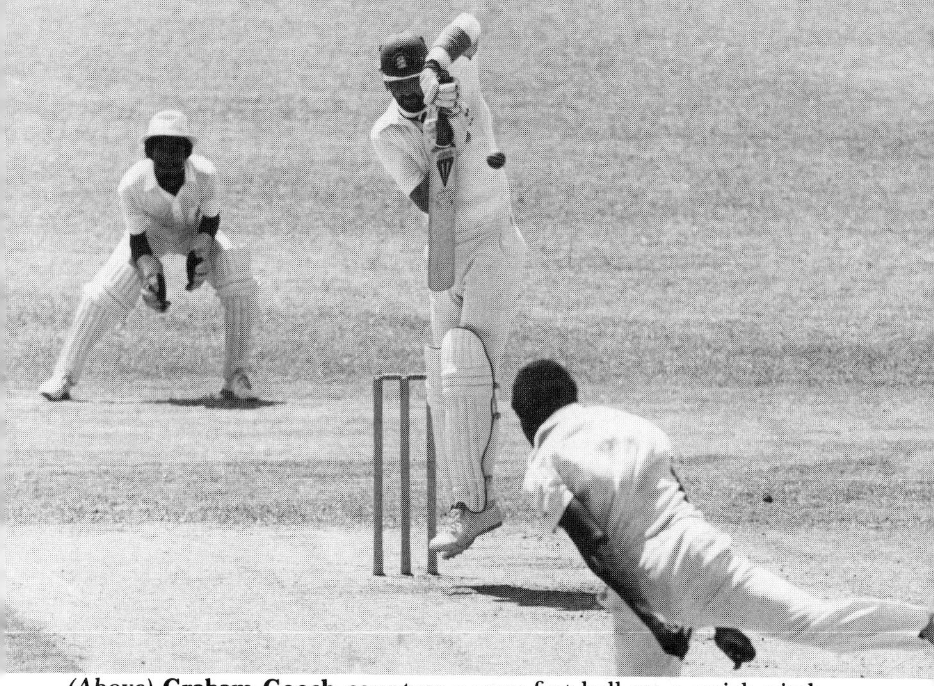

(Above) **Graham Gooch** counters a very fast ball on a quick pitch as it rises more steeply than expected. He solves it here by using a fine back defensive, but in order to play the ball down and not give a catch, he has to be airborne at the moment of contact.

(Below) **Javed Miandad.** The conclusion of a full-blooded straight drive off the front foot. The violence of the stroke has meant that his body has opened up after contact. Note how both legs are bent.

David Gower. The Gower waft (semi-steer, semi-cut) to a ball outside the off stump played from the half-cock position has brought about his downfall on many occasions, but also brought him numerous runs.

Allan Border uses his feet against Emburey and pushes him through a gap in the mid-wicket area.

Imran Khan. The follow-through off a back-foot drive. Notice how Imran has given himself more time by moving his right foot well back, while the position of his right toe, pointing towards cover, has enabled him to hit the ball from sideways-on, before becoming chest-on to the bowler *after* completing the shot. *(Below).* An unsuccessful chorus led by the captain, and very well supported!

Ian Botham. After the completion of a boisterous hook, he is continuing to watch the ball. His head has remained still even though the effort he has put into the stroke has almost swung him off his feet. *(Below)* A Botham bouncer. This has proved over the years to be a great wicket-taker. Here the batsman, Dujon, has been caught off his gloves.

Mike Procter. The square drive or cover slash off the front foot, a hybrid of the drive and cut. *(Below)* The open-chested action of a 'hopper', in which the left foot points at the batsman and the left arm plays little part in the body action.

Richard Hadlee. The position of the left shoulder indicates a good body action; that of the right shoulder a good follow-through. Hadlee's right arm has chased his left arm across the body until it has been checked by his left hip as he moves into his follow-through with the left arm beautifully high, and his head and eyes still concentrating on their target. *(Below)* Hadlee hooking a poorly directed bouncer not very elegantly, but effectively. Although he has moved inside the line and is a long way back, a purist would prefer to see his left leg in front of the middle stump.

Kapil Dev. He provides a perfect example of getting the left shoulder right round in his body action, so that it is almost pointing at fine leg and is ideal for bowling the away-swinger. *(Below)* The finish of an off-drive by Kapil. Note the top-of-the-handle grip with both hands working in unison.

(Above) **Stumped Knott,** bowled Underwood. Very fast and very neat — only one bail has been removed, and Rowe is on his way back to the pavilion for 70.

(Below, left) **Bishan Bedi.** It is all there in the moment before delivery: the braced front leg, with the toe pointing towards third man, and the wrist and fingers cocked to produce the break.

(Below, right) **Derek Underwood.** Classic sideways-on body action suitable for all types of bowling.

(Above, left) **Dennis Lillee** descending from his pre-delivery leap with his left shoulder and his head beautifully positioned.

(Above, right) **Andy Roberts.** A somersaulting off stump to emphasise that it does pay when the batsman (Greig) misses if the ball hits the wicket.

(Below) **Tony Greig.** As a skipper he always led from the front. Here he can hardly be much closer to the action. Notice how he is moving forward, and not on the retreat.

(Right) **Joel Garner.** His action may be a shade too open for the purist, with the right foot a little too straight; but it clearly suited Joel and that is what really matters.

(Left) **Malcolm Marshall.** His left foot has started turning and the ball has just been released from *very* close to the stumps.

(Right) **Abdul Qadir.** The timeless question. Will it break right, break left, or carry straight on? The answer: when in doubt, push out!

(Above) **Mike Brearley** directs proceedings for John Emburey, a bowler who is extremely punctilious about field placements.

(Below) **Ian Chappell.** The Australian captain certainly knows his cars, and displays the sartorial elegance of the 1970s.

Michael Holding flowing in to bowl. 'Poetry in motion.'

quite ordinary side. My one criticism on that tour was that his Press conferences were inclined to be a shade too condescending, though it must have been difficult to treat some of the questions seriously. I am sure that I would have enjoyed playing under David. All I ever wanted or expected from a skipper was a tactical awareness, ability as a player and occasional suggestions, allowing me to do my job to the best of my ability without interference. David's laid-back style would have suited my temperament admirably.

In some respects David Gower is a throw-back to the amateur of the past. His approach to life reminds me of that of Colin Ingleby-Mackenzie, who led Hampshire from 1958–65 with gaiety, humour, and considerable charm. His much-quoted recipe for the success of his team, his insistence that his players be back in the hotel in time for breakfast, would have appealed to David. Although Colin, again like David, gave the appearance of being a carefree cavalier, underneath there was a hard, realist centre. Both were of course, flamboyant and somewhat unconventional left-handers, but whereas Colin was no more than a lively middle-order county player, as a career average of nearly 25 shows, David is a high-class international batsman. Both are very good company with great joie-de-vivre, who consider good parties an essential and who open a magnum of champagne with the easy nonchalance that stems from dexterity and practice.

Neither believed in giving anything to the opposition, their tactics were never over-generous, and their field settings often tight and distinctly frugal. Both did lose their wickets from time to time with an over-ambitious stroke, but it is unlikely in the long term that they would have made more runs with more cautious methods which were foreign to their nature.

ALLAN BORDER

Little man, big heart

Just before the end of Allan Border's first season with Essex (1986), I asked Keith Fletcher for his opinion of his ability as a batsman. He thought for a moment and said that Allan was the best player he had ever batted with. That is an enormous tribute when one takes into account the number of outstanding batsmen Keith has partnered at the crease in over twenty years of first-class cricket. In addition, Keith Fletcher, like most top-class cricketers, is chary in making assessments; but his view of Allan Border certainly substantiated my own belief that the Australian is a truly great batsman, who has not always received sufficient recognition because his style is practical rather than spectacular, and rugged rather than beautiful.

At Colchester, while Allan was hitting a chanceless, almost faultless, undefeated 130 against Nottinghamshire in 1988, Graham Gooch voiced similar admiration for one master craftsman by another. He believed that Allan's success stemmed from his careful selection – he literally treats every ball on its merits. He would inspect each delivery before taking the appropriate action, whether to drive, to block, to sway, to hook or to cut, which reduced his chance of making a mistake. Another major virtue for which both Essex captains were especially appreciative and, as outstanding batsmen themselves, could appreciate better than most, was Allan's ability to make runs and come up with the big innings when it was most wanted. This is exactly what he did at Castle Park against Notts. Apart from Gooch, who had contributed an effortless 36, all the front-line Essex batsmen struggled, eventually settled, played an inappropriate shot and then departed, but Border not only prospered, he made batting look – which it certainly was not – an easy, uncomplicated business. In so doing, he underlined why he has scored, and will continue to score, so heavily and regularly. Everything about his batting is well organised and technically correct, starting with a stance with his weight equally balanced on both feet. This helps him to move either forward or back easily, which he does, like most of the finest players, very late and also ensures that his head is in alignment, and still, at the moment when bat hits ball.

One of the charms of watching Allan Border at the crease, which was especially noticeable in this particular innings, was the way he, having first assessed each delivery, obtained his runs all round the wicket, in that wide obtuse angle stretching from fine leg to third man, with sound text-book strokes. He would be quite content to play a maiden over and await the arrival of a ball, not necessarily a bad one, from which he could score without risk. Like many small men, though not so many left-handers, Allan is a marvellous square-cutter. It is not merely the power of the stroke, but the correct footwork and the way he places the shot, so that one was able to predict with confidence a boundary whenever Eddie Hemmings dropped one fractionally short outside his off stump. It was to be expected that he should be strong off his legs whether pushing, clipping the ball to mid-wicket, hooking, pulling, glancing or sweeping, as these come easily to a small, high-class left-hander. What is surprising, however, is the quality and the straightness of his driving, not of a full toss, or half-volley, but a ball which is only fractionally over-pitched. It is his driving along the ground using a full swing of the bat which makes him so difficult to contain. Another asset is the speed of his footwork which enables him to reach the slow bowlers on the full pitch or the half-volley, and explains why he is so effective against the spinners and, indeed, is not unreminiscent of Neil Harvey in his prime.

Although Australians possess probably the two finest coaches in the world, climate and space, they have an inbuilt competitive streak, and this last characteristic is why, per head of the population and including all sports, they are probably the finest sporting nation in the world. It is this attitude which fires Allan Border, makes each innings a personal challenge and helps to explain his desire for large scores. He still has an insatiable appetite for runs, which is seen in the way he scampers between the wickets in an effort to turn ones into twos, and twos into threes, irrespective of whether the shot has been played by himself or by his partner.

The respect and affection with which Allan Border is held in Essex was increased by his performance at Edgbaston on one of those notorious 'there will be no need for any declarations, and it should end early' types of pitch, which were among the least satisfactory features of 1988. He was hit on the head by a bouncer from Merrick and required fourteen stitches in his ear. I can think of a number of cricketers who would have then called it a day, but very few who would not only have come back, let alone a guest player, to win his personal battle with the bowler by scoring a remarkable century. That took more than ability, that took strength and depth of character.

At the time of writing Allan has played in 100 Tests, over 150 one-day internationals and has led Australia to victory in the Reliance World Cup in Calcutta, which was almost as big a surprise in 1987 as when India won it in England in 1983. By no stretch of the imagination were the Australians the strongest side in the tournament, and Allan Border himself is relatively more effective in first-class cricket than in the limited-overs game, for in the former he can afford to treat each ball on its merits and does not need to improvise. This does not mean that he has failed to score heavily in one-day matches, for his ability to hit all round the wicket makes containment difficult. His off-side repertoire includes the run-down through the gulley area, the genuine cut off both front and back foot, the square-drive off the back foot, the cover slash, the cover drive and the straight drive, while his on-side range is similarly extensive. Even so, his basic technique and his temperament are even better suited to Test cricket, where he has an average of over 50, despite the handicap of playing a high percentage of his matches for a weak and struggling Australia.

Australia has never had the same belief in born and raised-to-be captains which was derived from the Victorian Public School system, as England. Their selectors pick what they consider to be the strongest combination, and then decide the most appropriate skipper, working on the assumption that one of the group should be able to do a reasonable job. Sometimes they have been unfortunate, though rarely; while they have always avoided the danger of including a captain who could not justify his place as a player. Allan is not a natural leader in the Richie Benaud or Ian Chappell moulds, but he takes his cricket very seriously, is liked and respected by his compatriots and has had the considerable advantage of being easily the best batsman in a team which, at the highest level, was short of class players. It is hard to think of a much weaker Australian side (except when most of their best players had climbed aboard the Packer bandwagon), than the one beaten by England on their 1986–87 tour. However, Australian selectors are noticeably more tolerant than their English counterparts of lack of success in terms of matches lost by their skipper. They realised that waving a magic wand and changing their captain would not bring about an improvement, in fact it could have made matters worse as none of the alternative captains was likely to do any better. The reason for their lack of success, as was true of England when they played sixteen Tests without a victory, was due to an indifferent team, not a poor captain. The Australians had their reward for sticking with Allan Border when Australia won the Reliance World Cup. The manager and coach handled all the off-the-field problems which arise these days, and this allowed Allan to concentrate entirely upon events on the pitch.

Although I would prefer to watch David Gower batting I would want to have Allan in my side because, from the moment he walks out to bat after early wickets have tumbled and the bowling looks full of menace, one feels that here is the man to rescue the situation with a big innings, a fighter who revels in the challenge and who possesses the technique and the temperament to claw back the ground lost. How often opposing Test captains must have said, 'We had Australia on the floor, and then in came Border'!

3

ALL-ROUNDERS

2

THE ALL-ROUNDER

My definition of an all-rounder is a player who is able to command a place in his side for either his batting or his bowling. There is no shortage of this category in school, village or club cricket, but he becomes increasingly rare as the standard rises. The schoolboy all-rounder is in a similar position to the leading athlete who does well in every event and becomes the Victor Ludorum. However, as the competition becomes fiercer, both will probably need to specialise if they are to reach the top. In cricket it is not too physically demanding making runs and taking wickets once or twice a week, but it is different when one is competing not only at a higher level, but often every day of the week. In addition, the all-rounder has to match his skills against those of the specialist batsman and the specialist bowler.

The all-rounder knows that he will not in the long term make as many runs as a specialist batsman with the same ability, or take as many wickets as a specialist bowler of the same class. It is easy to understand, therefore, why so many first-class cricketers possessing all-round skill, especially in England where the season is so demanding, turn into either a batsman who can take wickets, or a bowler who can make runs. Nevertheless there will, fortunately, always be some players who will attempt to reach first-class standard as a genuine all-rounder, but even those who are successful could well miss being selected for their country as they have become useful 'bits and pieces' players who are not quite good enough in one department or the other, usually both, for international cricket. The value of a genuine 'bits and pieces' player to a county has been increased by the importance of limited-overs cricket. The most common, and popular, is the dependable seamer and useful middle-order bat, who is able to win the occasional one-day game with a lively forty, or fifty, and outstanding all-round fielder, as exemplified by Stuart Turner of Essex.

The value of a class all-rounder to any team is enormous, because he provides the balance which is so necessary at all levels of the game, but especially in limited-overs and international cricket. In the former five bowlers are essential, while in the latter they are highly desirable because the ideal team contains five bowlers, five batsmen and a wicket-keeper. A side which has only five batsmen is likely to be short of runs which is, of course, why Test selectors so often weaken their attacks and go for the safety of a sixth batsman. What they would like are two all-rounders who would not weaken the bowling and would strengthen the batting. The problem is that the complete all-rounder who is proficient enough in both departments to justify selection as either – Keith Miller is a prime example – is even more rare at international level, so that selectors are usually forced to rely on a specialist batsman who can bowl, like Wally Hammond or Ted Dexter, or a bowler who can make runs, like Maurice Tate or Ray Lindwall.

Despite the acute shortage of all-rounders of international calibre throughout history, rather strangely five great ones have emerged in the past twenty years: Mike Procter, Imran Khan, Richard Hadlee, Ian Botham and Kapil Dev. This distinguished quintet has three qualities in common: all were right-arm fast or fast-medium bowlers, naturally attacking batsmen, and excellent fieldsmen; they all excelled in limited-overs cricket at a time when that was becoming increasingly important; and, most remarkable of all, they could all claim to be the finest all-rounder their country has ever produced.

The all-rounder's job, especially when he is a seam bowler, is very demanding. Every player in this group, with the exception of Mike Procter, has suffered from the big increase in the number of Test matches played, let alone the seemingly endless flow of one-day internationals. On the other hand, it could also be argued, against that disadvantage, that the standard of the cricket in many of the matches was low. What batsmen would not have fancied making runs against Sri Lanka, or against Australia in 1986; and what bowlers could have failed to enjoy bowling at England or New Zealand in 1988? There is no doubt, however, that these five players would have excelled in any era, but their figures have undoubtedly been helped by their having participated in several sub-standard series, and by playing in so many Tests when they were at their peak.

IMRAN KHAN

The Islamic Paladin

Four of the best post-second world war England captains have been Sir Len Hutton, Ray Illingworth, Tony Greig and Mike Brearley; yet it would have been inconceivable, had any of them, at the height of their achievements, decided to retire, if the Queen, or Mrs Thatcher, had personally requested them to re-consider that decision, or that any cricket followers would have been stupid enough to threaten suicide if they had not changed their minds. However, this is what happened with Imran Khan, the greatest all-rounder that Pakistan has produced. It caused him to come out of retirement to lead his country against the West Indies in what proved to be one of the best series in the last decade. It underlined the difference in outlook which exists between our two countries for, in Pakistan, cricket is regarded as more than a game, and has become a political vehicle. It also illustrates that the ability of a captain to be successful does not only depend on the quality of his players, but also on how his particular brand of leadership is received by those under his command. For Pakistan Imran Khan was the ideal leader, and it could be that he will make more come-backs than Frank Sinatra.

Imran Khan's cousin, Majid Khan, was one of the finest, arguably the finest, of the post-war Cambridge University captains; but his laid-back style, which went down so well with the undergraduates, did not succeed at Glamorgan. His talents as skipper were also largely ignored by his country, perhaps because Pakistani cricketers respond better to a more positive form of leadership, which Imran Khan supplied with great success in 1987, when he became the first Pakistan skipper to win a series in England. He could have achieved this back in 1982, when England won a close three-match series by two Tests to one, but that was the first time he had led his country. Not surprisingly he made several mistakes, though as an individual he had a splendid tour. Captains, like wine, tend to improve with the years, and in 1982 Imran's inexperience showed, though he was desperately unlucky to lose the services of Sarfraz Nawaz. If Imran had been able to share the new ball with him, instead of with Ehtesham-ud-Din, who at gentle medium pace was totally unsuited to conditions which were tailor-made for high-quality seam bowling, Pakistan must have won the final Test. Nevertheless, the failure of Imran to realise how useful Mudassar could be with the ball in these circumstances was a surprising error, especially as he had picked up six wickets for 32 in the previous Test. However, his biggest mistake occurred in the first Test at Edgbaston, when he allowed the England tail to stage a rally through persistent short-pitched bowling, which seemed more interested in scoring direct hits on the two Bobs, Taylor and Willis, than in bowling them out. Imran also allowed himself to become embroiled in umpiring protests, which achieved nothing apart from controversy, but he never spared himself and his efforts in all three departments were outstanding by any standards.

It was a much more mature Imran who led Pakistan in 1987. In addition to his being the most accomplished player of the side, he had the advantage of also being the senior, the most experienced, and the best educated as well as coming from one of the great cricketing families which, unlike that of Hanif Mohammad, a former captain, was also wealthy. His background was upper-class. His forebears had been brought up to rule. As a result, making decisions and issuing orders came naturally to him, and were accepted by his team in rather the same way as a private automatically obeys the orders of the officer in charge. Imran was in complete and unquestioned control, and his manager was always at hand to carry out his instructions. He certainly possessed more power than any England captain since the war; indeed his position might almost be termed feudal, not unreminiscent of Lord Tennyson in the 1920s. Also, because Imran never abused his authority, he commanded from his players far more affection, awe and respect than any England captain could expect, or indeed hope, to obtain. One gained the impression that many of his side regarded him almost as a god, and he certainly possessed the features of a classical hero, an extremely handsome head supported by a magnificent physique. Tall and perfectly proportioned, he was an outstanding athlete, with the grace and the strength of a tiger, which inevitably attracted the most discerning females. One can imagine him leading a magnificent, explosive charge of Saracens during the Crusades, while the competition to join his royal harem was bound to have been fierce.

Like Mike Procter, Imran's stock delivery was the late in-swinger, but unlike Procter's, whose in-swing was the result of being very open-chested at the moment of delivery, he had a copybook action, with his body turning sideways during his high jump, with his eyes looking over his left shoulder, before he came down on his right foot and moved into an orthodox delivery stride. This made his pronounced in-swing unexpected, though not unknown, as Alec Bedser also bowled in-swingers using a classical action. The big advantage of Imran's technique was that it allowed him also to move the odd ball away from the bat, or at least to hold its own, which gave him greater variety than Procter. His exceptional speed was derived from a long, fast approach, a good but slightly complicated body action and perfect timing at the moment of ball release. When this last factor did not co-ordinate his line and length was liable to stray. He never achieved the grooved action and the discipline of Dennis Lillee or Richard Hadlee in their later years. Imran has also suffered from insufficient support and consequently was often used in long spells, even though he was more effective when employed in short bursts.

One can never finally tell what Ian Botham will achieve, and he might still become a great, as distinct from a spectacular, batsman. At the moment of writing, however, I would rate

Imran Khan as the most accomplished batsman of these five superb all-rounders, yet he will be remembered most for his feats as a fast bowler, despite playing some magnificent innings, especially when Pakistan were in trouble, including his first Test century against the West Indies in Lahore in 1980–81, and a memorable and undefeated 72 at Melbourne in 1983–84 after making 83 in the first innings.

This failure to appreciate fully his batting skills has been due to four factors. First, a great fast bowler will usually play a more decisive part in winning Test matches than a great batsman. Second, Imran is, to date, the only outstanding fast bowler from Pakistan, whereas they have produced a number of outstanding batsmen. Third, their team, on good pitches, has seldom been short of runs, so that it has often been unnecessary for Imran to play a big Test innings, or indeed feasible, as so many runs were on the board by the time he arrived at the crease. I have no doubt, however, that if Imran had concentrated solely on his batting he would have gone down in history as one of the finest, possibly the finest, Pakistani batsman. As it is, his present Test career batting average of 31.50 is unremarkable until one puts his 7319 runs alongside his 334 wickets at an average of 21.91 and the fact that he has taken five wickets in an innings on twenty-three occasions, and ten or more wickets in a match on six occasions. Fourth and last, the strain of being a genuine fast bowler, often with inadequate support, meant that Imran was frequently overbowled, so that he was often physically and mentally exhausted by the time he went out to bat. It is certainly very satisfying to send down 30 overs and take 5 wickets for 70, but it does not constitute the ideal preparation for a Test-match century.

This factor especially applied to Imran, because he takes so much out of himself when he is bowling flat out. All genuine fast bowlers, of which he is one, require a run-up to provide their body action with the impetus to produce great pace, but few depend quite so much upon it as Imran. Frank Tyson, for example, was as fast off thirteen paces, as well as being more accurate than off thirty, while Fred Trueman, Richard Hadlee and Andy Roberts were at their peak using a controlled approach. However, Imran is one of the group of those who, like Bob Willis, needed a long, hectic gallop up to the stumps to reach maximum speed. This was very exhausting and, combined with his high leap into the air, was why Imran damaged his leg and why he had problems if he was expected to send down 800 overs in a county season. This explains why he has usually looked far more formidable in Test cricket than for Sussex, where the stage and the audience were both too small to show him at his best.

IAN BOTHAM

'Both'

The first time I heard the name of Ian Botham was in Chalkwell Park, from the lips of Brian Close, then captain of Somerset. Apart from Close's expertise on every aspect of cricket, he had at seventeen been the most naturally gifted cricketer I ever encountered at that age, which gave him an obvious advantage when assessing a teenage player, as he was able to use himself as a yardstick. When Brian Close spoke in such glowing terms of Ian Botham's potential, I knew that he had to be very special, and this was, of course, more than borne out by his deeds for Somerset, and later England. Like most great players he established himself as an integral part of the National XI by the time he was twenty-one, and he soon became the best all-rounder in the world.

As a former all-rounder myself, I have followed Ian Botham's career with especial interest, and have been able to appreciate his combined skills more than most. It is not merely the wickets he captured, the runs he scored and the catches he took, but the grand manner in which these were achieved that made him unique and explains his immense popular appeal. I have always been among his greatest supporters because, in addition to his enormous ability, he has shown in his cricket certain virtues which I admire and salute – courage, determination and unselfishness. Unlike so many pace bowlers, Ian has never been frightened by bouncers when batting, and is prepared equally to give and to receive. He does not let minor considerations – such as a bruised and bloody toe when bowling, or a chipped finger when batting – prevent him performing. He has always been a team man, willing to sacrifice his wicket. The numerous records he has acquired have occurred in the natural context of matches, not by calculated pursuit.

In addition to his love for all sport, but especially cricket and football, Ian believes that life is for living. In his somewhat boisterous pursuit of happiness, he has almost become to cricket what Errol Flynn was to Hollywood. This inevitably has led to a number of clashes with authorities, who understandably have found his joie de vivre excessive, while too often he makes the headlines for the wrong reasons. What worries his supporters is that anyone with his generosity, loyalty to friends, and exceptional ability should be in trouble quite so often. One reason seems to be that, although he plays cricket largely by instinct, off the field it is usually wiser, certainly safer, to think carefully before pursuing a course of action. The other, and more disastrous reason, is that he has frequently been unwise in the company he has chosen or acquired, who have exploited his inability to resist a challenge.

As an all-rounder cricketer Ian Botham has more than enough work to do and, although the captaincy would have been an additional load, I believe he could have made a good England captain, certainly a better one than several of those who have followed, and will follow him. The problem was that our selectors entrusted him with that job at entirely the wrong time, when he was not only too immature, but had little experience of leading a side in the field. He was also given the impossible task of beating the West Indies with an indifferent side, so that the outcome was a predictable disaster, a perfect example of asking too much too soon.

If Botham had only been made captain of England at thirty, it might have been so different. He would still have been hungry for the supreme honour in the game, but far more experienced. He might have done well, as a flamboyant leader from the front, for he possesses a much deeper knowledge of the game and its tactics than is generally realised. The responsibility at thirty might also have curtailed, or at least reduced, the number of off-the-field incidents. Even Ian might have realised that a captain of England cannot afford to become involved in too many brawls and bacchanalian parties, though it must be admitted, sadly, that his record over the past decade hardly supports that view, and he still shows few signs of growing up. When, as an unknown nineteen-year-old he was reported as having 'thumped' Ian Chappell, then captain of Australia, nobody was especially concerned, indeed many were distinctly amused. However brawling on an aeroplane, damaging property, and hitting an over-zealous policeman, reveal flaws which darken his brilliance as a sportsman, and cannot be camouflaged by his great fund-raising efforts for leukaemia research.

Raising money for charity is a very worthwhile exercise. In the process, providing it receives sufficient support from television and the rest of the media, it will also make the front-man more famous and popular. Bob Geldorf's efforts, for example, on behalf of the starving in Africa turned him from another rock star into an international celebrity, almost a saint, albeit a plaster one. The 'Botham Walks' have provided vast sums for leukaemia research and more coverage than many England teams would receive, or indeed have deserved, on tour.

In addition to several instances of lack of control, Ian has become over-sensitive to criticism, and appears to believe he is the innocent victim of media plots. It has been said that if you live by the sword, you must expect to die by the sword. As the media, especially television, are stronger than the sword, anyone who depends as much on them as Ian does should expect to be attacked by them if ever he steps off the 'straight and narrow'. It may be unfair, but Ian's attitude of 'get stuffed' in answer to attacks hardly helps. It was difficult to avoid a wry smile on hearing that, after his contract with Queensland had been cancelled, he said that it would allow him to spend more time with his wife next winter.

Since he made his debut for England in 1977 Ian Botham was, for the next decade, by far the most important member of the side, and certainly the one most likely to win a Test match. He has been England's most successful all-rounder in international cricket in this century, with the figures to support that claim. At the time of writing he has made 5057 runs, taken 373 wickets and held 109 catches. However, my assessment is not made just on the basis of statistical records. For example, Ian Botham has captured more wickets than any other English bowler in Test cricket, yet not by the widest stretch of the imagination was he the finest bowler we have produced since the war, let alone since 1900. In addition, he has already scored more runs than Patsy Hendren, Maurice Leyland and Tom Graveney, without being as good a batsman. On the other hand, at his peak he was certainly England's best all-rounder, a match-winner, worth his place for both his bowling and his batting.

The outstanding feature of Ian's bowling has not been the size of his haul of wickets, but his high striking rate. This was noticeable from the outset of his international career. In his first Test at Trent Bridge, in July 1977, when England beat Australia by seven wickets, he took 5 wickets for 74 runs in 20 overs. In his second, which was won even more handsomely, he, in the role of third seamer, took 5 for 21 in only 11 overs. What put him so far ahead of the other accomplished fast-medium bowlers at that time, like Mike Hendrick, Chris Old and John Lever was the number of times that he secured five or more wickets in an innings, something which Hendrick failed to achieve in twenty-three Tests.

There were five reasons for Ian's striking rate in terms of wickets per overs bowled, for which he has been called the 'man with the golden arm'. First, he has always been essentially an attacking bowler whose main objective has been to remove, rather than to contain, batsmen, an increasingly rare virtue in the age of limited-overs cricket. This, incidentally, explains why he has been relatively more effective as a bowler in Tests than in the one-day game.

Second, in his early years Ian not only possessed a late out-swinger, but also appreciated that it paid to bowl a full length; the half-volley which swung late might be driven for four runs, but it was also far more likely to take a wicket than a ball which pitched just short of a length, a lesson which Ray Lindwall had also learned. In addition, Ian acquired a very good in-swinger, so, unlike the typical English seamer who depended largely on movement off the seam, he had the ability to swerve the ball in the air. This was especially valuable, as had been demonstrated earlier by the two Australians, Bob Massie and Gary Gilmour, as batsmen do not encounter many bowlers able to swing the ball late, either way.

Third, Ian has an exceptional physique which, combined with an economical run-up, has meant that he has been able to maintain his pace for long periods; indeed, when he was taking wickets (and sometimes even when he was not) it appeared very difficult to prise the ball from his hand. One can only take wickets when one is bowling!

Fourth, due to his Rambo-style image, and some of the less savoury incidents in which he has been involved, there has been a tendency to underestimate Ian's intelligence. This is a mistake for, though Ian is a natural cricketer, he thinks about the game and knows a great deal about it. When bowling, he is always eager to experiment in the hope of taking a wicket, even if in the process he concedes some runs. He has a well-disguised slower ball, uses the crease, changes his pace and, although his bouncer is certainly not the most lethal in the business, it has, perhaps because of this, brought him a remarkable number of victims. So many batsmen have been unable to resist the bait and paid the penalty.

Finally, and perhaps most important of all, is Ian's confidence in his own ability and his belief that he will dismiss batsmen. This is why I would always be tempted to put him on when all seems lost. A classic example occurred in the Edgbaston Test in 1981 when the Australians appeared to be cruising home; Botham was given the ball and took the last five wickets for 1 run in 28 balls.

A combination of a lifestyle not entirely conducive to sport at the highest level, increasing age, the strain of trying to demonstrate for year after year that he is the best all-rounder in the world – which he probably was for five years – and too many international matches and tours have inevitably taken their toll. It is fair to say he is no longer the force he once was as a bowler. I noticed the decline for the first time during the 1982–83 Australian tour, when his out-swing was not moving, his bouncer had lost its snap and, on the few occasions when he did beat the bat, the ball was not hitting Bob Taylor's gloves with a real thwack. I wondered what was wrong.

The answer was obvious. After a marathon spell, in which he never once moved the ball away in the air although the conditions were favourable, he used an abbreviated run-up and, at little more than medium pace, immediately swung the ball away. His problem was that he had simply lost his timing, so that he was not releasing the ball at the right moment and his body was opening up too soon. Foolishly, some people immediately wrote him off. He answered them by coming back after a winter's rest, in the summer of 1985 against the Australians, not in his normal role as third seamer, but, Bob Willis having retired, as England's fastest bowler. He charged up to the wicket relying on his strength, and though he did not move the ball as much as he had done in the past, as his body was less supple, he was consistently quicker than at any other time, finishing with 31 wickets and sending down more overs than anybody else. He was never fast in the sense that Michael Holding or Malcolm Marshall were fast, but he was distinctly sharp. On the other hand, I believe he would have found it impossible to have maintained that pace if he had to bowl a large number of overs, as there is a considerable difference between bowling flat out for, shall we say, 300 overs in a season and maintaining that speed over, say, 900 overs in a season. Since then his bowling has been noticeably less effective, and it was sad to see him struggling, though bravely as always, against Pakistan in the final Test at The Oval in 1987, when he not only became the first Englishman to concede over 200 runs in one innings of a Test, with his three wickets costing 217 runs, but the runs flowed at more than four per over.

As a batsman, Ian Botham is one of the few players who

has the ability to change the course of a Test in a short time against a reputable attack by orthodox aggression, not slogging. There is invariably a hum of excitement whenever he walks to the crease, as the crowd hope that they are about to see Ian unleash one of his major assaults which offer marvellous, unforgettable entertainment. In my opinion, Ian Botham is likely to be remembered more for his batting even than for his all-round skill, because he is a pure-bred hitter, an even rarer species in international cricket than great all-rounders.

I term Ian a 'pure-bred hitter' because he is a technically sound player who uses correct footwork and the full face of the bat in both attack and defence. He should never be confused with a slogger, who swings across the line. Because of this correctness, Ian hits centuries as well as exhilarating thirties, the two finest examples being against Australia at Headingley in 1981, when all seemed irretrievably lost, and at Old Trafford in the fifth match of the same series. It also should be remembered that, in 1985, he scored five flamboyant hundreds for Somerset. The nearest England has had to a batsman-cum-hitter capable of contributing major innings at both Test and county level was Gilbert Jessop before the first world war.

This immediately invites two questions. Why has Ian been so successful and why have not more players become orthodox hitters, as their match-winning potential is so valuable? There are several reasons. First, Ian's success stems precisely from his being a technically correct player with a sound defence, and exceptional ability. He finds it hard to resist a challenge, which can be seen in his instinctive reaction to a bouncer and his fondness for the reverse sweep. He enjoys living dangerously, but in the main he hits straight.

Second, as an all-rounder who normally bats in the middle of the order, failure to make runs is of less importance than to a specialist batsman, who must produce the figures if he is to hold his place. Also, in the middle order there is less chance of playing a big, long innings, because, if the pitch is easy the early batsmen should have already climbed aboard that run-galleon. It follows that any sensible captain will encourage a hard-hitting middle-order all-rounder, because he is ideal for pressing home an advantage from a position of strength, chasing runs against the clock, and capable also of occasionally producing a major innings which can win a match.

Third, the spread of limited-overs cricket has not only increased the value of the genuine hitter, but has also exposed the vulnerability of good bowlers when subjected to an uninhibited attack by a high-class stroke-player on the rampage. This applies just as much in Test matches as in the one-day game, perhaps more so because it is far rarer. Ian's aggressive approach, combined with his ability to hit boundaries off good-length balls, upsets a bowler's rhythm and, after only one four, it has often caused opposing captains to switch immediately to the defensive.

Fourth, Ian is exceptionally strong, and this, combined with his sense of timing, means that he is able to hit a ball considerably harder and further than most batsmen. It also reduces the risk in hitting sixes, for which he has a distinct partiality, as he showed by striking the highest number ever of sixes in an English first-class season. To reach the boundary full toss on a reasonably sized ground most batsmen require to hit and time the ball perfectly, otherwise there is a danger of holing out in the deep. This is why Sir Donald Bradman, who, of course, played at a time when boundaries were bigger, largely removed the six from his repertoire as an unacceptable risk. Because of his physique, combined with his very heavy bat, Ian is able to mis-hit a six, as he demonstrated so well when he once top-edged his sweep at Headingley, but the ball still sailed into the crowd. On the many occasions that Ian middles a hit, it does not just drop over the boundary, it will soar high into the stand, even on a big Australian oval, while on the postage-stamp ground at Taunton, it is liable to disappear into the town. Sixes have a primitive appeal and the ability of Ian to supply them in quantity is yet another reason for his box-office success.

Fifth, for a decade with Somerset Ian had the fortune to

play alongside Vivian Richards, who on numerous occasions gave practical demonstrations of how to destroy an opposing attack.

Finally, Ian was born in an era of limited-overs cricket, which requires the extravagant strokemaker. Runs have to be gathered quickly, and when this happens it is noticeable that the bowlers do not bowl so well.

In addition to his attacking bowling and batting, Ian is a superb fieldsman with remarkable agility for a big man, extremely fast reactions, and a very dependable pair of hands. In the slips he has brought off many brilliant catches off the pace bowlers, and made them look easy, but he is also outstanding when fielding to the slow bowlers, which is far more difficult. A purist might fault him for adopting a half-bend position with the palms of his hands resting on his knees, and though no coach would advocate this stance, as long as Ian keeps catching the ball nobody can really complain. At second slip to the quickies, he stands very close, frequently ahead of his wicket-keeper, which means that it is possible for him to take the catch which would not have carried if he had adopted the normal position. Conversely, though, it must make a very fast edged ball more difficult to see. Inevitably, he is an expert, and fearless in the suicidal 'bat-pad' position. Anticipation combined with a fast, accurate throw means that he is very good either at 'saving one', or out in the deep, where he is far faster over the ground than one expects. Like most bowlers, he is superb when fielding to his own bowling; indeed it is difficult to think of any bowler who has been his superior.

Ian Botham would have made an enormous impact on the game whatever the era, because his all-round skill, physique and presence gives him special star quality; but he also arrived on the scene in what might be termed the age of the sporting personality. This has enabled sportsmen, not just cricketers, to exploit their ability commercially on a much larger, and more rewarding scale than had been the case previously. The outcome was that Ian became not only England's finest all-rounder, but also the biggest name in cricket since W. G.

Grace in the previous century and Sir Donald Bradman before the last war. His fame was not entirely due to cricketing prowess, however, as Sir Gary Sobers, who was an even more distinguished all-rounder, never acquired as much international recognition and received far, far less money.

The new lucrative world which has opened to top athletes has stemmed from a combination of sports sponsorship, heavy marketing, the media, above all the 'box'. Television has turned news-readers, chat-show hosts and even weathermen into instantly recognisable personalities able to command large fees for personal appearances and endorsing goods, and it has done exactly the same for sportsmen and women. The more frequently they appear on the screen, the greater the demand to endorse, to promote and to become involved in an array of highly remunerative extra-curricular activities, including television advertising, which then increases exposure still further. Non-cricket-lovers will recognise Ian Botham immediately, not for his skill with bat and ball, but for the difficulty he experienced with that third Shredded Wheat, while the general public has been so well fed by the press, including the paper for whom he provided a ghosted column about his activities both on and off the field, that he has become a household name. He can afford a lifestyle very different from that of his cricketing predecessors, none of whom could have afforded to take a personal suite at a hotel during an overseas tour, or employ a virtual 'minder', nor would they have dreamed of so doing.

These are the results of the increased fame and fortune now available, but there is a price to pay which, strangely, a number of our cricketing stars, including Ian Botham and Bob Willis, have strongly resented. They cannot understand that their private, as well as their sporting lives, have become general news, and they become incensed by the criticism they receive for incidents which occur outside cricket. What, it seems to me, they never took fully into account was that England's playing record over the past decade has, in the main, been disappointing. When a team does badly the media will attempt to provide some reasons, in addition to lack of ability. The players must automatically then expect to be censured for such things as anti-social behaviour, lack of discipline, failure to practise, indulging in parties and 'la dolce vita' generally. In contrast, the side that is perpetually winning can 'get away with murder'. A batsman who arrives at the ground in his dinner jacket and scores a century is a hero, but woe betide him if he fails. The same applies to the bowler who captures seven wickets to win the match, even if he has been involved in an all-night party. Bad news usually commands bigger headlines than good news. '*Botham batters hundred in 45 minutes to win game*' would receive less coverage than '*Botham batters Beauty in burlesque brawl*'.

MIKE PROCTER

Proctershire

Where and when a cricketer is born can play a vital part in his career, and Mike Procter had the misfortune to be at his peak when South Africa were probably the best, and most exciting, team in the world, but had been banned from international cricket. If he had been born in any of the other Test Match countries he would probably have returned figures comparable with any of the other four all-rounders, as he was unquestionably a world-class opening bowler and a fine forceful batsman who could have earned a place in any country in either capacity. His Test career, however, was confined to a mere seven Tests, all against Australia. His figures are distinctly impressive though – 41 wickets at 15.02 runs apiece, and 226 runs with an average of 25.11 – but his ability has to be judged largely on his performances in first-class cricket in England and South Africa. These are outstanding – nearly 1400 wickets at under 20 runs each, and over 21,000 runs averaging more than 36, with 319 catches added for good measure.

The majority of the finest genuinely fast bowlers have had actions which either enabled them to make the ball leave the bat, like Dennis Lillee or Fred Trueman, or, like Frank Tyson, they have bowled straight, relying for success on occasional movement off the seam combined with sheer pace through the air. Although there have been some with rather open-chested actions, such as Bob Willis and Colin Croft, who have tended to push the ball into right-hand batsmen, there have been very few who have been genuine in-swingers, yet both Imran Khan and Mike Procter bowled really big 'in-dippers'. Unlike Imran, whose stylish body action did occasionally make the ball leave the bat, Mike Procter's in-swing was derived directly by what was perhaps best described as a 'hopper's' action. He was the only truly quick bowler I have encountered who employed this particular form of delivery.

A 'hopper' gives the impression of bowling off the wrong foot, but this is only an illusion as all right-arm bowlers release the ball off their left foot. The difference is that most bowlers either jump, spring or drag into their delivery stride and then release the ball off their left foot, whereas the 'hopper' lands on his right foot a stride early, and hops on to it again before releasing the ball off his left. This method is quite common in junior cricket, and boys who use it often appear to have 'nip off the pitch', but it is seldom encountered at higher levels, no doubt because some well-intentioned coach has made the 'hopper' change his style. I have a horrid suspicion that, if Mike Procter had been brought up in England, he might never have developed into a great fast bowler as his action would have been changed. However the 'hopper' method does have two weaknesses. First, the bowler has to rely almost entirely on his right arm and run-up for his pace, and, unlike in a text-book action, the left arm is unimportant. Second, bowling fast as a 'hopper' puts a great strain on the leg, right shoulder and knees. Mike could never have lasted as long as he did without the build and the physique of a bull. The in-swing and in-slant fast bowlers, like Bob Willis and Mike Procter, require a long charge up to the wicket to generate the speed, whereas those with classical body actions, like Dennis Lillee, Mike Holding, Fred Trueman and Richard Hadlee can afford to reduce their run-up, and remain great bowlers well into their thirties; indeed all four were better at thirty than twenty.

Using a long, spectacular straight approach prior to a disconcerting whirl of arms and legs, Mike made his debut for South Africa as what could be described as a 'tearaway' fast bowler, exceptionally quick and inclined to be erratic, but his speed through the air was such that an indifferent delivery often went unpunished. He was also fast enough to alarm the timid. Like all 'hoppers' his right arm was very high at the moment of delivery, which helped to make the ball bounce, while, like Imran Khan but even more so, he made the ball dip in late and move a very long way. As the only two top-class in-swing fast bowlers post-war, both had the added advantage that batsmen were unaccustomed to facing their particular style of menace.

The best example of the effectiveness, and the amount, of Mike's swerve occurred against Essex in Chalkwell Park in 1972, when he took four wickets in 27 balls, including the hat-trick. The fascinating feature was that all his victims were given out lbw and he was bowling round the wicket, rather like an off-spinner on a 'turner'. Mike also possessed a good bouncer, which tended to chase the right-hander who took evasive action.

As a batsman Mike was an exciting, but essentially correct stroke-maker, who, like so many South Africans, had benefited from good coaching at an early age and thus been guided out of bad habits. His ability to drive powerfully off both his front and his back foot enable him to score runs safely and quickly. Even though his bowling exertions meant that he normally batted in the middle order, he still managed to score 47 centuries in first-class cricket and his big innings were invariably entertaining. There were, occasions, however, when, confronted by exceptional pace bowling, he looked, like so many other fast bowlers, fallible.

His performances with bat, ball and in the field for his adopted county, Gloucestershire, were legendary, so that for many years the club was known as 'Proctershire'. After all, he was their most accomplished batsman as well as the player most capable and likely to produce a match-winning innings in a limited-overs game. He was also their main match-winning and feared bowler. 'Keep Procky out for his first six overs and we'll take runs at the other end' were the normal tactics.

In addition to his immense contributions as an all-rounder, he proved an inspiring captain. Like so many South Africans, he retained his schoolboy enthusiasm for the game and never acquired that overt cynicism frequently adopted by county skippers. It is background, not coincidence, that has ensured that the Greig brothers, Tony and Ian, Clive Rice, Eddie Barlow and Mike Procter all turned out to be efficient, effective and inspiring county captains. Although Mike was never a deep thinker, and lacked the subtlety needed to become a master commander at the highest level, he did a splendid job for Gloucestershire, leading from the front by personal example. If his charges into the enemy ranks may sometimes have lacked such tactical considerations as a pre-charge bombardment, covering fire or a smoke screen, they were invariably gallant and colourful.

RICHARD HADLEE

'The Hit Man'

Richard Hadlee, the finest and the fastest bowler in the history of New Zealand cricket, has captured the highest number of wickets in a Test, in a Test innings and in Test cricket. At the time of writing he is also the leading Test wicket-taker and could well be the first to capture 400 wickets in Test matches.

Originally I would have classified him as a world-class bowler who could score runs, rather than as an all-rounder as, like so many members of the pace-bowling clan, he was unhappy and uncomfortable when facing fast bowling. It became almost standard practice to bring on a quickie immediately he arrived at the crease, even if the spinners were creating problems and taking wickets. However, in addition to his ability as a cricketer, he was above all else a professional, who dedicated himself to maximising his talents as batsman, bowler and fielder, through hard work. It has paid rich dividends in terms of runs, wickets and catches, and large financial rewards too. From a happy hitter in the late order, he turned himself into a very dangerous batsman, who not only became the first Kiwi to complete the double in Test cricket of 1000 runs and 100 wickets, but in 1979–80 he scored one of the game's more improbable centuries in 92 balls against the West Indian pace quartet of Roberts, Holding, Garner and Croft on a lively pitch, which earned him a place among the great all-rounders.

He enjoyed the advantages of coming from a great cricketing family. His father Walter Hadlee was a fine stroke-maker, who captained New Zealand on their 1949 tour to England, and who went on to become Chairman of their Board of Control and the most influential person in New Zealand cricket. His five sons were all talented cricketers. In addition to Richard,

Dayle took 71 Test wickets and Barry played for his country in the Prudential World Cup.

In 1973 when Richard Hadlee first toured England as a young, erratic paceman with an enormously long run-up, whose action and speed suggested that he wanted to become a high-class fast bowler, few thought of his developing into an all-rounder, despite his hammering 46 on his debut in Test cricket against Pakistan in the same year. His batting has always been adventurous and, like most tall left-handers, his driving off his front foot between mid-off and cover was very powerful and he was not afraid to loft the ball over the boundary. His ability to gather runs quickly has been especially valuable in limited-overs cricket, and in county cricket when either Nottinghamshire was chasing a target, or needed sufficient time to remove the opposition. In 1984 he also did the double for Notts, which is an outstanding feat these days because of the big reduction in the number of first-class matches. If he had been playing for Notts in the 1950s he would merely have considered it par for the course.

Of these five world-class all-rounders, I would rate Richard Hadlee as the most formidable bowler; on occasions the others, especially Imran Khan and Botham might return more spectacular figures, but day-in-and-day-out over a decade, for both New Zealand, where the bowling in his support was limited, and for Notts, he stands out on his own in all forms of the game. Like Fred Trueman and Dennis Lillee he has improved with the years. Like them he developed into a relatively better bowler at thirty than at twenty, and for exactly the same reasons – a perfect sideways-on, disciplined action and a sensible, economical run-up. These virtues have enabled him to move the ball away from the bat, and bring the odd delivery back sharply; he did not have to strain for extra pace, and he has seldom broken down. He turned himself into the perfect bowling machine, who never wastes his energy, but bowls at the stumps and makes the batsman play, varies his pace and has a lethal bouncer which is made the more deadly because, with maturity, he does not over-use it.

Like the other members of this distinguished quintet, Richard Hadlee has been blessed with a fine physique and stamina. Handsome, with an imposing presence, he stands out and is a great asset to any team because of his ability, professionalism and reliability. He is such a good, and respected bowler that in limited-overs cricket opposing batsmen, as with Mike Procter, have usually been prepared to try and see Richard off in his opening spell and take runs at the other end. But although greatly respected, he does not possess as much warmth, charisma and sparkle as the other four. One could imagine him as a gambler on a Mississippi paddle boat in the nineteenth century, immaculate in morning suit and black hat, with a Derringer – highly professional, a winner, financially astute, a loner, and rightly feared.

Richard's approach has been similar to that of a pre-war England professional for whom the game is a serious business and, unlike that of most New Zealanders, who normally have a more amateur and cavalier approach. Richard's professionalism, combined with his determination to capitalise fully on his skill, has led inevitably to some clashes with his own Board of Control, who have been prepared to accept him on his terms, because he has been for many years their greatest asset. This helps to explain why spectators are inclined to admire him as a player, rather than to love him as a person. His contract with Nottinghamshire has also meant that his relationship with other Kiwi players has not been as close as it might have been if he had spent more time in New Zealand domestic cricket, which also applied to Glenn Turner.

Richard Hadlee has taken more wickets than anyone in the history of Test cricket at an average cost per wicket which is considerably lower than that of Ian Botham and Kapil Dev. It represents a superb performance, especially as the back-up bowling was unexceptional, unlike that of the West Indian pace bowlers, while Dennis Lillee clearly benefited by having Jeff Thomson and Max Walker in support.

What are the type of problems which confront a batsman when receiving an over from Hadlee on a pitch giving him a little help, such as at Trent Bridge? The first ball pitches on a length just outside the off stump and moves away late. The second is a replica and the unfortunate batsman is grateful that he was not a good enough player to get a touch. The third ball lands on about the same spot, but instead of going away nips back sharply. It is, of course, the fear that this might have happened to either of the two previous deliveries which forced the batsman to play at them. The fourth ball could well come straight through pitching off stump and, as a result of the line of flight, hitting the leg. The fifth might well pitch about the same spot and hold its own because of the angle it hit the seam combined with Hadlee's high classical action. If this delicious assortment has failed to produce a wicket, he could well try an excellent yorker. It will be appreciated that the ball does not always behave for Richard as intended; in other words the out-swinger could well turn out to be a 'nip-backer'; and, as they once said about Maurice Tate, if he did not know which way the ball would move off the seam, what price the batsman?

At the end of a hostile Hadlee over the batsman will not only be grateful to still be there, but will probably discover that the knuckle on the first finger of his bottom hand has been jarred by the bat handle each time the ball has hit the bat. Hadlee bowls straight, he varies his pace and he believes in making the batsman play. To him wasting effort by being off-line is an offence.

KAPIL DEV

Romantic Hero

Kapil Dev has the looks of a hero in a romantic costume drama in that never-never-land of mediaeval chivalry, where dragons are slain, castles stormed and maidens rescued. His face and laughing brown eyes are too open for the deceit and sordidness let alone the corruption to be found in most Indian films about the present day. Like his cricket, he is without subterfuge, and as gloriously irresponsible as Denis Compton.

As a result of his all-round ability, he has received enormous coverage in the media of his country, more indeed than an English cricketer of the same stature. In particular, television has meant that the shy lad from Chandigarh now has one of the best-known faces in the whole of India, and is exceptionally popular. He has done far better materially than he could have foreseen when first picked for his country in 1978–79. Visible signs of his prosperity include his handsome house and hotel, complete with a bar which has the unusual though appropriate name of 'the Sixer'. Both are in Chandigarh, one of the best designed and modern cities in the land.

When Kapil's first-class cricket began, and he was chosen to tour East Africa, he was far less sophisticated, and far better behaved, than most English cricketers of the same age, who not infrequently seem to be under the impression that they know it all and are convinced they deserve to be highly rewarded. Even when, after the retirement of Sunil Gavaskar, he became the most famous cricketer in India, Kapil retained his natural modesty, and it is pleasing to hear him still say, 'I owe everything to cricket and the game has given me immense pleasure as well as privileges'.

There has always been a shortage of fast bowling in India.

The climate and the pitches, combined with the build, temperament and diet of a high percentage of the population, are simply not conducive to speed, and in the 1960s the main job of their new-ball bowlers was often to remove the shine. But if India were to hold their own in Test cricket throughout a world in which so many pitches were sympathetic to seam bowling, and also in the one-day internationals which were becoming increasingly important, this had to change. India was blessed in the mid-1970s by the arrival of Kapil Dev.

Kapil Dev is not only the most successful all-rounder in Indian cricket, but also their best new-ball bowler; indeed the only world-class one they have produced since the 1939–45 war. I deliberately use the term 'new-ball', rather than fast, because Kapil is essentially a great fast-medium bowler, who has never been sufficiently quick to blast out opponents with sheer pace. He was sensible enough to realise this early in his career, and he only occasionally employs the bouncer. He would probably have bowled more of them if he had been brought up in England, where they are so profitable, because the quality of hooking is so much worse and the bounce less even.

Although not genuinely fast, Kapil is sharp enough and tall enough to force most batsmen to play him half-cock, or off their back foot, unless the pitch is very slow and easy. His height, combined with his classical, graceful, flowing action enables him to achieve lift, but his most important asset has always been a natural late away-swing, derived directly from his basic action. This explains why he has been so effective with the new ball. On occasions, in the Reliance World Cup in 1987 for example, he has failed to swing the ball as much as expected. This happens when his timing, at the moment he releases the ball, is slightly 'out'. Like all natural away-swing bowlers, he will also make the odd ball nip back off the seam, sometimes deliberately, sometimes unintentionally; but he goes so far round in his action that he has never been able to bowl a late in-swinger. I have experienced the same problem, and Kapil has solved it in the same way, by relying on in-slant, the pushed 'inner', and by use of the crease. It is possible to bowl the in-swinger by bringing the left foot to the left, rather than to the right, of the back foot, but in Kapil's case it would probably ruin the intricate machinery of what is a beautiful action.

Kapil's control, so essential for a fast-medium bowler, is no divine gift from Shiva, Rama, or Krishnan, but stems directly from hours of practice in his formative years. He also owes much to the advice, encouragement and suggestions he received from D. P. Azad in his early days at the Chandigarh cricket club, for he knew the correct way to coach a bowler at that stage: the bowler has to discover what suits him, his coach merely unlocks the door. D. P. Azad also recognised Kapil's batting ability, and made sure that his desire to hit the ball was not restricted by insisting that he adhered to the coaching manual. A young batsman's penchant for depositing good-length deliveries into the crowd should never be discouraged.

In addition to a smooth, elegant approach, delivery and follow-through, Kapil possesses a fine physique and stamina, without which he would never have taken more wickets than any other Indian in Test cricket. The overall standard of seam bowling in India has in fact greatly improved since Kapil arrived on the first-class scene. This was clearly illustrated in the summer of 1986 when, under his captaincy, they won the Texaco Cup and then beat England 2–0 in conditions which assisted seamers. Nevertheless, Kapil has never enjoyed the support and the penetration of a West Indian paceman, so consequently he has often had to keep bowling for very long spells and take over the role of a stock, rather than a shock, bowler. His greatest year was in 1979 when in 18 Tests he took a remarkable 74 wickets. It was a marvellous performance, but one cannot help wondering why any cricketer should, in twelve months, be asked to play 18 Tests plus a seemingly endless number of one-day internationals. It automatically devalues the standards and the importance of international cricket. It also makes a mockery of the record book. In twelve months Kapil was able to capture 74 wickets, only four less than Harold Larwood, unquestionably a greater bowler, captured in his whole Test career!

The first appearance of Kapil in a Test match was as a nineteen-year-old on the 1978–79 Indian tour to Pakistan, when the visitors were well beaten. At that time he was primarily a bowler, even though his seven wickets cost 60 runs apiece; nor did the no. 8 position in the batting order – with Prasanna, Bedi and Chandrasekhar to follow – suggest big scores. However, in the same year back home against the West Indies he not only took 17 wickets, but also averaged 65.80 with the bat and became the youngest Indian to make a century in a Test. These feats confirmed the arrival of a world-class all-rounder, but there has always been a mercurial quality about Kapil's batting. As a result he has experienced some prolonged bad patches, and has never made as many big scores as his ability warrants. At the time of writing he has made only three Test centuries, whereas Ian Botham, also a genuine hitter, has made twelve.

The inconsistency of Kapil's batting is best demonstrated by his performance on his first tour to England in 1979, and to Australia in 1980–81. In England he averaged 7.50 in 6 innings over 4 Tests, and in Australia and New Zealand combined he averaged under 10 – which hardly makes sense when one considers the runs he has scored both before and since. What were the reasons for this slump? On his visit to England he became too worried about the way the ball was liable to deviate off the seam, and although he obviously enjoyed bowling in these conditions, as a batsman he could not make up his mind whether to follow his natural inclination to attack, or to concentrate more on defence. He simply fell between the two. This probably applied to some extent in Australasia and, combined with a loss of confidence, proved disastrous. Ian Botham has also experienced batting failures, especially against the West Indies, but never on that scale. The reason stems from Ian being basically a *correct* hitter. He uses the full face of the bat for his attacking strokes more than does Kapil, whose extravagant cross-bat shots are among the most exciting in the game, while nobody else plays so well the pick-up with an angled straight bat which dispatches the ball for six over square leg with no apparent effort. It is also true that Kapil has usually played for a stronger batting side than Ian Botham, so there has been less need for his runs, but there are also many similarities between them. The most important is the way the mere sight of them walking to the crease is sufficient to fill the ground with expectation and to waken sleepers and quieten chatterers. In addition to being great all-rounders, both men are great entertainers, while their natural inclination to play their strokes and take risks has been encouraged by limited-overs cricket. If Kapil had reached the top in the 1950s and 1960s, when there were no one-day internationals and fewer Tests, so that each match had more significance than it does today, his batting would probably have been more restrained and less uninhibited. The odds are that it would have brought him more runs, but conversely provided less excitement and possibly fewer victories.

When Kapil Dev and Ian Botham were asked to captain their respective countries for the first time, they both found themselves up against the West Indies, and both came close to winning, Ian failing by two wickets at Trent Bridge and Kapil by four wickets at Sabina Park. With a little more experience each might have made the ideal start, which could have extended Ian's reign. It was inevitable, however, that Kapil would eventually become a victim of the musical chairs system favoured by the Indian selectors. Like English football directors, whenever the Indian team experiences a lean spell, they sack the captain, conveniently forgetting the occasions when they hailed him as an outstanding leader. This was the eventual fate of Kapil, but not before India had achieved two historic triumphs under his command. The first, and the more unlikely, was winning the Prudential World Cup in 1983, which emphasises the uncertainty of limited-overs cricket, because India was not the most formidable side in that tournament.

On the Saturday before the final I was at Lord's when

the news came through that India were 17 for 5 wickets at Tunbridge Wells against Zimbabwe and seemed certain to be eliminated before the semi-final stages. It was then that Kapil chose to play the most spectacular innings of his life, 175 not out in a total of 266 for 8, having gone in at no. 6 and with nobody else reaching 30. I then watched the Indians follow this up by beating Australia at Chelmsford on the Monday, England on the Thursday at Old Trafford, and the West Indies at Lord's in the final on the Saturday. It was a remarkable performance, as they started as 66–1 outsiders (and I would have wanted 100–1!) In that last week they caused three major upsets, in which their three seam-bowling all-rounders – Kapil Dev, Roger Binney and Mohinder Amarnath – all contributed major performances. This, combined with depth in batting and splendid fielding, meant that the team played above itself to achieve an entirely unexpected triumph.

In 1986 India, under the captaincy of Kapil, won the Texaco Cup and then beat England 2–0 in the three-match Test series in conditions which favoured seam bowling, something which no previous Indian team could have achieved. Although it underlined how Indian seam bowling had improved, one would need to go back to the late 1940s to find the standard of English pace bowling quite so anaemic. Kapil eventually lost his crown in 1987 when India were knocked out of the Reliance Cup in the semi-final by England, and when Australia, even more surprisingly, beat Pakistan in the other semi-final.

What does the future hold for Kapil Dev apart from more wickets, more runs, and more catches? It is difficult, indeed impossible, to forecast because, like with Ian Botham, there is that mercurial genius about his cricket which is always liable to upset predictions. Logic suggests that his bowling will become less effective – he has never been truly fast and, temperamentally, it is hard to imagine him reducing his pace and run-up, like Lillee and Hadlee, and remaining a world-class bowler. Also, his batting depends so much on eye and lacks the technique of a Gavaskar or Boycott, who could go on scoring runs into their forties and probably their fifties. Whatever the outcome the one certainty about Kapil is that he will always be treasured by those lucky enough to have seen or, even more, played against him. He brought to the game, which sometimes takes itself too seriously, a twinkling effervescence. Whether bowling, batting, or fielding he sparkled and bubbled like vintage champagne; and his smile was devastating.

4

WICKET-KEEPERS

[illegible]

No [illegible] can [illegible] a good [illegible]. Because good [illegible]
[illegible] it is [illegible] the most important person in the [illegible]
[illegible] more [illegible] qualities to [illegible]
[illegible]

WICKET-KEEPERS AND WICKET-KEEPING

No team can afford a poor wicket-keeper, because good fielding is vital and he is by far the most important person in the field. The keeper has many more opportunities to take catches during a season than anyone else, infinitely more chance to prevent runs; he is the key to most run-outs and can bring off a number of stumpings; he is, in short, the hub around which the fielding side revolves. In addition, a wicket-keeper can put a shine on the performance of his colleagues by swiftly intercepting an indifferent return and camouflaging a mistake, though he will from time to time forcibly indicate that he wants the ball to arrive over the top of the stumps.

A bad wicket-keeper is a disaster; consequently the standard in county cricket is very high. In the same way there are very few poor goalkeepers in League Football. No county can afford to have an indifferent performer behind the stumps. However, this does not mean that a great wicket-keeper, like a great batsman or bowler, does not stand out, though he does so less obviously. It is easy to appreciate an outstanding innings, or a fine spell of bowling, but a wicket-keeper can keep perfectly for six hours without a catch or stumping, having few balls to stop and no possible run-outs. In contrast, taking seven catches in an innings might well have no significance beyond the record book, if they were all straightforward ones.

The introduction of limited-overs cricket and an increased emphasis on the importance of physical fitness led to a marked improvement in the overall standard of fielding in first-class cricket; but this can hardly be said to apply to the wicket-keeping if one judges it by the performance of the keepers in the eight national teams for the 1987 Reliance World Cup. This excellent tournament witnessed much brilliant batting and the fielding was excellent, but the bowling was no more than average, often showing a surprising lack of accuracy, while the wicket-keeping was distinctly sub-standard. If I had been asked to select the strongest team out of all the contestants, I would have picked as wicket-keeper, on the form shown in that tournament, D. Houghton from Zimbabwe. Although he was a good performer and also an accomplished batsman, I would have placed him in the highly competent county category, rather than as an exceptional international. This supported my view that, one-day cricket for first-class and international cricketers has lowered the standard of wicket-keeping. In place of craftsmen, it has produced a breed of athletic fieldsmen with gloves on, who do a highly professional job of coping with fast, fast-medium and medium-paced bowling when standing back. This trend has, of course, been further encouraged by a decline in the number of slow bowlers, as well as genuine spinners.

The real test for the man behind the stumps is how he performs standing up to the wicket. How does he cope with a leg-break and googly bowler on a dusty pitch, an off-spinner on a 'sticky' or a bowler like Alec Bedser, who bowled in-swingers and leg-cutters at about the same pace as Max Walker? Bedser wanted his wicket-keeper to stand up, and I have seen Godfrey Evans catch, airborne and one-handed, a genuine leg-glide by Neil Harvey off him, a feat made all the more remarkable by Neil being left-handed.

The fact that a modern-day wicket-keeper would have difficulty dealing with these problems is not his fault, as they do not arise in his world. The leg-spinner has become almost an anachronism, at least in England; few slow bowlers spin the ball sufficiently to worry a keeper, 'sticky' wickets no longer occur, and present-day keepers automatically stand back to take even medium-paced seamers. It is easy to understand why seam bowlers and captains prefer to have their keeper standing back – his two main tasks are to take catches and to prevent byes. It is much easier to do these standing back than standing up. In addition, standing back automatically widens the catching zone behind the stumps, not only effectively providing another slip, but also simplifying the task of all the slip fielders on either side of the wicket by giving them an earlier sight of the edged shot. I used to favour my first slip standing rather wide with the wicket-keeper going for everything, as the chances of a catch by someone with gloves on diving to his right were better than those of first slip taking it low and left-handed; and that is now standard practice.

However, a truly great wicket-keeper must be consistently brilliant standing up to the wicket as well as back, which means that I cannot place any present-day keeper into this category; and over the past twenty years only Alan Knott and Bob Taylor fall into that class. I also have had to exclude Rodney Marsh, who achieved more dismissals – 302 in 83 Tests – than any other wicket-keeper. This was a marvellous feat in itself, but it was in no small way due to being behind the stumps when Lillee, Thomson and Walker were destroying opponents with bowling which naturally produced a large number of catches behind the wicket. At the start of his international career Rodney was christened 'Iron Gloves', but he improved enormously and did a magnificent job for his country as keeper, competitor and batsman; but purely in terms of wicket-keeping ability I would rate both Don Tallon and Wally Grout superior.

West Indian wicket-keepers for the past decade have spent most of their existence standing a long way back to a succession of very fast bowlers, so that their prime requirement was to possess a safe pair of hands and to be agile and fast-moving: in other words, an athletic slip fieldsman, assisted by gloves and pads, and typified by Jeff Dujon, who moves with the sinewy grace of a panther. However, for me, Jackie Hendriks was, by a considerable margin, the most accomplished keeper from the Caribbean, a judgement I make which stems very largely from having watched how he took the bowling, especially down the leg-side, when the ball turned and the bounce was uneven.

Probably the best keeper from the Asian continent, certainly the most charismatic, was Farouk Engineer, who had the good fortune, and the challenge, of operating when the three finest contrasting spinners in the world at that time were in action, often on unreliable pitches – Prasanna, Bedi and Chandrasekhar. Nevertheless, during Engineer's spell with Lancashire, although he was clearly one of the best keepers on the county circuit, he did not measure up to the standard of either Alan Knott or Bob Taylor, and this applies, in my opinion, to all the other men behind the timbers between the late 1960s and the present time. I am doubtful whether we shall see two such complete wicket-keepers again, not because those currently playing, and those yet to come, do not possess as much ability, but simply because they are unlikely to have the same opportunity, or to be set the same problems. Both Alan Knott and Bob Taylor served their apprenticeship before limited-overs cricket had imposed its stranglehold, when the pitches were uncovered, and spinners were essential and also regular match winners. This enabled them to become master craftsmen, each in his own very individual way.

As a wicket-keeper and, in his later days as a batsman too, Alan Knott was, like his Kent and England predecessor, Godfrey Evans, a 'one-off'. Alan's father had kept wicket, and he himself had done a certain amount as a schoolboy, but he joined Kent primarily as an off-spinner and chance played a considerable part in his becoming a wicket-keeper. His first appearance for Kent 2nd XI was not behind the stumps – though he did have several games for their Club and Ground in that capacity – but in a county which had produced so many outstanding exponents his potential was soon recognised. His assets were nimbleness, which enabled him to move quicker than anybody else, an instinct which enabled him to be in the right place at the right time, and a wonderful pair of hands. He often put me in mind of a small, bouncy puppet, manipulated by a genius. He seldom made a mistake, yet was still able to bring off catches and stumpings which other keepers would hardly have considered to be chances. He had style, but it was very much his own, and which he had adopted because it suited himself and his build.

In contrast, Bob Taylor had wanted to be a wicket-keeper since he was nine years old, and he arrived at Derbyshire as a nineteen-year-old to become understudy to George Dawkes, having represented the Minor Counties in first-class cricket, and after four years with Staffordshire under the guidance of Jack Ikin. When he joined Derbyshire it seemed that he would have to serve a long apprenticeship in their 2nd XI, but an injury to George Dawkes soon gave him the opportunity to take over, and he stayed for the next twenty years. He became the most stylish wicket-keeper in the country – the perfect model for anyone considering taking up a career behind the stumps, for he made even the most difficult tasks look simple. I have only seen two other wicket-keepers who were able to turn what is essentially a hard and very demanding job into such a graceful art form, Don Tallon, and Keith Andrew, who was unlucky not to have been given more international recognition.

It was the perfection of his methods which enabled Bob Taylor to improve with age so that he was a better keeper in his late thirties than in his early twenties, rather in the converse way as an unorthodox batsman, such as Denis Compton or David Gower, could find runs harder to come by in their late thirties than the text-book masters, like Sir Jack Hobbs and Geoff Boycott, who lasted well into their forties.

Alan Knott, because he was so dependent upon his agility, found it harder than Bob Taylor to maintain his peak of performance which he reckons to have been during his early and mid-twenties. He realised that he was losing a certain amount of his youthful mobility with the passing years, and he also damaged his neck in a car accident, but he largely overcame these problems by constant physical exercises designed to retain suppleness, combined with the thoughtful professionalism, which played such an important part in his career. Although he was unable to do certain things in his thirties which he could do in his twenties, it never showed because he did not attempt the impossible, while his positioning, like that of Peter Shilton in goal, improved so that he was even less likely to make a mistake. There are several similarities between keeping wicket and keeping goal, including the need for fast reactions, agility and plenty of 'guts' (in the Royal Marines termed 'moral fibre'), but by far the most important was less bringing off that brilliant catch, but *never, or hardly ever making an avoidable error.* As a result, Alan Knott became an integral part of the England team, and remained an automatic selection until he joined World Series Cricket and, later, went on that rebel tour to South Africa. This was when Bob Taylor, for so long his understudy, was given the opportunity to take over as star, a role he played with distinction and style.

A top-class international cricketer has always had to spend a large portion of his life away from his home and, though this is a marvellous experience for a fun-loving bachelor, it inevitably puts some strain on a marriage. Both Alan and Bob were helped to avoid this particular problem by their both being religious. Yet, like in their style of keeping, there is a considerable difference in their choice of faiths, Alan being a born-again Christian and Bob embracing the more disciplined Roman Catholic Church as a convert. Their faith helped achieve marriages which worked, though the most important factor undoubtedly lay in their choice of partners.

Going on tour and having to remain on the sidelines for the major matches is a depressing experience for anyone, but it is far worse for the second keeper in the party, as he knows that his chance of selection is most unlikely to occur unless the first choice is injured. Bob accepted this thankless role with the grace which typified his skill, underlining that, in addition to being the number two keeper in the world, he was, and has remained, one of cricket's gentlemen. He has shown that it is possible to remain unaffected by fame and fortune. I was particularly impressed by the way, when rain held up play in a Benson & Hedges game in Scotland, he spent his free time coaching youngsters. However, if I was picking one keeper for my World XI from this period, it would have to be Alan Knott; after all, for more than a decade he was the first choice of the England selectors and captains, because initially he was a shade better, he kept regularly to Derek Underwood and, above all, was a very good batsman at Test level.

ALAN KNOTT

'Mr Callisthenics'

In 1984 I watched Kent beat Glamorgan by 52 runs in a one-day encounter at Canterbury on a pitch giving all types of bowler some encouragement without ever being difficult. It was not an especially distinguished match, but it was made memorable for me by Alan Knott, who, though nearing the end of his career, gave a performance which could not have been equalled by any other keeper in the world.

Although Kent possessed a powerful batting line-up, on this occasion none of their front-line players was able to provide a major innings and, until Alan arrived at the crease at no. 6, it did not look as if they would score sufficient runs. By clever improvisation, plus belligerent support from Richard Ellison, he enabled his county to pass the 200, which was always likely to be beyond Glamorgan's reach. During their reply, he took two wonderful diving catches, both in front of a non-existent second slip, made a lightning leg-side stumping off Derek Underwood, and was perfectly positioned when he ran out Davis. I gave the Gold Award to Richard Ellison, who was the top scorer with an undefeated 58 and the most successful bowler with 4 for 28, but I still regret that I did not ignore figures, and hand the award to Alan for his magic behind the stumps. His performance confirmed my belief that, day in and day out, he was the most accomplished of all the wicket-keepers I have seen since the war, and it also underlined his value as a batsman.

I had first realised Alan Knott's potential as a wicket-keeper when he came with the Rothman Cavaliers side, which I was captaining, to the West Indies in 1965. He was no. 2 to Godfrey Evans, and my team contained several other promising youngsters, including Keith Fletcher, John Hampshire and Ron Headley. What impressed me about Alan was his determination and dedication. He realised that this was an opportunity to improve his cricket and understood why I used him as a night watchman when Wes Hall was bowling on a quick wicket, always an awesome prospect. At the end of the trip I had no hesitation in telling him that the next time he went to the Caribbean, it would be with the MCC, and so it proved.

People often ask me who was the finer wicket-keeper, Godfrey Evans or Alan Knott? It is not an easy question to answer. Quite apart from the fact that they were both world-class performers, they were entirely different in method, character, build, and approach to life and the game itself. Godfrey was a breezy, bouncy extrovert, who avidly sought the good life, adored parties, particularly those which never ended, enjoyed gambling, found twenty-four hours in a day insufficient, had the ability to cat-nap in the pavilion during the lunch interval, wanted to make a million pounds, but preferably in a week, was a supreme optimist and a natural showman. He was not only very powerful, but he also possessed such exceptional vitality that he was as lively at the close of a day spent in the field with the temperature around 100°F as at the start. He thrived on the big occasion.

Alan, on the other hand, was small, rather shy, and a fitness fanatic, so that he was forever doing exercises throughout every game. An ancient panama hat, sleeves rolled down and floppy pads meant that he did not look immaculate like, for example, Keith Andrew or Bob Taylor, but he was extremely nimble and had superb reflexes, which enabled him to change direction. Despite having moved towards the off he would still manage to take a full-length catch off the inside edge outside the leg stump. He was very much a family man, as well as a Christian, did not drink, and was cautious by nature.

Quite apart from the financial aspect, Alan Knott was one of the few players who really enjoyed his two seasons of World Series Cricket in Australia. He was not bored by constantly meeting the same opposition or being in a scratch team of talented mercenaries. Although the overall standard was higher, it lacked the stimulation provided by representing England abroad, but then touring never had the same appeal for Alan as it had for Godfrey, because the latter found the off-the-field activities on tour almost as pleasurable as the cricket and he was a tonic, often a gin and tonic, for the rest of the party. What appealed to Alan about World Series Cricket was that, unlike an MCC trip, he was able to have his wife, Jan, and his son with him throughout, while the organisers looked after the wives and children far better than most Boards of Control who have always, understandably, regarded them as a nuisance. In addition, Alan's approach to wicket-keeping was so professional that he was able to maintain the highest standard whatever the game. Alan, day in and day out for Kent, was a better keeper than Godfrey Evans, but for the big occasion, and with his adrenalin flowing, I would pick Godfrey. After all, he missed nothing in five Tests on the 1950–51 tour to Australia, even though he was standing up to Alec Bedser and taking catches down the leg-side; yet in the anti-climax of touring New Zealand afterwards he showed that he was mortal.

Like every good wicket-keeper, and some quite ordinary ones, Alan Knott was brilliant standing back, where he made some of the most brilliant diving catches I have ever seen because he was so agile and quick. However, when I first saw him at close quarters, I was most impressed by how he took Derek Underwood on a genuine 'sticky' against Essex. Derek was not only turning the ball viciously, but what made the conditions really difficult for both batsman and wicket-keeper was the unevenness of the bounce. Despite this problem Alan's hands, body and pads always seemed to be in the right place at the right moment. Playing for both Kent and England for so long together meant that he and Underwood established a complete understanding, and there is no question that Alan's reliability behind the stumps was an important reason for Derek's success on all types of pitch and in many different countries, while his fine spin bowling consistently provided Alan with a large number of victims.

Each of the three great Kent and England wicket-keepers – Leslie Ames, Godfrey Evans and Alan Knott – worked with a master slow bowler, Leslie with 'Tich' Freeman, Godfrey with Doug Wright, and Alan with Derek Underwood, but there was one difference. A regular feature in any pre-war Kent scorecard was 'Stumped Ames, bowled Freeman'. After the war, though not so often, a Kent scorecard would read 'Stumped Evans, bowled Wright'; then later, even less frequently, 'Stumped Knott, bowled Underwood'. This does not mean that Alan was a less able stumper than his two predecessors, but that he had far fewer opportunities. This was due to the increase in the number of batsmen who chose to play spinners from the safety of the crease. In addition, both Derek and Doug Wright bowled at what a club cricketer would describe as a lively medium-pace, whereas 'Tich' Freeman gave the ball far more air, so that it was essential to use one's feet against him. A high percentage of the stumpings which Alan made off Derek occurred when the batsman had lifted or dragged his back foot. However, the main reason that the career Test records of Alan and Les Ames are so different – Knott: 95 Tests; 269 dismissals, 250 catches, but only 19 stumpings; Ames: 47 Tests; 97 dismissals, 74 catches, and 23 stumpings – was the big increase in the amount of seam bowling.

Although I always advocate selecting the best wicket-keeper available, it is an obvious advantage if he is also able to bat well, because this gives his side the equivalent of another all-rounder. In Test cricket Alan not only made five centuries, but also scored 4389 runs, including 30 fifties and an average of 32.75. He was, in fact, the ideal person to come in at the top half of the lower order.

He had three special qualities: first and foremost, he positively relished a crisis and possessed the moral fibre and the ability to frustrate the most hostile pace bowling. He demonstrated this against Australia in 1974–75, when he scored 638 runs and withstood the Lillee and Thomson barrage more effectively than anybody, apart from Tony Greig and

John Edrich. Second, he had the skill and temperament to 'drop anchor' when required. Third, he was also capable of scoring runs very quickly, not by hitting but by brilliant, often positively impish improvisation, as he showed in winning the Walter Lawrence Trophy for the fastest century of the 1976 summer against Sussex at Canterbury.

Like his keeping, but far more so, his batting style was highly individual and unorthodox. As a thinking and intelligent professional, he simply worked out methods which were the most suitable for him. The fact that these did not appear in most coaching manuals meant that they made bowling against him more difficult and frustrating.

In batting Alan Knott employed an unusual grip. The *palm* of his left hand, rather than the back of his left hand, faced up the pitch, which meant that he relied very largely on his right hand to supply the power for his strokes. Like many small men he was very quick on his feet, and unlike most of his colleagues, he was prepared to attack the Indian spinners by going down the pitch against them, refusing to allow Bedi and Prasanna to dictate, while like most keepers he was skilled at picking the googly early. His grip enabled him to give with his left hand against the sharply rising ball and to drop it dead, sometimes when both his feet were off the ground. His right hand being guide and master meant that he became not only an especially good cutter, who was able to answer the threat of a ring of encircling slips and gulleys by deliberately steering the ball over the top, but he was a master of on-side placement.

Alan has always been a thinking cricketer. If I ever wanted a judgement on the ability of a batsman, bowler, or a wicket-keeper, he would give an assessment which would be accurate, concise and scrupulously fair. He is certainly the type of person who, although he has retired, still has much to offer to the game. He has probably forgotten more about first-class cricket than many of our county coaches have ever known. I believe he would make a very good selector.

5

BOWLERS

BISHAN BEDI

Ageless magician

As a child it seemed to me that left-handers were not only different, they were also more elegant. Left-hand batsmen all appeared to possess an attractive follow-through, and the bowlers had aesthetically pleasing actions. Maybe I was lucky to see Frank Woolley, Bill Voce, Nobby Clark and Hedley Verity before the war, but afterwards this belief persisted even when it did not always apply. Beautiful was hardly an appropriate description of 'Slasher' Mackay of Australia at the crease, while Alf Valentine's bowling action was positively crab-like; but there were still sufficient left-handers around to support my view – Alan Davidson, Dick Howarth, George Tribe and now Wasim Akram with the ball; Neil Harvey and David Gower with the bat; and the most graceful of all-rounders, Gary Sobers. It was certainly more than borne out too by Bishan Bedi, who represents my 'dream' left-hand slow bowler.

Everything about Bedi's bowling, his effortless sidle up to the stumps, his classical body action and his style, were a joy to behold. His method and his skills were ageless, a subtle mixture of spin, flight and change of pace, combined with precision in line and length, so that although the game had changed in many ways, he still took wickets, and indeed would have taken wickets in any era. Bishan Bedi would have been just as at home in the 'Golden Age', when Colin Blythe, Wilfred Rhodes and Frank Woolley were weaving their spells as in the 1970s, possibly more so because back in those days the game and the outlook of the players was more romantic and adventurous. His ability to deceive batsmen stemmed from the clever way he was able to disguise the exact moment he released the ball, so that until it was on its way they were uncertain as to its length and pace.

Although Bishan could be deadly on any pitch giving him assistance, he was unlike Derek Underwood, for example, in that he was more feared on a dry wicket where the top was wearing away than on a wet one. However, as he was raised on what in the main were good firm covered pitches, he was, relatively speaking, most at home in conditions which favoured the bat, especially as he had the imagination which never allowed him to settle for the role of a negative stock bowler whose sole aim was to record another maiden over in the scorebook. His outlook occasionally resulted in arguments with some of his captains, who were inclined to think in terms of dot-balls. What they wanted was a 'Bapu' Nadkarni, because although Bedi was never less than very tidy, he was essentially an attacking bowler. This meant that he schemed, and was sometimes successful at achieving the downfall of very good players on an honest wicket, and, even when he was bent on containment, he still wanted to set traps for the unwary. If I was given the choice of being a finger spinner at any time in the history of the game, I would choose to come back as Bishan Bedi, because he was as close to perfection as anyone I have seen.

Bishan Bedi's pedigree was recognisable at a very early age. He did not require a decade to learn his intricate and delicate craft, making his first-class debut in 1961–62 when he was only fifteen, and being selected for India in 1966 at twenty. He went on to play in 67 Tests, in which he captured 266 wickets at 28.71 apiece and, if the cost may appear rather high, it should be remembered that most of these wickets were obtained on good batting pitches in high-scoring, frequently drawn games, while to average four wickets per Test is very good for a slow bowler, especially in his case, when he usually operated with two more high-class spinners who also were major wicket-takers. He was the first Indian to take 200 Test wickets.

Between 1972–77 Bishan played for Northants with considerable success, even though the home pitch was then one of the best in county cricket. In his second season his adopted county managed to finish third in the Championship, which was in no small way due to the hundred wickets he captured. He himself was fourth in the national averages and with a stronger batting line-up they could well have taken the title. Although in 1974 he again captured over a hundred wickets, a considerable number were in his capacity as a tourist for India. His total haul for the Midland county was an impressive 434 at 20 runs apiece, as, although there were more slow bowlers on the circuit during this period than at present and fewer pitches especially designed for seamers, the trend had already commenced. Strangely, Bishan will probably be best remembered for his unexpected and unwelcome contribution which happened during their first honour, the Gillette Cup in 1976, when they just beat Lancashire in the penultimate over. They would have won by a considerable margin if their captain, Mushtaq Mohammed, had not displayed tactical naivety by almost allowing his opponents to escape after his bowlers had given him control. There has always been a place for quality spin bowling in limited-overs cricket, but surely never in the final over when the team batting first has wickets in hand, had not scored as heavily as they wanted, and possessed a hard-hitting batsman at the crease. This fundamental error resulted in 26 runs being plundered off Bedi who, until that moment, had bowled quite beautifully. What made it all the more peculiar was that Dye, who had probably never bowled better in his life, had sent down only 7 overs for a mere 9 runs. There was no way that even the redoubtable Hughes would have smeared 26 runs off him with a well set field, especially as in those days there was no fielding-circle limitation.

The heavy casualty rate experienced by England cricket captains in recent years underlines that leading an international team, especially against superior opposition, is a hard, precarious and often a thankless occupation. Assessing Bishan's ability as a skipper is made even more difficult, because in addition to the many problems and pressures facing all Test captains, India is closer to a continent than a country, while over the years he was involved in several fierce rows with the hierarchy controlling the game. The most bitter was with the President, Rungata, after the disastrous tour to England in 1974, when he had so many disagreements with his captain, Wadekar. Although Hinduism is one of the more tolerant and gentle religions, being the only Sikh in a team largely composed of Hindus must surely have been something of a handicap, which was not helped by Bedi's conviction that his decisions were invariably correct and by his willingness to defend them. As a leader he was sometimes too close to those immediately under his command, and many of the minor squabbles could easily have been avoided if he had been more remote, or diplomatic. Therefore, it was no surprise that in his 22 Tests as captain incidents did take place. The most bizarre occurred in the fourth Test against the West Indies at Sabina Park in 1976. Having seen three of his batsmen seriously injured by persistent fast, short-pitched bowling on a lively wicket and unable therefore to take any further part in the contest, he declared his first innings closed with six wickets down, as a protest. He denied that he declared in the second innings, but the West Indies only had to claim five wickets as, in addition to the three casualties, nos. 10 and 11 failed to arrive at the crease, and West Indies won by ten wickets with over two days to spare. He also created something of a record in that all seventeen members of his touring party fielded during what must have been one of the most unhappy Tests in history.

Tactically Bedi proved astute and considerably more adventurous and positive in outlook than most Indian captains as might have been expected from a bowler whose main objective had always been to dismiss batsmen rather than to keep them quiet, and starve them into a false stroke through the denial of runs.

There is a real danger that a bowler captain will either over-bowl or under-bowl himself. Ray Illingworth was sometimes accused of the latter, occasionally with justification, while it was said that there were occasions when J. W. H. T. Douglas would simply forget that he was still bowling. To avoid the error of being on at the wrong time – and any true bowler should always want to bowl even when the conditions are unsuitable – I used to rely on the advice of my second-in-command. Bishan's judgement of when to bring himself on and when to take himself off was very good, though he was to some extent assisted by an acute shortage of alternatives. This was certainly the case during what was his best tour as captain, in Australia in 1977–78, a close and absorbing series, which, although India eventually lost by three Tests to two, was their most successful venture 'down under'.

However, Australia that year had lost many of their most accomplished cricketers to Kerry Packer, including nearly all their leading pace bowlers. They were forced to recall the veteran Bobby Simpson to captain their side, which he did with considerable success both as player and leader. Australian batsmen had then had little experience of playing top-class spin bowling, and it was left to their captain to demonstrate what might almost be termed a lost art. Their selectors also failed to realise, until the last Test, the advantage of including left-handed batsmen against a wrist-spinner and a slow left-hander. Bedi proved to be the main wicket-taker and the most effective bowler on the tour, with 31 wickets at 23.87 apiece in the Tests.

Bishan is a charming companion and his bowling was not only a joy to watch, but his many patkas, which he changed each session, helped to enliven the proceedings with an extra splash of colour.

DEREK UNDERWOOD

'Deadly'

It is a bonus to be different from most other bowlers, who tend to fall into a few basic categories, and it was this difference which helped to make Derek Underwood so deadly. 'Deadly' will be remembered as a great left-hand spinner with figures which more than substantiate his reputation. In over twenty years of first-class cricket, from 1963–1987, he captured more than 2000 wickets at under 19 runs apiece, while his haul at Test match level was 297 wickets in 86 Tests, which included five wickets in an innings 17 times and ten or more wickets in a match six times – very unusual for a finger-spinner. His international career included eight overseas tours, which makes a nonsense of the criticism that he was not effective abroad: a great bowler will take wickets anywhere. Derek naturally was far more dangerous on a wet pitch in England than in normal conditions at Kensington Oval in Barbados, just as Richie Benaud was more formidable in Australia than in England, while it is considerably easier facing Richard Hadlee in Madras than at Trent Bridge.

Derek Underwood would have played in many more Tests and might well have finished with over 400 Test wickets, if he had not joined Kerry Packer for two years or, later, accompanied Graham Gooch's unofficial tour to South Africa. It should, perhaps, be mentioned that the big money paid to Test cricketers did not commence until after the Packer affair, and was the result of the big influx of commercial sponsorship. This meant that, although Derek enjoyed his international cricket and tours, he never received the financial rewards which are now available. It is easy, therefore, to understand why one of the most delightful people in the game became involved in World Series Cricket. Although he had enjoyed the fun, companionship and glory of being an automatic choice for England for more than ten years, these were not nearly as rewarding in monetary terms as his 'unofficial' visits to Australia and South Africa.

The finest slow left-hand spinners – Robert Peel, Colin Blythe, Wilfred Rhodes and Hedley Verity – have all been treble-purpose bowlers. First, on a pitch that provided them with some assistance they were match-winners. Second, they could be relied upon to be economical, and were used in the role of a stock bowler, because of their complete command of line and length. Third, in addition to their control, they had acquired all the subtleties, including flight, change of pace, the arm-ball and full use of the crease, which meant that they were still effective against good batsmen even when batting conditions were perfect. These three attributes also applied to Derek Underwood, but where he differed was that his pace was medium rather than slow, his trajectory much flatter, and his break owed more to cut than to finger-spin. This aspect of his bowling first dawned on me when Derek came on a somewhat improbable tour to Cyprus and Malta with the Cricketers Club team, which I captained. We were playing against Service teams on mat pitches and, though economical as always, Derek was not causing the problems I expected, because the ball was tending to skid off the surface. My own cutters were obtaining more deviation, while a very occasional wrist-spinner was making the ball bounce and turn. I suggested to Derek that he might experiment with the occasional much slower delivery which, if successful, could provide him with an additional weapon in more serious cricket. The idea appealed to Derek, but it did not work, because at a slower pace his break did not increase, while that late dip, which the big finger-spinner obtains, was missing.

In addition to the first-class game, Derek was an immediate success in limited-overs cricket where he became probably the best 'brake-bowler' in the business. On countless occasions he would come on to bowl midway through an innings and restrain the batting side so effectively that they either dropped well behind the required run rate, or would be forced into fatal indiscretions when attempting to increase the tempo.

Derek's unusual style of bowling stemmed directly from his early, and equally unusual, arrival on the first-class scene. I first batted against him for Essex at Maidstone in 1963, when he was only eighteen. In those days he bowled medium-pace from over the wicket, tending to move the ball into the right-handed batsman and drift, or cut, some deliveries away. It was a form of attack seldom encountered in first-class cricket. In addition to the novelty, it was economical. I always found medium-paced left-handers from over the wicket – like Trevor Goddard of South Africa, Ernie Toshack of Australia, or Don Smith of Sussex – hard to score against. In our first encounter, Derek trapped me lbw for 0, and returned the impressive figures of 33–12–77–4 in an Essex total of 293 for 8 declared. Our next meeting was in the return match at Leyton, where I was able to make a prolonged examination of him as my 78 runs took me some four and a half hours to acquire. I was most impressed. Here was a young bowler who possessed the two essentials; he was economical and penetrating.

Although there were some judges, including several on the Kent committee, who failed to realise Derek's worth immediately, I was convinced that somebody very special had arrived. From the outset he 'gobbled up' batsmen quickly and cheaply. He was not only the youngest bowler to capture a hundred wickets on the circuit in his first season, but by the time he was twenty-five, in 1970–71, his total wickets in first-class cricket exceeded 1000 – a truly remarkable feat, which only George Lohmann and Wilfred Rhodes managed to achieve at an earlier age and in a very different era. It seems safe to predict that nobody will equal that particular feat; but it also underlines that not all spinners need to play county cricket for ten years before they have mastered their trade!

Derek started as a medium-pace left-armer from over the wicket with a classical sideways-on body action. Gradually he developed into a brisk spinner who operated from around the wicket and employed quite a long jog up to the stumps. He had a flat trajectory because of his pace through the air, and on good pitches he relied on a combination of unerring accuracy, slight variation of pace and a particularly effective arm-ball, a legacy from his days as a seamer. He did not turn the ball much in these conditions because of his dependence upon cut, relying more for break upon a fast-turning wrist rather than on his first finger, but batsmen always feared that he might make the odd delivery do just enough to find the edge of the bat.

On a pitch which gave him some assistance, especially if it was very wet, he more than lived up to that nickname of 'Deadly'. He could be virtually unplayable. A perfect example of the havoc that he could wreak in such circumstances occurred against Pakistan at Lord's in 1974. After a prolonged heavy shower the slope allowed water to creep under the covers on to the pitch. As a commentator for *Test Match Special*, I was able to predict not only how he would destroy the opposition, but the exact time when the pitch was ready for him to be brought on. In 6.3 overs he took 6 wickets for 2 runs, and finished with 13 wickets in the match for 71 runs.

Of all the left-hand spinners I have seen and faced on a wet pitch, Derek was the most dangerous. These even include Tony Lock in his bent-arm period, when he was faster through the air and spun the ball considerably more. What was it that made 'Deadly' so devastating in these conditions? First, there was his absolute control of line and length. Second, because he was never a 'big' spinner, he never suffered from turning the ball too much or failing to find the edge, whereas Tony Lock was liable, on a bad wicket, to pitch on the leg stump and miss the off when bowling round the wicket. Third, Derek's pace through the air not only meant that, to hit him on the full toss, a batsman had to decide to go down the pitch before the ball left the bowler's hand, always a dangerous tactic; he was also far more effective on a pitch which, for the normal slow bowler, was too soggy and slow.

In 1968 Derek bowled England to victory at The Oval after

an enormous storm on the final day appeared literally to have washed away all hopes of a finish. This would indeed have been the case had the spectators not provided a couple of volunteers to assist the ground staff. Were they inspired by patriotism, or a desire for more cricket? I have my doubts whether they would have been quite so helpful if England had been batting, or Underwood had been playing for Australia! Be that as it may, Derek predictably obliged on that sodden strip, finishing with 7 for 50, with Inverarity, who had opened the Australian innings, being last out playing no stroke to the arm-ball and providing one of the outstanding cricket photographs of all time, as it includes every member of the fielding side.

This arm-ball, one of the main weapons in Underwood's armoury, derived directly from his text-book sideways-on action, and swept in so far from outside the off stump that an unwary batsman would often have decided to cut it, only to find himself attempting the stroke off his stumps, seldom a wise policy.

It was his ability to drift the ball into the right-hander and sometimes bring it back off the pitch, which made Derek noticeably more effective against right-hand than against left-handed batsmen. The left-hander found that the delivery which pitched only fractionally short outside his off stump was cuttable, or, when slightly over-pitched, drivable. From round the wicket the ball which pitched on or outside the left-hander's off stump was unlikely to break back sufficiently to be a threat. Derek would try to counter this by going over the wicket, and bowling into the rough area around the left-hander's off stump or outside, and employing one or two short-legs. But as with the majority of leg-break and left-hand spinners, he remained much more successful against the right-hander.

Any captain would welcome having a world-class left-arm bowler in his team, but, in the case of Derek there were several additional advantages. First, his behaviour was impeccable both on and off the field, a player who simply did not know how to give less than his best. Second, he was universally respected and liked by those with whom he came into contact. Third, he had considerably more determination than many bowlers who go in low down the order, with the result that he became a regular 'night watchman' for England, because he could be relied upon not to flinch against the most hostile fast bowling. Derek, indeed, enjoyed his batting, which relied largely on three strokes – the forward defensive, the cut and the 'Underwood special', in which he shovelled the ball out to the on-side, frequently in the air, using plenty of bottom-hand. He did, in fact, once, in his later years, score a century for Kent, which surely indicated a marked decline in bowling standards! Finally, although he was never a fast mover, he became a very dependable fieldsman with a safe pair of hands and an accurate throw. Rather typically, he could never understand why any player – mind you, he did rather more work than most – should want to be a captain. If I was asked to name a model for anyone to copy in his attitude towards the game, I can think of nobody better than Derek Underwood.

DENNIS LILLEE

The Menace

The greatest fast bowlers – like Ray Lindwall, Fred Trueman, Mike Holding and Richard Hadlee – have all possessed qualities more than sheer speed, which enable them, as with good wine, to improve with age; and Dennis Lillee is no exception. They all possessed outstanding body actions, yet all were very different; Lindwall and Trueman dragged, Holding glided through his action, so that his leap passed almost unnoticed, while both Hadlee and Lillee jumped quite high before coming down on that right foot with the body sideways-on and the head looking round a high left arm. Their actions helped to provide them with pace, but also gave them control, the ability to move the ball both in the air and off the pitch, and variety. With time they all became very intelligent bowlers who were able to think batsmen out, not merely blast them out. As a result, day-in and day-out, on all types of wickets and in all types of conditions, they were at their most effective in their mid-twenties and early thirties.

In the cases of Hadlee and Lillee, both drastically cut down what had always appeared to be excessively long run-ups, although at the time they were in fashion. Certain bowlers do benefit from starting from near the sight screen, and this applied to Wes Hall, Mike Holding and Bob Willis, but the majority would be just as fast, take less out of themselves, and have more control off a shorter approach. One of the more absurd spectacles in county cricket is to see a bowler, whose pace is nearer to medium than to fast, using a run-up which is twice as far as that of Malcolm Marshall.

In addition to reducing his approach, Dennis Lillee amended his running action by holding his hands much higher in front of his chest. He found that this not only gave him more smoothness, but it was also easier for him to move into his high and spectacular body action.

With 355 wickets to his credit Dennis is one of the leading wicket-takers in Test cricket. What, of course, is the most significant feature of Dennis' performance is that it was achieved in only 70 matches, giving him a strike rate of over five wickets per Test. He also took five or more wickets in an innings 23 times, and on 7 occasions captured ten or more wickets in a match, despite the time he lost recovering from his back injury and the two years he spent in World Series Cricket. But for these interruptions his final tally would surely have been well in excess of 400 wickets.

Great fast bowlers, like heavyweight boxers, have always attracted headlines, and none more than Dennis, who had, in addition to his ability, exactly the right appearance for television, over six feet tall, heavily moustached and instantly recognisable. He became an Australian folk hero and had the business acumen to capitalise on it in an age when it paid to be controversial. He seemed to realise that a 'bad guy' image and constant disputes with the establishment, was financially rewarding, views which his principal captain, Ian Chappell, understood only too well.

How did Dennis compare with Ray Lindwall? Although Rodney Marsh, who from behind the stumps was better placed to judge Dennis' ability than anyone else, claimed that he did not bowl an outstanding yorker, something which Lindwall certainly possessed, and was noticeably less effective against left-handers, I am inclined to feel that in all conditions he was possibly even more formidable, because his action was steeper, though not with a new ball, which Ray used to swing more. Ray, despite having a good command of the vernacular, never engaged in verbal abuse, which became an accepted part of the Lillee scene, nor could one even imagine him participating in the Javed Miandad incident or the aluminium bat affair, but he did not play when television sponsorship and controversy were considered so important and profitable.

Fast bowlers have always been an aggressive breed, and Dennis Lillee was unquestionably both one of the most aggressive and one of the greatest. He did not merely dislike opposing batsmen, he regarded them as General Sherman regarded Red Indians, 'the only good Injun is a dead Injun'. This was summed up in a book, *Back to the Mark*, which appeared under Lillee's name, in which he stated that his bouncer was intended to hit the opposing batsman and to make him wonder whether it was sensible to continue, always assuming that he was capable of so doing. Not that there was anything new about his attitude or his hatred of batsmen – a good bouncer *should* hit the opposing batsman, unless he takes evasive action, fends the ball down with his bat, or hooks it successfully. The bouncer which simply flies past a batsman's head is both a waste of time and effort. The instinctive reaction of many fast bowlers has been to answer the insult of a boundary scored against them with a delivery aimed at the perpetrator's head – which is not very subtle, as one knows what to expect, but then fast bowlers have never been famed for their kindness or their intellect. I treasure the comment of a pre-war fast left-armer nearing the end of his career who, having been struck for a violent four by my partner, followed up with a bumper which was inevitably an innocuous one and which received the same treatment. His words were: 'If I was only ten f . . . (adjective) years younger, I would have pinned that f . . . (noun) to that f . . . (adjective) sight-screen.' The passion and hate remained, but the pace had gone.

Quickies have always capitalised on their ability to frighten some players, because being struck by a cricket ball travelling at anywhere between 65mph and 90mph can be a painful experience. There have been some good batsmen who never made any runs against very fast bowling, unless the pitch had been doped. One county player who scored between 1500 and 2000 runs every summer invariably failed against Yorkshire, because Fred Trueman simply rolled him over every time he ran up to bowl, but immediately Fred was omitted he produced a double-century. It is also understandable why so many tail-enders are apprehensive of anything much over medium pace, as they lack the technique to cope. The timid batsman understandably prefers to acquire a duck to being a sitting one – which he certainly would be against a bowler of Dennis Lillee's pace, accuracy and approach.

By giving in print his views on bouncers, however, Dennis did little more than provide extra ammunition for those who wish to see the bouncer eradicated from the game. It was rather like a very hard, strong tackler at football who, in the course of a season, usually manages to notch up a couple of broken legs, saying that, in addition to winning the ball when he tackles, he aims to slow down, stop, and sometimes completely terrify the opposition.

Dennis Lillee made his debut for Australia in 1970–71 in a fairly high-scoring draw at Adelaide in which the opening pair, Boycott and Edrich, shared two three-figure partnerships, but he still managed to take five wickets in the first innings. I saw him for the first time in the following Test, the seventh in that series, at Sydney, which Ray Illingworth's team won by 62 runs to capture the Ashes, and when Ian Chappell made his debut as captain of Australia. Having called correctly, Ian invited England to bat on a pitch which was tailor-made for pace bowling and, if Lillee had been mature, he would have won the match. As it was, he sprayed the ball about and tried to bowl too quickly, instead of letting the wicket do the damage; yet he was still a marvellous prospect because he possessed real pace and a beautiful action. In the following summer he signed for Haslingden in Lancashire, where his figures were unremarkable and certainly did not compare with those of numerous West Indian fast bowlers, but he learned two things which were to prove important when he came to England under Ian Chappell in 1972 – that it was necessary to bowl a fuller length, and that on a slow pitch speed alone was not sufficient. The result was that, although only twenty-two, he became the finest fast bowler in the world, taking 31 wickets in the five Tests at 17.67. What made his performance all the more remarkable was that he did not have much pace support other than Bob Massie. As a result Ian Chappell was forced often to use him in very long spells, even though he walked back 46 paces and did not spare himself in an extremely energetic run-up, body action and follow-through. It is true that his captain made sure that he did not have to bowl too much in the other matches, but only an exceptionally fit man could have maintained his speed over such lengthy periods, and the physical strain which it imposed was probably responsible for his breakdown later. I said at the time that, in my opinion, his approach was too long, but how can one criticise a bowler who produces figures like he did that summer?

What partly worried me was that children naturally like to imitate their heroes and there was a danger that we might be breeding marathon runners rather than fast bowlers. My comments on *Test Match Special* resulted in my receiving the following delightful postcard: 'You are absolutely right. My grandson, Shaun, aged three, now runs from seventeen yards before releasing the ball from three paces'. It was signed 'Worried Grandma'!

My next encounter with Dennis Lillee was in the Caribbean in 1972–73, when Australia was touring the West Indies. Although I have always been impressed by his bowling, on this occasion I was even more impressed with him as a man and the way he tackled disaster. The situation was that his previous partner, Massie, had lost his ability to swing the ball which meant that Ian Chappell had to rely upon the penetration of his leading bowler. It did not work out that way, as Dennis finished with 0 for 132 in the first Test and a damaged back prevented him taking any further part in the series. In the second Test he found himself relegated to the sidelines, a depressing position for anybody, let alone for somebody who had been hailed as the fast bowling hope his country had lacked since the retirement of Alan Davidson.

In those circumstances my reaction, I must confess, would have been to enjoy myself as much as possible, but Dennis displayed admirable character by refusing to accept, as seemed probable at the time, that his career was over before it had really begun. He was helped by always having been a fitness fanatic, and he began by undertaking every day a very long solitary jog from the hotel to the ground and back again. His injury was eventually diagnosed as stressed fractures in his back and, after a lengthy period in plaster, he was told by his doctor in his home town that the only way he could possibly return to the first-class game was literally through hours of painful body-building exercises. These would have defeated most people, but Dennis was prepared to accept them. It required enormous self-discipline as well as dedication, as there was no guarantee of success.

His return to the game could hardly have come at a better or more dramatic time than in 1974–75 when England were expected to retain the Ashes but Australia discovered a fearsome virtually unknown partner for a revitalised Lillee, Jeff Thomson (although they had opened together once previously, against Pakistan in 1972–73).

Together Lillee and Thomson sank Mike Denness and his team with a barrage of pace which would have destroyed a much stronger and braver batting line-up. It is hard to conceive of a better demolition job. Australia won four out of five Tests by large margins, with Lillee capturing 25 wickets at 23 apiece and Thomson 33 wickets at 17.93 apiece. Although England took the sixth and final Test by an innings, Thomson was absent injured, and Lillee was only able to send down six overs, and this further underlined the damage inflicted by this pair. I never encountered an England team quite so demoralised by pace until the 1980s. It would be no exaggeration to say that some of our batsmen were so shell-shocked when they returned home that they never again batted with the assurance they had possessed before that disastrous tour.

The mayhem that Lillee and Thomson created was the outcome of exceptionally fast bowling of the highest quality, but they were assisted by several other factors. First, and probably most important, was that the majority of the Test pitches were not only fast, but had an uneven bounce, which automatically made batting against quick bowling both difficult and dangerous. Second, the umpires had not read, or chose to ignore, Law 42/8 because they allowed far too many bouncers from both sides. Third, England suffered from a number of key players having bones broken. The most serious loss was John Edrich, who was injured twice, because he possessed the determination and ability to stand up to pace bowling in these conditions which several of his colleagues lacked. Finally, the crowds chanting Lill . . . Lee, Lill . . . Lee, Lill . . . Lee every time he ran up to bowl, and baying for 'Pommy' blood, produced a gladiatorial atmosphere. The Australian crowds were too like Roman spectators, in a different setting and at a different time, for comfort.

In his prime Dennis was controversial, provocative, and aquisitive. He became involved in so many incidents, including that aluminium bat and his logo-infested headband, that some people tend to forget that, in addition to being one of the great fast bowlers of all time, he also possessed a deep love for the game.

In 1988 he was signed on as an overseas player for Northamptonshire, a decision which surprised and rather baffled me because, in Winston Davis, they had a fast bowler of international calibre, and Lillee himself had retired from the first-class game several seasons earlier. Also, it seems morally wrong to spend money on two imports when only one can play at the same time for a county club. Surely it would be wiser to use it in developing local talent? True, Dennis had made a come-back with Tasmania, but to be a success in county cricket when the nip, if not gone, was not nearly as sharp as it once had been, was asking a great deal. Although batsmen and slow bowlers can flourish in their late thirties and forties, and, indeed, into their fifties, seamers, as I discovered, lose their edge. The bowling arm in pursuit of extra pace is inclined to drop a fraction, but even more irritating is that the perfect 'nip-backer', which a few years earlier would have claimed an lbw, now finds the inside edge.

We shall never know just how successful Dennis would have been as a bowler with Northants, as he broke down with a serious knee injury early in the season. He was written off medically for the rest of the summer, but, again demonstrating his remarkable determination to overcome a serious physical handicap, he was able to play in the last few matches. His final figures of 20 wickets at 36.55 were unimpressive, especially as in the 1988 season so many pitches were substandard, and Winston Davis took 73 wickets at 22.10. An initial inspection would suggest that Northants had made a mistake, which was certainly my original view, but this was one of the occasions when I am delighted to confess that I was wrong. Although Dennis did not have the opportunity to win matches for his adopted county, he still proved to be a marvellous, infectious tonic. He was a splendid coach, and his enthusiasm breathed fresh ideas and new life into the members of both the first and second elevens. His bubbling vitality, and keenness to help, proved irresistible, and the big improvement made by the young Northants quickie, Mark Robinson, owed much to Lillee's advice and encouragement which has transformed Mark into one of the best fast-bowling prospects in the land.

Dennis' final first-class appearance in 1988 was for Northamptonshire against Essex at Chelmsford. I had the good fortune – no, I must put it higher than that – I was privileged to see him bowling for the last time, the shortened but still spectacular run-up, the dramatic action and follow-through, the occasional ball which left the bat so late that even Graham Gooch played and missed, were all still there. On a slow, flat pitch and nearly forty years old, Lillee still looked the most menacing bowler on either side, which included the two England and Essex seamers, Foster and Pringle. His enthusiasm was so intense that it was easy to understand why he had been able to inspire the Northants players; and I enjoyed the way in which Allan Lamb, from his position in the slips, would from time to time indicate to Dennis that his arm had dropped just a fraction, and that it needed to be a shade higher to obtain that late out-swing which still threatened despite increasing years and a docile pitch.

ANDY ROBERTS

'Mean, moody, magnificent'

Three adjectives which describe the bowling of Andy Roberts, as they used to describe a certain film star, are 'mean, moody and magnificent'. Unlike Dennis Lillee or Colin Croft, Andy Roberts never allowed himself to be carried away by anger, frustration or jubilation, yet in his own quiet way he exuded menace, so that between 1974 and 1980 he was the most apparently malevolent of all the fast bowlers. He reminded me of an ultra-professional 'eliminator', because his expression never seemed to change – a black Charles Bronson. He certainly dropped plenty of opponents with his classical bouncer, which was always feared by batsmen. What made it so formidable was that it was not used too frequently, was nearly always well directed, and very fast.

Andy's run-up was comparatively short and straight. He belligerently bustled up, rather than ran, to the stumps. In his action his left arm was kept lower than is advocated in the textbooks, but he turned sideways in his leap and his right arm came over very high. Although possibly a shade too open-chested for text-book satisfaction, this clearly suited him, and that is what counts. It also enabled him to swing the ball away late, and to make it nip back sharply off the seam. He was essentially an economical bowler, not merely because his control of line and length was very good, but it could also be seen in his run-up, body action and follow-through. These were without extravagance or frills, and designed to achieve maximum effectiveness as simply as possible, like a bullet, and as deadly.

Like most of the great fast bowlers, he was able to resist the challenge for his virtually permanent place in the West Indies team from highly talented younger pacemen, because he had learned not to rely on speed through the air alone for his success. He could provide change of pace, including a well-camouflaged slower ball, movement both in the air and off the wicket, a very quick yorker, that vicious bouncer, and a high strike rate in terms of both wickets and felled batsmen.

Fred Trueman, in fact, claims that Andy possessed two different bouncers, giving this example from a World Series Cricket match for which Fred was providing the television commentary: Andy was bowling against Barry Richards, who, apart from being a world-class batsman, had played regularly with Andy for Hampshire. From his position in the slips, Barry had learned more about Andy's bowling and what he did than anybody else. Andy suddenly produced a bouncer which Barry swayed back from and cut down to third man. The next ball appeared to be an exact replica, but it was a yard faster, and struck Barry on the glove while he was swaying back and attempting to repeat the stroke. Before he returned to the pavilion he examined where the ball had pitched, and found that it had landed in almost the identical spot as the previous bouncer.

I watched Andy Roberts make his international debut, in the third Test at Bridgetown in 1974, on what is best described as a typical Barbadian pitch, at least up until the last ten years, in cricket parlance 'an absolute belter', which unlike today was what one expected to find at the Kennington Oval. The West Indies made 596 for 8, Lawrence Rowe scored a triple hundred, and Tony Greig gave what was surely the best all-round performance in Test cricket. Andy Roberts, who had begun his first-class career for Antigua four years earlier as a nineteen-year-old, looked, even on that featherbed, an outstanding prospect, who was appreciably faster than Holder and Julien, the other two pacemen. In these circumstances, it was surprising that the West Indies selectors should have discarded him for the rest of the series, but he came from Antigua, not yet considered a national nursery, indeed he was the first Antiguan to represent the West Indies.

In his next nineteen Tests he was to take a hundred wickets in under three years, a quicker haul than anyone's until Ian Botham's. He captured a high percentage of these wickets on pitches not designed for seam bowling and without the class support he was to receive from other quick bowlers later in his career. However, in some respects his most important contribution to West Indian cricket was that he put Antigua on the map, and this not only helped to raise the standard of the game in his island, but on the other smaller islands as well. Up until then West Indian selectors had picked their teams almost exclusively from the four principal centres, Jamaica, Barbados, Guyana and Trinidad.

Quiet and undemonstrative both on and off the field, Andy was a teetotaller, which among fast bowlers is unusual. He was the antithesis of that lively, noisy, fun-loving, Calypso-singing, rum-drinking Caribbean cricketing cavalier, who does not exist these days at Test level outside the media. West Indians have to take their cricket very seriously, otherwise they would never have produced so many outstanding players or been world champions in a competitive world. The game provides the most talented with fame and fortune, as well as an escape route from comparative poverty, so that it is played very hard. Nevertheless, the majority of the professional cricketers from the West Indies still love playing and endlessly talking about the game, but Andy Roberts was an exception here too. To him, cricket became a job and he contributed little to the gaiety and noise which is to be heard in every West Indian dressing-room. He became a fast-bowling machine who could be relied upon to take wickets, though it was noticeable that, after a couple of years or so with Hampshire, he was more menacing when playing for the West Indies than for his adopted county. There was always competition for places in the West Indian side, whereas Roberts on half-throttle was still a more formidable prospect for opposing batsmen than any of his Hampshire colleagues. His greatest value to the county was usually in one-day matches, when he knew exactly the number of overs he would send down, while he could also be a dangerous hitter in a final assault. There was, in fact, a suggestion of a machine, though of a very different type, about his batting which had a distinctive, jerky, robot-like, stop-stop-biff-biff-stop-bang rhythm.

Withdrawn and lacking the warmth and the laughter normally associated with West Indian cricketers, when Andy walked out on Hampshire in the middle of the 1978 summer, apart from his ability as a player he was hardly missed by his colleagues or the county's supporters. Rather strangely and sadly, though for different reasons, the same might be said to have applied to Barry Richards, who also walked out on Hampshire that same summer. The team's reaction to the departure of these two most talented cricketers provided the perfect response. They won the John Player League.

By 1978 the strain of fast bowling for the West Indies and Hampshire had taken its toll on Andy Roberts, even though, after that wonderful first season of 1974, his effectiveness for his adopted county had noticeably decreased. In that summer, he was the only bowler to capture over one hundred wickets and he comfortably topped the national averages at 13.62, while in county Championship games his figures were:

658.4 overs 178 maidens 1493 runs 111 wickets av. 13.45,

unquestionably one of the outstanding feats ever of fast bowling in county cricket.

There were several reasons why he was so devastating in 1974 County matches. First and foremost, he was a world-class bowler at the peak of his form. Second, it was his first season on the circuit, and few of the batsmen had faced him before. Third, he was keen to make a good impression. Fourth, Hampshire – having rather surprisingly carried off the Championship in the previous season, in spite of the fact that their attack lacked penetration – were expected, with Roberts in the team to provide that extra bite, to repeat the performance. Until August they carried all before them, only to be robbed most cruelly in the closing stages by the weather. The situation meant that even two 'mercenaries' such as Andy Roberts and Barry Richards had to be affected by the enormous enthusiasm displayed by the other players and their supporters. The club was unaccustomed to being considered the best team in the land, which, though it finished second, it undoubtedly was, so that everyone fancied its chances again for 1975. Surely even English weather could not prove quite so unkind again? But both Roberts and Greenidge joined the West Indies for their Prudential Cup campaign, in which period the county lost two out of three games and, even more important, Roberts was absent injured for their last three matches, of which two, against Derbyshire and Sussex, would surely have been comfortably won with him in the side. This would have been more than enough for them to have gained the Championship. As it was, they finished third, and had to settle for the John Player Trophy, reaching the semi-final of the Benson & Hedges Cup and the quarter-finals of the Gillette Cup.

That really marked the end of Hampshire as a serious threat for the Championship pennant. Roberts and Greenidge were not available in 1976, as they were touring with the West Indies, and from then on the former seemed somewhat disinterested, never again performing with the total commitment expected from such an outstanding bowler.

MICHAEL HOLDING

Poetry in motion

Fast bowlers come in all shapes and sizes, but most of the really quick ones have been powerfully built. Wayne Daniel and Charlie Griffith used to remind me of heavyweight boxers as they lumbered up to the wicket; Frank Tyson had exceptionally broad shoulders; Fred Trueman possessed a well padded posterior and Ray Lindwall, although under six feet, weighed around twelve stone of solid muscle, someone you definitely wanted on your side in a punch-up. But Michael Holding was different. He might have modelled for a statue of a Greek god or an Olympic athlete, and he was unquestionably the most beautiful fast bowler I have encountered, 'poetry in motion'. Everything about him pleased the eye, a tall, handsome, slimly built man of just over six feet, who possessed the grace of, and indeed had been, a fine runner. His smooth approach flowed into a body action of elegance, coupled with a perfect follow-through, which all combined to produce deliveries of lightning speed. Although his run-up was, until towards the end of his career, exceptionally long, it was so silky that it was aesthetically stimulating. He was such a good mover that it was impossible to imagine him doing anything which did not have style.

When I first saw Holding bowl he, like Frank Tyson, relied mainly on sheer speed through the air for his success; but unlike Frank, and like Fred Trueman, Ray Lindwall and Richard Hadlee, he became a more complete bowler in the second half of his career. During the first era he sent down two of the fastest overs I have witnessed, and he also provided the finest sustained spells of pure pace throughout the course of a Test match.

On a pitch at Bridgetown in 1980–81, which gave assistance to the bowlers on the first day but became easier as the match progressed, the West Indies were allowed to make 265 in their first innings. When Geoff Boycott and Graham Gooch came out to begin England's reply, one could feel, almost hear, the atmosphere in the packed stadium. Michael Holding rose to the occasion with a new-ball first over of shattering speed. Before he knocked out the Yorkshireman's off-stump he had twice had him playing and missing. Later in the proceedings the England captain, Ian Botham, for a short time threatened to regain the initiative, until Clive Lloyd recalled Michael, who instantly responded with a first over at him of similar venom in which he had Ian caught at the wicket. An indication how the pitch had by now eased was provided by the West Indian second innings, which was declared at 379 for 7, though it must be admitted that Dilley, Botham and Jackman were neither as fast, nor as hostile as Holding, Roberts, Croft and Garner. Any real hope of England saving this match was, despite a fine century by Gooch, virtually ended when Boycott, though managing to escape the ignominy of a 'pair', fenced hesitantly at Holding and was caught in his first over. Holding then, with his next delivery, clean bowled Mike Gatting, who was still on the down swing with his bat as his stumps were shattered.

To understand and appreciate why I rate Michael Holding's bowling against England in the fifth Test at The Oval in 1976 so highly, it is necessary to take into account the ultra-docile pitch and the lack of success achieved by all the other fast and medium-fast bowlers in the same match. At this period the Oval wicket was a slow featherbed and, indeed, it was later relaid. The previous summer when Lillee, Thomson and Walker had been carrying all before them, England were forced to follow on 341 runs behind, but were able without too much trouble to make 538 runs at their second attempt.

In Michael Holding's match, as that is how it should always be known, the West Indies' first innings total was 687 for 8 declared, and their second innings 182 for 0, off a mere 32 overs. Their second effort was so belligerent that Bob Willis was reduced to a field which would have been considered over-defensive in the final stages of a limited-overs game. Faced by the formidable West Indian total, England replied with a highly respectable 435.

Once they had avoided the follow-on, they looked certain to save the match, as the pitch was playing even more easily and especially as it seemed probable that the only serious threat, Mike Holding – who in the first innings had returned the tremendous figures of 33.9 overs, 9 maidens, 92 runs, 8 wickets – must surely have taken something out of himself as he had bowled at top speed throughout; but it was not to be. Much to my surprise, Mike came storming in once more to bowl his side to an improbable victory by 231 runs with six wickets for 57 in 20.4 overs on a pitch which was slow, docile and made for batting and big scores.

Holding's bowling in this game provided the classic example of what can be achieved by exceptional pace even in conditions totally unsuited to fast bowling. An examination of the figures of the other quick and medium fast seamers of both teams in that game are revealing and emphasise this point. Willis took 1 wicket for 121 runs in 22 overs; Selvey 0 for 110 in 24 overs; Woolmer 0 for 74 in 14 overs; and Greig, though this includes some overs of off-spin, 2 for 107 in 36 overs. Holding's own colleagues were not much more successful – Roberts 1 for 139 in 40 overs; Holder 3 for 106 in 41.5 overs; Daniel 0 for 30 in 10 overs; and King 1 for 39 in 13 overs. Personally, I doubt whether Holding would have been able to cause quite so much devastation in these circumstances later in his career, when he was both a more experienced and, in some respects, a more accomplished performer, because he would not have believed it was possible. Charging windmills is an occupation only for those who are without cynicism, young and very fit.

It is doubtful whether, in his early years, Holding would have been able to last a full season of county cricket. During his spells with Lancashire and Derbyshire, he only played in about half the matches, as only one overseas player was allowed at a time. His first taste of county cricket was in 1981, with Lancashire, when his appearances were restricted by his week-end contract in the Lancashire League. Despite the weather he still comfortably headed the bowling averages, taking 40 wickets at just under 18 runs apiece, something he repeated when he joined Derbyshire in 1983. This proved for him a very abbreviated summer, as he was injured during the crowd invasion at the end of the Prudential World Cup against India and was unable to appear until mid-August when his 21 wickets worked out at a remarkable 12.47 runs each. In 1984 he played a leading part in England's rout by the West Indies in the role of third seamer rather than as the main strike bowler, to suggest that he was approaching the end of his international career. However this lay, in fact, several tours away, following the gradual arrival of the new pacemen, Patterson, Walsh, Davis, Ambrose and Bishop. In 1985 and 1986 he captured 50 and 52 wickets for his adopted county at a cost which was far cheaper than any of his colleagues, but in the following seasons for the first time he had to settle for second place, and an almost identical haul. It would be very wrong, though, to judge Holding's services to Derbyshire cricket purely in terms of his many great bowling feats, several spectacular assaults with the bat and numerous catches be-cause his contribution as guide, philosopher and friend to the other members of the staff has been very valuable. He was particularly helpful to their army of seamers and their captain. Michael, in fact, is an intelligent and highly respected per-former who more than justified the standing ovation he re-ceived on his last appearance at Perth in Australia early in 1987.

For most of his international career he was fortunate that he was part of a four-man pace quartet, and therefore his spells were shorter than for teams which carried three, which used to be the norm, while the number of overs he was expected to deliver in a day was considerably less. His physique was not ideal to take the strain of being a *very* fast bowler. Inevitably he has suffered a considerable number of injuries, which he overcame by a combination of determination and the hard slog of strengthening his muscles by exercises. He also learned how to bowl off a shorter run, and although this led to a slight decrease in speed, he gained in control and the ability to move the ball much more off the seam and in the air. The outcome was that it enabled him to play first-class cricket for far longer than had once seemed probable.

As one would expect from such a perfectly balanced athlete, Mike Holding's fielding, especially in the deep, was sheer joy to behold – it had pace, beauty and his returns came back like rockets. Also, like most tail-enders from the Caribbean, he was always liable to strike some spectacular boundaries, which were especially useful in limited-overs cricket, and he has also recorded a number of fifties in Test cricket.

JOEL GARNER

'The Big Bird'

The best way to teach children under ten to play back correctly is for the coach to throw short deliveries at them from a *kneeling position*. This method provides the accuracy, the necessary pace and a realistic trajectory. The coach who bowls overarm at a small boy is not only liable to frighten him, but he will also achieve too much bounce, while the trajectory will have no similarity with what the pupil will encounter from bowlers of his own age. A similar problem is experienced by adult batsmen when facing Joel Garner for the first time. Joel's exceptional height – 6ft 8in. – has played a considerable part in transforming him from another excellent seamer from the Caribbean into a great bowler for the West Indies and Somerset.

His body action was not beautiful and might be described as functional, while his run-up looked rather ungainly, a mixture of massive, steadily moving arms and legs, plus enormous strides which covered the ground more quickly than it first appeared; but it suited Joel. In addition his right arm, when he released the ball, was very high, so that it was propelled quickly at the unfortunate batsman from a height of over ten feet. This gave him a disconcerting, and an unusually steep delivery, which made picking his length so difficult, especially the yorker, while he also made the ball lift far more sharply than other bowlers.

Of all the West Indian pacemen, I would have found facing 'the Big Bird' (presumably a pterodactyl?) the most disconcerting, because even on a good pitch he was always liable to make a good length ball rise higher and more steeply than expected. Although he was not as fast through the air as Roberts or

Holding or Marshall, he was still able to pitch his bouncer further up than they, but it was the ball he made rise to around hip high from only fractionally short of a length which worried every batsman.

In addition to the advantage which his height gave him, he was also less profligate than many of his pace bowling colleagues in terms of no-balls and wides. His control was always good, which made him particularly valuable in limited-overs cricket, where he proved the most consistently effective performer in two World Cups. Whenever Joel opened the bowling for Somerset, opposing counties were only too happy to settle for existence during his first spell and to seek runs at the other end until the final slog, when the two most productive and rewarding shots against him were unintentional outside, and inside, edges.

Throughout history fast bowlers have tended to be fiery-tempered, a mean and moody, aggressive breed, who disliked all batsmen, especially live ones. Joel Garner was, however, an exception. Like many big men, he is essentially a gentle giant, who was liked and respected by both his team-mates and his opponents. The control he invariably displayed on the field was also reflected by his lifestyle, one of the game's foremost gentlemen who was especially good with children, as well as one of the best fast bowlers.

Although lift, accuracy and pace were Joel's chief weapons, he was able to move the ball off the seam and sometimes in the air, though not as acutely nor as late as a number of other bowlers. Andy Roberts, for example, did more off the pitch, and Botham swung the ball more. But there is no question that Garner was one of the finest bowlers, and for several seasons in the late 1970s he would have been my first choice as a bowler for any Test or limited-overs series. To support this assessment, let us examine his figures for Somerset, after he had joined them full-time in 1979, alongside those of Ian Botham, England's leading wicket-taker in Test cricket. As bowlers usually win Test matches, it also helps to explain the West Indian domination.

1979	Garner	393.1 overs	55 wickets	average 13.83
	Botham	257.0 overs	26 wickets	average 32.53
1980	West Indian Tour			
1981	Garner	583.4 overs	81 wickets	average 15.08
	Botham	279.5 overs	31 wickets	average 31.48
1982	Garner	259.1 overs	33 wickets	average 17.65
	Botham	247.2 overs	39 wickets	average 18.43
1983	Garner	256 overs	34 wickets	average 19.83
	Botham	119.3 overs	12 wickets	average 32.32
1984	West Indian Tour			
1985	Garner	295.4 overs	31 wickets	average 23.83
	Botham	134.4 overs	11 wickets	average 42.18
1986	Garner	419 overs	47 wickets	average 23.21
	Botham	285.1 overs	22 wickets	average 43.68

Averages never tell the full story, but with two bowlers playing for the same team over a number of years they provide a fairly accurate guide in terms of their penetration and effectiveness, yet only once in six years did Botham's figures approach those of 'the Big Bird'. It is also noticeable that Joel's wickets became gradually more expensive. Although this was to some extent the result of increased age and injuries, the main reason was surely that county batsmen gradually became accustomed to that disconcerting trajectory. Somerset certainly would never have dispensed with his services in the early 1980s as they finally did in 1986.

In addition to coming out well ahead of the other international class bowler in the Somerset side, Joel's record alongside the other great West Indian fast bowlers is also very impressive, perhaps more so. (Marshall, whose figures are correct to end-summer 1988, has now taken over 300 test wickets.)

Garner	56 Tests	2112 overs	247 wickets	average 21.16
Holding	59 Tests	2076 overs	249 wickets	average 23.28
Roberts	47 Tests	1856 overs	202 wickets	average 25.61
Marshall	58 Tests	2174 overs	290 wickets	average 20.41

In nearly the same number of Tests, Joel has taken almost the same number of wickets as Michael Holding, whom I would unhesitatingly place among the finest fast bowlers in the world, but he has been more economical, costing over two runs per wicket less. Andy Roberts also took over 200 Test wickets, and though he was in every sense the complete fast bowler, his cost per wicket was even higher. There are several reasons for this, the main being that, in his early years, he did not enjoy the support bowling of the same high quality that Joel has had and provided throughout his international career. The only great West Indian fast bowler who has been as inexpensive and also has an even higher strike rate is Malcolm Marshall, currently the fastest and best paceman in the world. What makes Joel's record so remarkable is that he has been as successful in terms of both wickets taken and their cost as three West Indian colleagues, even though he was *seldom* given the new ball and the first opportunity of exploiting the initial life to be found in so many pitches against two new batsmen. This suggests that Joel was the most deadly with the old ball, which surely must make him the finest third seamer in history.

Joel Garner's final Test bowling figures are also statistically superior to those of the three great West Indian pacemen of the early 1960s, Wes Hall, Charlie Griffith and Sir Gary Sobers. Hall finished with 192 wickets at 26, Griffith with 94 wickets at 28, and Sobers with 235 at 34. However, it should be stressed that in those days there were fewer Tests per year, and the pitches, especially in the West Indies, Asia and Australia, were far better than they are today. Neither the shine nor the seam lasted as long, and there were fewer opportunities to pick up easy wickets by frequently meeting opposition which was not of true international quality.

The similarity between Garner and Holding is stressed again

by their respective records in one-day internationals. Garner played in 85 matches, and took 129 wickets at 18.25 runs apiece; and Holding played 96 matches, and took 135 wickets at 21.27 apiece. Both were outstanding bowlers in limited-overs cricket, effective and economical, they did not panic under pressure, and they maintained control of line, length and pace which was sufficient to upset any batsman. Once again it is noticeable that Garner was less costly, as he also was in Test cricket. A major cause of this was the steepness of his delivery, which meant that batsmen found the ball would hit their bat further up than they wanted, and this made him very difficult to attack. I have watched Joel bowling on numerous occasions, and have seldom seen him harshly treated. Once, on a very slow pitch at Chelmsford, Graham Gooch did pull him for three fours in one over, but that stands out in my memory like an oasis in a desert.

Despite being an exceptionally tall man, Joel Garner still was an outstanding close fieldsman, helped by his enormous hands and surprising agility. In the jobs outside cricket listed in the 1987 *Cricketers' Who's Who*, he was included as a telegraph operator. I always visualise him repairing a line without requiring a ladder.

MALCOLM MARSHALL

The Liquidator

When the West Indies arrived for their 1988 tour of England, there were hopes that, despite the length of time since England had last achieved a Test victory, they would be able to avoid a repetition of the disasters which befell them in 1984, and during their painful expedition to the Caribbean in 1985–86. This optimism was based on the failure of Vivian Richards' side to reach the semi-finals of the Reliance World Cup in 1987, and the way it had been forced to struggle early in 1988 at home against Pakistan, rather than on any evidence that an England revival was imminent. Nevertheless, after England had deservedly won the three one-day matches for the Texaco Trophy, everything suggested that it would be a close series; not only did the West Indian batting look suspect, but, even more important, only Malcolm Marshall remained from the great pace quartets which had dominated the previous series. Marshall had also missed the winter's tour to Pakistan and the World Cup, through injury, and though his record supported his claim to be the finest fast bowler in the world, there was a feeling that he might have lost his edge. However, he proved that this was far from being the case by capturing 35 wickets at 12.65 apiece in five Tests, and on three occasions taking five or more wickets in an innings. As was to be expected from a party which could afford to omit fast bowlers of the calibre of Winston Davis and George Ferris, who would certainly have gained a place in any other international team, Marshall was splendidly supported by the new generation of West Indian pacemen, who look more than capable of dominating world cricket for the next decade.

What made Malcolm Marshall's success so intriguing was

that it was achieved not so much by speed – because the Test pitches were not especially quick, so that there were comparatively few short-pitched deliveries – but by swerve. His ability to swing the ball both away from, and into the bat at a pace varying between fast-medium and fast, defeated England's batsmen. The surprising feature of Malcolm's swerve was the amount. It often started early, but it went a very long way, much further than that of most genuinely quick bowlers. The only true fast bowler I have seen who could swing the ball, both out and in, to the same extent, was Ray Lindwall. There were occasions after the initial shine had worn off the ball when Malcolm made it move almost as much, though earlier, as Bob Massie had done in his one remarkable summer of 1972; but, of course, the Australian's pace was slower.

In addition to his prowess as a swerve bowler, Malcolm does not fit into the three usual categories of West Indian pacemen: the tall giants such as Joel Garner; the human tanks with the build of heavyweight boxers like Wayne Daniel; or the tall, svelte athletes in the Michael Holding mould, who seemingly glide up to bowl. Malcolm was born in Barbados in 1958 and, although he has put on some weight recently, he was initially wiry and comparatively short and slight. He really attacks the bowling crease, sprinting up to it, jumping high, and finally coming down hard on his left foot. He releases the ball with a slightly open-chested action, which aids his in-swinger, and flashes past the umpire and into his follow-through. His sensibly short run-up is slightly angled, which helps him to get close to the stumps, but it also explains why he is sometimes cautioned for running down the pitch, as he has difficulty in moving away quickly enough.

I have never seen Malcolm swing the ball as often and as much as he did in the 1988 Test series. At times he reduced both his pace and his run-up to great effect. On previous tours his main weapon was his pace and for five years he was considered to be the fastest bowler in the world, but he was never just a 'tear-away' quickie, because he has a cricket brain and has learned how to think out, as well as blast out, opposing batsmen. Few spinners, let alone pacemen, are more punctilious than he is about the exact position of his close fielders. Although it does take time, I enjoy those little interludes which are liable to occur when Malcolm is playing for Hampshire. It normally starts when he waves to his captain, Mark Nicholas, at the commencement of his run. This is followed by a series of gestures and a request in Bajan, a language which I find the most difficult to understand of all the West Indian dialects, but which Mark has mastered and now speaks fairly fluently. Malcolm is not content merely to have a bat-pad specialist, preferably inside the batsman's trouser pocket, the fieldsman has to be minutely adjusted, but over the years it has so often produced a wicket, not infrequently from the next ball, that it clearly pays to carry out his wishes. One of the most satisfying moments in bowling is to trap a batsman with a carefully worked out ploy, something which Malcolm does frequently to the delight of his colleagues, and which must give him enormous satisfaction and happiness. His natural ball has been the away-swinger which he worked in close conjunction with a deadly 'nip-backer'. As he was shorter than the other members of the pace quartet, his bouncer was not as steep, but in some respects was more unpleasant because on a fast pitch and at his speed, the ball tended to skid through at just over rib-cage height, difficult to play, too fast to pull, unsuitable for the hook, and potentially painful.

Malcolm made his debut for Barbados in 1977–78. In the following season he toured India and Sri Lanka with a West Indian team which was minus most of its stars who were engaged in World Series Cricket, and he played his first Test at Bangalore. Any doubts that he was destined to become the natural successor to Andy Roberts, the oldest of their first pace quartet, were removed in the 1978–79 Shell Shield series in which, with Sylvester Clarke as his partner, he was largely responsible for the success of Barbados, and captured 25 wickets. In the summer of 1979 he was chosen as one of the reserve West Indian quickies for the Prudential World Cup, also joined Hampshire as their overseas replacement for Roberts, and topped their bowling averages. The following summer he returned with the West Indies for a full tour, when he established himself as an integral part of their team for the next decade. Apart from those seasons when on duty with the West Indies, Malcolm has been an enormous asset for his adopted county as a world-class, devastating, and very inexpensive fast bowler. Twice, in 1982 and 1986, he achieved a three-figure haul. What was impressive about both feats was the low cost. On the first occasion his wickets cost 15.73, while his colleagues were collecting theirs for between 21 and 30 runs each. The second season illustrated even more clearly the gap between a great Test bowler and good county bowlers. His 100 wickets worked out at just over 15 runs each, whereas the least expensive members of the Hampshire attack averaged over 28, and the wickets of the remainder cost between 32 and 34.

In addition to his numerous match-winning feats with the ball, Malcolm has become an extremely useful stroke-making batsman, who could undoubtedly make many more runs but, with a strong batting line-up, Hampshire has wisely allowed him to concentrate on his bowling. Although the county has benefited enormously from the services of this splendid all-rounder, it should not be forgotten that Malcolm has also gained considerably from this happy association, on the cricket as well as the financial side. Playing with Hampshire has turned him into a more complete bowler who has learned to become effective on all types of pitches, not merely those with pace. Although he demonstrated this so superbly in the summer of 1988, it was evident even in the 1984 series, when he produced my two favourite examples of his quality and his character.

At Leeds on the first morning, a powerful stroke by Broad caused a double fracture to his left thumb. This was expected to put him out of the game for at least a fortnight; however, he came in at no. 11 and batted one-handed, which enabled Larry Gomes to reach his century, as well as adding some useful runs for the last wicket. He then secured three of the six wickets to fall during the latter part of the Saturday and, on the Monday morning, gobbled up the remaining four wickets, with a lovely spell of genuine swing bowling.

He missed the fourth Test owing to his injury, much to the relief of the English batsmen, but returned for the fifth at The Oval on a pitch which had some pace. The West Indians were dismissed for 190, their lowest total of the tour, but Marshall, perhaps irritated by his duck, bowled almost as quickly as Michael Holding had done on a much slower wicket eight years earlier. He scythed his way through the England first innings, taking 5 for 35 in 17.5 overs of a spell of frighteningly fast bowling which probably contained too many short-pitched, lethal deliveries. It was one of those occasions when I was happier, and far, far safer, in the commentary box than I would have been out in the middle!

It is only a matter of time before Malcolm Marshall takes his 300th Test wicket and soon afterwards passes Lance Gibbs' record West Indian haul. Although he has obviously been helped by always having very penetrative pace support and thus enjoys more opportunities to polish off opposing tails than the bowlers from other countries, conversely his colleagues are more likely to grab victims than those who back up Hadlee, or McDermott, or Kapil Dev.

ABDUL QADIR

The Spinning Mystic

Of all forms of bowling the most fun to bowl is the leg-break and its close associates, the top-spinner, the flipper and the googly. In an era which has seen, mainly as a result of limited-overs cricket, an acute shortage of slow bowlers and an increase in the importance of the dot-ball – the ball off which no run is scored – the genuine wrist-spinner has been in danger of becoming as extinct as the lob bowler. The wrist-spinner is, of course, more expensive than the finger-spinner, because he is likely to bowl more loose deliveries, as it is far more difficult to control the ball. Fortunately there are some signs that the leg-break bowler is returning to the game, and even in England, which has not produced a great wrist-spinner since before the 1939 war, Andy Clarke, essentially an accurate club 'roller', did well for Sussex in his first season in 1988. He was responsible for an hilarious cameo when bowling at Derek Pringle at Ilford. He tied Pringle up in knots for fifteen minutes of farce containing unsuccessful attempts to off-drive, sweep, charge, pull, cut and push. It ended when the Essex all-rounder was bowled attempting a mighty heave over mid-on to emphasise the laughter which this type of bowling generates. However, it has been the success of Abdul Qadir of Pakistan, combined with the inability of batsmen to cope with this style of attack – which many of them had never encountered – that has ensured the wrist-spinner will not become obsolete. The consternation Qadir has from time to time caused among English batsmen must be similar to what occurred when the googly was first introduced into the game at the beginning of this century.

Like many slow bowlers, Qadir began his career as a seam

bowler and a rather conventional opening batsman. If he had been born in England it is a fair bet that he would have finished as the 'bits and pieces' player who is so handy in county cricket but would achieve little in Pakistan. In the nets Qadir discovered by chance that he had the ability to deliver a leg-break which had sufficient dip and turn to worry his colleagues. Although his fingers and wrist enabled him to break the ball sufficiently on a true surface, he also had an action which, with his lack of height, combined naturally to produce that loop which makes his flight more dangerous. These gifts are not, on their own, sufficient to make a serious impact at first-class level, let alone in Tests. They have to be carefully honed and cultivated, requiring hour upon hour of practice and experiment. Abdul Qadir succeeded, because he attacked the task with the fervour and dedication of a novice who has entered a monastery convinced of his calling. The outcome is that he has become the most exciting and feared slow bowler of the last decade, and the only one who has frequently decided the fate of Test matches.

Like a great fast bowler, Abdul has the ability to trouble good batsmen in all conditions. On a pitch responsive to spin he is a deadly executioner; on a good pitch he is always liable to take wickets, and even on a 'feather bed' he can be effective. An example of his skill in the last category occurred at The Oval in 1987. The pitch was so friendly that Pakistan amassed over 700 runs. The wicket virtually emasculated the seamers and the finger-spinners, but a genuinely fast bowler or a high class wrist-spinner could still prove effective. This was the ideal situation for a bowler of Abdul Qadir's type. His captain, Imran Khan, had runs aplenty to spare and could afford to use him for long spells supported by attacking fields. If Tauseef Ahmed, who had done very little bowling on the tour, had provided better support and Wasim Akram had not been forced to depart to hospital with appendicitis, Abdul would almost certainly have won the match for Pakistan.

As a non-drinking, non-smoking, devout Moslem with a sense of humour, who never swears when fieldsmen drop a catch off his bowling, even if he may mentally condemn them to a particularly unpleasant fate, Abdul looks an unlikely player to be caught up in a series of major incidents. In New Zealand, after he had been taken off by his captain, he was fined for sulking. He not only refused to pay, but criticised his colleagues on television with the result that he was sent home in disgrace. The surprise is that the selectors were prepared to pick him again. Then there was his punch-up with a spectator in the Caribbean. He has been fortunate that there has been no serious contender for his place and, perhaps even more important, that Imran Khan appreciates his genius with the ball, and knows how to handle him. Imran so wanted Abdul Qadir in his team that he was prepared to await his late arrival on the 1987 tour which, like the visits of India and New Zealand in 1986 and the West Indies in 1988, England lost.

Why should such a sensitive person as Abdul Qadir have experienced so many clashes during his successful career? As cricket has been responsible for raising his standard of living and status in life, he naturally has taken the game very seriously. To him, leg-spin bowling is an art form of which he has become a master, a magician even, who does not welcome advice, even from the chosen few who have graduated in the art. In addition, he is easily upset. He requires a captain who is sympathetic, encouraging, understanding and yet allows him freedom of expression when he is bowling. He would have had difficulty fitting into county cricket where there is a shortage of such skippers.

It is over ten years since Abdul Qadir first played against England during the 1977–78 tour, when he was an immediate success and topped the bowling averages. Like so many post-war wrist-spinners, however, he made little impression when he came to England in the following summer, played in no Tests, and finished with only six highly expensive wickets. He was a member then of a sub-standard Pakistan party because their most accomplished players were involved in World Series Cricket. As a result he received neither the special treatment nor the encouragement he needed. On his second tour in 1982, Imran Khan was at the helm, and he knew how to get the best out of Abdul. In terms of figures, he did not enjoy an outstanding visit, which was hardly surprising as all three Tests were played on pitches which encouraged seam to such an extent that of the 45 Pakistan wickets to fall in the series, only five were claimed by the England slow bowlers. He had to be content with ten wickets in three Tests, but he did leave a lasting impression because of the way he bamboozled so many England batsmen, even when they scored runs. Derek Randall's innings at Edgbaston, in which he never succeeded in picking Abdul's googly, even though he scored a century, provided a fascinating example.

His late arrival, combined with the slow pitches, meant that Abdul's bowling on the 1987 tour to England did not prove as dramatic as expected until the Oval Test, when, once again, he showed that in ideal batting conditions he was, by a considerable margin, the best attacking slow bowler in the world. His style may not be beautiful, but it is instantly recognisable, a stuttery, bouncy, rolling, almost nautical approach, followed by a powerful body action in which he does not use his full height, opens up early, and, ideally speaking, is too square-on at the moment of delivery. However, more important is that his run-up, action and follow-through allow him to purvey a mixture of leg-breaks, top-spinners and googlies, which have baffled and confused batsmen on all types of pitch. His control is very good for a wrist-spinner, and his lack of height helps in producing the ball which looks like a tempting half-volley but so often drops a shade shorter, and turns. The outcome, when a batsman attempts a drive, is frequently fatal.

Abdul Qadir loves bowling which, for him, has become an intricate craft, almost in itself a mystic way of life. Unlike some slow bowlers, he is still keen to continue even when he is being heavily punished. He is convinced he will eventually out-manoeuvre the batsman, and he also knows that he cannot take wickets unless he continues to bowl.

He is, of course, very dependent upon his wicket-keeper and fieldsmen; and he is at his happiest when he can encircle his intended victim with close catchers. This is fine when there are plenty of runs to play with, a new batsman has just arrived, or the pitch is taking spin; but there have been occasions when a less attacking field would have not only reduced the runs scored, but might also have increased the chances of taking wickets.

In a period which has been dominated largely by pace, seam and flat finger-spinners who are more interested in keeping the runs down than taking wickets, the arrival of Abdul Qadir has been a tonic. Once again we have been treated to the sight of a bowler who tantalises and deceives batsmen in the air and off the pitch. That skill makes the game infinitely more interesting to play and to watch; I only hope that Abdul Qadir's success will inspire others to emulate him.

6

CAPTAINS

CAPTAINS AND CAPTAINCY

In England there is a tendency to cloak captaincy with a social mystique stemming from the days of 'officers and gentlemen'. Captains then were automatically drawn from the amateurs, the vast majority educated at public school and university. The amateur captain did, in fact, enjoy several practical advantages apart from his class and station in life, the most important being that, because he was not paid by his county, he had independence and could afford to ignore his club committee – usually a well-meaning, if somewhat nebulous bunch of men – providing he was doing reasonably well and had the support of the three members who had experience of first-class cricket. He was often appointed to the job at an early age, with the tacit acceptance, if not the approval, of the players, who would certainly have opposed him if he had been a professional; while if he failed to do well he could be removed without the danger of losing a high-quality player, who had cost money to develop, to another county, as is liable to happen with a professional captain, for example, Tom Graveney and Chris Tavaré. He had usually the experience of captaincy at school and university level, which helped, and the advantage of being slightly removed from his troops, and indeed he often had his own dressing-room, which made maintaining discipline easier. This does not mean that amateur captains were invariably good, quite the reverse, as some of the worst skippers in first-class cricket came from the amateur ranks, but they did enjoy some other practical pluses, not the least being a background which encouraged the confidence so helpful to those in command.

In addition to being directly employed by the club, today's

county captain faces more pressure, because winning and success is far more important. Now there are four 'Honours' – the County Championship, the NatWest Trophy, the Benson & Hedges Cup, and the Sunday League – 'up for grabs' – which produce not only honour and glory but are worth a great deal of money to himself, his players and his county. In consequence, if his team repeatedly misses out, he will lose his job, which explains the casualty rate among Derbyshire, Yorkshire and Lancashire skippers; indeed the job of the county cricket captain is very similar to that of a football player-manager except that no Board of Directors, however stupid, would ever appoint a player-manager who would automatically miss half the matches in a season. This is what occurs, of course, when a county appoints a regular member of the National XI as its captain. Logically, no county captain should be playing regularly for England, because he misses too many matches. This destroys that continuity of command which is so important – though one might not think so judging by the 'musical chairs' played with the England captains by the selectors in the summer of 1988.

Selectors will naturally argue that, if current England players do not lead county teams, how can they gain sufficient experience to lead England? Although they have a point, I do not believe that they chose Willis, Gower, Gatting or Gooch, let alone Botham, for the way they led their respective counties. All were primarily selected for their ability and experience as Test cricketers. It should also be remembered that two of England's finest post-war captains, Sir Len Hutton and Ray Illingworth, had no real experience of leading a county, but they possessed what is far more important, an exceptional knowledge and understanding of the game at every level, as well as being outstanding performers.

A captain, like a football manager, is judged, often unfairly, on results, so it follows that the first requirement for both is a powerful side, or inept opposition. Having to lead England against the West Indies during the last decade was virtually the kiss of death for any England skipper, and nobody was surprised when the guillotine fell on Denness, Botham, Gower, Gatting, Emburey and Cowdrey. However brilliant each had been as tactician, inspired leader and motivator, he was bound to fail against opponents who bowled, fielded and batted so much better. Even a captaining genius would have been hard put to it in 1988 to dismiss the West Indies twice at Headingley with an attack consisting of Dilley, Foster, Pringle and Cowdrey, and at Old Trafford with Dilley, De Freitas, Capel and Childs, or to score sufficient runs with a batting line-up as weak as the one given to Graham Gooch at The Oval. In these circumstances it is easy to understand Graham Gooch's statement after yet another crushing defeat. He was merely admitting the obvious when he said that a team is only as good as its players; but this clearly did not concur with the more romantic views of Ted Dexter, a former England captain, who wrote: 'No wonder the England team is in such a sorry state if that is the general atmosphere in the dressing-room'. He went on to blame Gooch for leaving Matthew Maynard and Robin Bailey to their own devices, and for not leading a flamboyant counter-attack himself in the second innings, rather than staging a brave defensive rearguard which simply required adequate support from two players to have come off.

Ted Dexter never faced the problem of leading a very weak England XI, but he was upset by Gooch's excuse: 'because I am being asked to believe that all my work in thirty Test matches as captain of England could just as well have been done by anyone else or nobody at all'. If Ted is saying that he was a better motivator than Graham who, after all, was the selectors' fourth choice as captain, that would be fair comment; but I do not believe that the England side under him, neither the most astute nor inspiring of post-war skippers, though the most autocratic, would have changed the outcome of the Oval Test in 1988. After Graham was re-appointed for the Lord's Test against Sri Lanka, Ted wrote further, 'Graham Gooch, to my utter amazement, has again been entrusted with the captaincy of England, this time against part-timers Sri Lanka at Lord's'; but as our selectors had already chosen that year four captains, and sufficient players for two teams, it should not have amazed him.

Ted goes on to say, which is true, 'Affable and easy-going as Gooch is, it is hard to see where the much-needed leadership is going to come from, unless it is by personal example with the bat. It is a long time since England benefited from a captain's innings', though he might be said to be overlooking a century by Mike Gatting at Adelaide, or David Gower's 90 against the West Indies in Trinidad. Ted then suggested Len Hutton's record with the bat when he became skipper as an example for Gooch to follow, but he was forgetting two factors: first, Len, also, had a much stronger side and, second, he was tactically superior though, like Graham, he was never a dashing commander. The real surprise was that Gooch should have been appointed to the captaincy for India after he had told the selectors he was unavailable and under contract in South Africa. A touring captain has different and much bigger responsibilities than leading in a home series, and it seemed strange to nominate someone who was reluctant to make the trip, unable to make up his own mind, and had demonstrated with Essex that leadership was not his natural forte.

What in many respects was even more baffling was the inability of the selectors to realise how appointing Graham Gooch in these circumstances was bound to jeopardise the entire tour, because it would look to many outside the cricket world as a deliberately provocative act, which it was not, just a naive, unintelligent one, like on the last occasion when England called off a tour because the government of the country we were visiting had decided that one of our players, Basil D'Oliveira, was unacceptable.

I have always believed that, if Basil had been included in the initial party, which was logical enough as he had scored a fine century in the last Test – having been summoned as a late replacement – the tour would have gone ahead. The reason given by the then chairman of the selectors for his omission was that, for an overseas tour, D'Oliveira was regarded as a batsman, not an all-rounder. Although this was difficult to believe, it was just about acceptable if one took into account Basil's lack of success with the ball in the Caribbean. What the South African government did not find acceptable was when Cartwright, a bowler, was forced to withdraw, that D'Oliveira should have been invited to take his place. It believed that the England selectors had given way to political pressure whereas they, like the 1988 selectors, had not realised that, sadly, it is impossible to divorce sport from politics. India had accepted Gooch and Lamb for the 1987 World Cup, because it was then politically and financially expedient.

Although the first requisite for a successful captain is a powerful side, or poor opposition, one must not under-rate what can be achieved by an outstanding skipper. He can transform a very limited side into a formidable combination, while poor captaincy can ruin even a good team, and make a bad team worse. The captain's job, like that of the football manager, is to maximise on the ability of those under his command, but how this will be achieved can vary enormously, from the quiet, thinking Mike Brearley to the flamboyant, follow-me-fellows-and-we-can-beat-anybody approach of Tony Greig. I admire Brian Clough, who for many years has done so well with quite ordinary material. He himself may be difficult at times, but he has repeatedly accomplished the impossible. The captain must be prepared to rule, for without discipline, chaos will reign. This is the responsibility of a captain both on and off the field, because ultimately he has to make the decisions on how the game is played. The type of discipline he imposes will vary with his character and the players under his command. The best results will only come if they respect and have confidence in him, but from the outset he must make it absolutely plain that he is the master, for there can only be one. Maintaining discipline these days is more difficult than in the past, when the rewards were less, and when players were not financially independent, and so could not afford to turn down tours, or hire their own advisers, and when county-swapping took far longer.

A captain cannot afford to be indecisive, but it does help if he has imagination, is prepared to do the unexpected, and take the occasional gamble, always remembering that no successful gambler ever bets on tram tickets.

Who have been the four finest international captains in the last decade? My choice, and in no particular order, would be Ian Chappell, who gave the appearance of a latter-day Ned Kelly, an anti-establishment rebel, and an outstanding player; Mike Brearley, the guru with a cricket brain; the Islamic paladin and superb all-rounder Imran Khan, whose qualities I have described earlier in the 'all-rounders' section of this book; and Tony Greig, a man with real presence, who could have sold snow to the Eskimos but who was also a more accomplished player than is usually realised. They all, in their very different ways, made the best possible use of the talent at their disposal, which is the hallmark of a good skipper.

It is safe to say that none of my selected four would have required – indeed they would have strongly resented – the presence of that new addition to cricket dressing-rooms, the team manager-cum-coach-cum-general-factotum such as Bobby Simpson, Glenn Turner or Micky Stewart. Naturally they had a traditional manager to administer the business and social sides of a tour, but they looked after the cricket side, and would certainly have found a team manager completely superfluous for a home series. In other words, a really good skipper does not need one of these new style managers.

The records of those international teams and county clubs which have employed 'cricket managers' have not been outstanding, although in most cases the sides were struggling before the appointment which was, of course, the main reason why the appointment was made. In this connection it is significant that the West Indies, who have easily the best Test playing record, have not required one. There is also, as yet, no suggestion that they are thinking of having a supremo to replace their selection committee, a move much favoured by certain sections of the English press during, and following the indecisiveness which was the outstanding feature of Peter May's reign as Chairman. Although a cricket supremo does have certain advantages, like a good captain he will not be successful without the players and, as can be seen in the football world, he is not an automatic recipe for success.

The weakness of a supremo, or indeed any permanent manager, is that he is liable to become too close to the players and not sufficiently objective – which presumably was one of the reasons for the blunders in Pakistan. Then there is the problem of what happens when a manager and captain do not meld – as was the case with David Clark and Ray Illingworth in Australia, although, in India, David had done a splendid job as manager with Mike Smith, a very different style of captain to Ray. Micky Stewart and Mike Gatting blended well together, but that could well not apply to several other England skippers.

My own solution for England would be a selection committee consisting of four plus the captain. Two would be former players and two would still be playing on the county circuit, but approaching the end of their first-class and international careers, like Jack Hobbs and Wilfred Rhodes who were chosen when professionals were first co-opted on to the Selection Committee in 1926, or such as Keith Fletcher and Derek Underwood. The Chairman could be either salaried or not, but would be given a maximum of four years in office.

It is not without significance that the West Indian managers who have assisted Clive Lloyd and Viv Richards as captain, have been distinguished former players like Clive Walcott, Jackie Hendriks and, at present, Clive Lloyd himself. It is hard to imagine West Indies ever appointing a full-time permanent manager, such as Peter Lush, whose practical knowledege of Test cricket is at second-hand.

Clive Lloyd, of course, was first and foremost a great player, whose batting and fielding would have been an enormous asset to any Test team, and I have so described him earlier in the 'batsmen' section. He is a most friendly person, who was also a little senior to the side which developed into the best in the world and which, with the odd exception, like the touring of New Zealand in 1979–80, he led with efficiency and charm. I would place Clive in the good, competent category of captain, but would not classify him as an outstanding one, for I think he would have had problems if he had been leading a weaker side, as was shown when he captained Lancashire for three rather indifferent seasons, 1981–83, when they finished in the lower half of the table.

TONY GREIG

Super-salesman

Although Tony Greig held a British passport, as his father was born in Scotland, he was raised and learned his cricket in South Africa. His outlook was essentially South African, which was one reason, I suspect, why he made such a fine captain of England. Like so many of his countrymen his basic enthusiasm for the game was greater than that of so many English captains. It was not mere coincidence that Mike Procter, Eddie Barlow and Clive Rice made such an impact on the county circuit. In addition to their ability, and all three were better players than Tony Greig, they possessed an almost schoolboy zeal and, indeed, must have been disappointed and rather surprised that so many of those under their command did not have the same fervour. They all managed to inspire their adopted counties and to a greater extent than Tony was able to do for Sussex, whom he led between 1973–77.

There were two major reasons for this: first, Tony was missing on Test duty for much of each season, whereas the other three could afford to concentrate entirely on domestic cricket. Second, the Sussex committee lacked drive and imagination, while the side itself was short on class, especially on the many occasions Tony was missing. Here was another example of how even good captaincy will not produce the results without the players; but it is also true that his record with bat and ball for his adopted country was much more impressive than for his adopted county. Big occasions and big crowds brought out the best in him, and these were rather rare in Sussex.

With the tall, rangy good looks of the hero of a Western, Tony had presence, all-round ability and a sharp, sometimes devious mind. Although he led from the front with the infectious verve of a gay cavalier, he was not always too fussy about how his objectives were obtained. In other words, despite all the outward charm, he had a ruthless streak which was especially noticeable when Ian Chappell was the opposing captain. No prisoners were to be taken. An instance of this was his running-out of Alvin Kallicharran after the close of play in the first Test in Trinidad, which caused a furore that permitted Tony's appeal to be withdrawn. Tony was vice-captain at that time and this act was done instinctively and without malice.

Tony was inclined to rely on instinct, and this led to him making several mistakes both on and off the field, which, with a moment's thought, could have been avoided. 'Grovel' was not the ideal word to use when announcing what he intended to make the West Indies do, while his decision in the fifth Test against the West Indies in 1976 to take off Willis after two overs with the new ball, during which he removed Greenidge for 0, and replace him with Underwood, does not make any more sense in retrospect. On that Oval featherbed, which saw the West Indies make 687 for 8 dec., and Vivian Richards 291, it can only be termed a tactical and psychological blunder, but it was part of the nature of a man who was forever experimenting. Sometimes his ideas worked brilliantly, but inevitably some were failures.

Greig reached his peak as captain on the 1976–77 tour to India when his team won the series by three Tests to one with one draw. He proved himself an outstanding tactician and a master diplomat. The fact that he was really a South African underlines just how brilliant he was in that important area. He used his great reach to smother the threat of world-class spin-bowling, and his charm to diffuse the problems which arise on any tour.

There is a tendency to underestimate Greig's prowess as an all-rounder, not at county level, but in the more rarefied and demanding atmosphere of international cricket. I watched him give his best all-round Test performance against the West Indies in Barbados on the Mike Denness tour in 1973–74.

Bowling off-cutters, rather than off-breaks, at nearly medium pace, he took 6 wickets for 164 in 46 overs, and caught Sobers for 0, diving full-length at first slip, out of a massive West Indian total of 596 for 8 declared, having previously batted at no. 6, making 148 out of a total of 395. In the final Test, which enabled England to draw the series, he finished with 13 wickets for 156, strangely proving himself a more effective bowler in the Caribbean than in England.

Personal courage is an essential ingredient for any Test captain, an attribute which Ian Chappell, Imran Khan and Mike Brearley also possessed, because the skipper who flinches against pace bowling cannot hope to engender confidence among the more timid or apprehensive members of his side. It is therefore not surprising to find that Tony scored more runs than anyone else when England were destroyed by the pace and hostility of Lillee and Thomson in 1974–75. In addition, he took as many wickets as anyone else during that ill-fated series, but the cost was high. His lack of fear could also be seen in his willingness to station himself in the more suicidal positions in the field, though his best place was at slip. He excelled in a crisis, and repeatedly came to England's rescue when all seemed lost, usually assisted by Alan Knott.

A natural extrovert, with expensive tastes and a rather flamboyant lifestyle, Tony inevitably had several clashes with cricket authorities whenever they tried to impose their style of discipline. He took them on with the charm of a cinema Robin Hood, but his tendency to act without thinking sometimes caused trouble when he was talking and writing. As a captain, however, he found that his experiences as a player, and as a sophisticated hell-raiser who had frequently been in dispute with authority, proved a distinct asset. He knew exactly how far to let his team go, a classic example of the poacher turned gamekeeper.

Another asset as captain was Tony's ability to handle press conferences. He was an exceptional public relations officer. To 'sweet talk' the Indian umpires (by complimenting them on their ability and saying how much he looked forward to seeing them in action), as a South African captain of England, before a ball has even been bowled, you have to be in the very top flight, and Tony certainly was (it also worked, as their umpiring *was* good); he had a quick mind, a clear delivery, and presence, but most important of all, he knew what people wanted to hear from him, and he gave it to them. Unlike some England captains, he was never supercilious when dealing with the more stupid of the media questions. The only Test skipper in the same communication league was Richie Benaud.

Tony was at the height of his powers both as a player and a captain when he led England against Australia in the unforgettable Centenary Test in 1977, and he would have been appointed for the Ashes series at home in the following summer if he had not decided, very shrewdly, that his future and his fortune lay with Kerry Packer and World Series Cricket. He returned to England, played in the series under Mike Brearley, and, at the same time, in his role of 'agent provocateur' for Packer, was discreetly signing as many England players as possible. He became Public Enemy No. 1 to the MCC and TCCB. It was not only because he had put the survival of Test cricket in some doubt, and was responsible for them becoming embroiled in an expensive law suit, which they predictably lost. They felt that, as the captain of England, he had been disloyal to those who appointed him. Tony himself argued that Test players would benefit financially and far more quickly than would have been the case without World Series Cricket, and he has been proved right. Whether it has benefited the game as a whole remains a moot point. Tony was not too concerned about either the ethics, or the financial rewards for professional cricketers in the future. He saw the coup, quite correctly, as an opportunity to make sufficient money to support his lifestyle and to settle in Australia, and, being a shrewd businessman, he immediately and instinctively hopped aboard the gravy-train. I cannot say that I blame him, and indeed I believe that some of the responsibility should lie with the establishment who appointed a 'mercenary' as captain, one who could not be expected to have the same loyalty as somebody born in this country.

If South Africa had not been banned from Test cricket, Tony would have played for the Springboks. He came to England to make money playing the game he loved, and hoping that it might also give him the opportunity of participating at the highest level, something which had become impossible in his own country. When he saw the chance of acquiring security for himself and his family, and living in Australia, he took it. I can think of several genuine England post-war captains who might have done the same thing, though probably not so well, because they could never have sold the idea to their colleagues so convincingly, or packaged the deal so attractively. In addition to being a very efficient and inspiring captain, Tony Greig is in a class by himself as a super-salesman.

MIKE BREARLEY

Cricketing Guru

Unlike Tony Greig, Ian Chappell and Imran Khan, Mike Brearley was not a charismatic captain who led from the front and inspired by his personal contribution as a player. He was a thinker who, in addition to obtaining a first-class Honours degree, also possessed a very shrewd cricket brain, a comparatively rare combination, of which C. B. Fry is probably the best example. Mike analysed every aspect of the game and became a master tactician. He was not always right, no captain ever is, but he made few mistakes and there was never a danger of his allowing his team to drift aimlessly because he had run out of ideas or lost interest. He was never afraid to consult with others which might confirm or alter a plan of action. He was always prepared to do the unusual, though in the main I would describe his captaincy as sound, sensible, and occasionally inspired.

In addition to the tactical side of the game, the captain of a county, or of a team on tour, has to maintain discipline and try to keep some fifteen very different people contented both on and off the field. Depending on the players, some of whom can be very difficult, this calls for a knowledge of man-management, on occasions 'petit dieu' management, and I have often thought it would help a captain if he were a qualified psychologist. In this area Mike excelled, because he was sensitive, which enabled him not only to find out what was worrying a member of his team, but also – something beyond the ken of most charismatic leaders – he understood why and sometimes even came up with a solution. In this he was obviously helped by the two winters he had spent working in a therapeutic community for the disturbed. However, he also had a strong determination to win; camouflaged by his scholarly and civilised appearance, there lay that ruthless streak which every successful captain requires.

As well as being a shrewd tactician and a quietly efficient leader, Mike had the good fortune to arrive on the scene at the right moment to take command. He was appointed captain of Middlesex in 1971, a side which had far more ability than its results had suggested, and was simply crying out for a leader capable of capitalising on the considerable talents available. He proved an immediate success as, in his first summer, his team moved from sixteenth to sixth place in the Championship table and, but for the bad weather in the closing stages of the season, would have finished even higher. He not only preached the importance of batting bonus points, which the club had tended to ignore, but pointed out that scoring more quickly also provided more time in which to dismiss the opposition. His bowlers, especially Latchman, a leg-spinner somewhat lacking in confidence, prospered from his encouragement and his meticulous attention to detail in field placings. He led Middlesex with distinction for twelve years in which they were always winning, or coming close to winning, one of the Honours available, which in no small way was due to Mike's skill. In county matches he benefited by being able to field a balanced attack, though he was handicapped by not being provided with those 'result' pitches – the pitches at Lord's are the responsibility of the MCC, not the county – which were deliberately designed to ensure a finish.

His years as county captain, combined with the tours he had made, had given him the right experience when he was appointed to lead England in 1977. This applied particularly overseas. In England the main requirements for a skipper are a good side and tactical ability, but on tour man-management is equally important, not forgetting that vital 'just a little bit of bloomin' luck'. In Mike Brearley's case it meant that his basic weakness – not being a sufficiently talented batsman at the highest level – as illustrated by an average of only 22 in 39 Tests, often against some limited attacks – was not felt as it would have been against the West Indies, or Australia at their peak. He also took over a team which was on the up-grade with the arrival of several outstanding young players, including the match-winning Botham and the dashing Gower.

In addition to the experience of captaincy he had gained with Middlesex, Mike Brearley had led Cambridge University, the England under-25 side in Pakistan, and he had been vice-captain to Tony Greig in India, whom he succeeded in 1977 when Tony joined Kerry Packer. Mike could hardly have had a more auspicious start to his international career as captain. He regained the Ashes by the wide margin of 3–0, with two draws, but he was again fortunate in three respects. First, most of the Australian side had secretly signed up for Packer, which split the party into two camps and cannot have helped when the news broke during the first Test. Second, the England fielding was superb and Mike showed his ability as a high-class slip whereas the Australians were as shoddy in this department as they were in their dress. Finally, Ian Botham brought additional fire to a formidable attack.

The World Series Cricket which followed ensured that the opposition was seriously weakened for most of Mike's reign as skipper. It obviously helped him to lead England to their ten wins and five draws before he suffered his first defeat in Melbourne, though he still returned with the Ashes. His one disastrous tour was a badly organised twin trip, in which all three Tests were lost and he received treatment from the Australian crowds which was not unlike what D. R. Jardine had been subjected to in 1932–33, though without reason apart from earlier successes he had enjoyed. However, he still had the last laugh when he was recalled to captain England against a full-strength Australia in England in 1981. He assumed command after two Tests, one lost and one drawn, and, demonstrating his exceptional value as a leader, took the series by 3–1. Although he owed much to the genius of Botham and one tremendous match-winning burst from Willis at Headingley, he did display exceptional control in tight situations which enabled him to win two matches that should have been, and indeed looked, lost.

Mike was not merely a quiet and reassuring leader, who remained unruffled in moments of tension. As captain of England he was helped by his age and his own interests keeping him slightly apart from the other players, and he was able to handle Botham expertly because he had first skippered him before he became the best all-rounder in the world. Although Mike had the traditional background of the amateur skipper, he was frequently anti-establishment in his attitude; he battled hard for increased rewards for players, firmly opposing any victimisation of those who had joined World Series Cricket, which helped him to gain the respect of those under his command. He was invariably fair, firm, and was their champion, indeed a very shrewd one when it came to negotiations with the powers-that-be. I have always felt that Mike would have made an outstanding trade union leader, with the considerable advantage of being more intelligent than the bosses, and just as determined.

IAN CHAPPELL

A latter-day Ned Kelly

If I had not included Ian Chappell as an outstanding captain, I would certainly have placed him in my section on great batsmen. Although he was not so naturally gifted as his brother Greg, personally I would prefer to have him coming to the crease when the going was very tough, because he was such a fighter, which also helped to make him an outstanding and effective captain. He had been well educated with a rather conservative and cricket-orientated background, which makes some of his more controversial actions surprising. At eighteen he became a regular member of the South Australian team, and he made his first international appearance against Pakistan when only twenty-one.

Like most of the best Australian batsmen, Ian was a backfoot player, but having learned how to adapt to English pitches in the Lancashire League, this did not prove the handicap it has been to some Australians on their first tour to this country. In 1968 he was their leading run-scorer in the Tests and topped their first-class averages. Although it sometimes proved his downfall, he was a very good, instinctive hooker, unquestionably one of the best cutters I have seen, and the safest of slip fielders. Utterly fearless, he thrived on fast bowling and was prepared to take on the quickest. This was to prove another advantage when he became captain.

He was appointed skipper for the first time for the final (seventh) Test of the 1970–71 England tour under Ray Illingworth. Chappell lost, but the match marked the start of an Australian renaissance. As Richie Benaud wrote: 'Australia's longest-ever Test Match sequence without victory, and then came Chappell'. It was here that Ian enjoyed the luck which every successful captain must have. He took over at the right time, when things had to improve and he capitalised on it. The Australian team which toured England in 1972 under his captaincy was expected to do badly, but it managed to draw the series, winning two Tests and surprising everybody by its performance. Although Ian himself did not have an exceptional tour, his captaincy was very astute, he made sure that the fielding was excellent, and he had another piece of luck, the arrival of Dennis Lillee on the international scene, while Bob Massie enjoyed his one brief summer of glory. Chappell followed this up in 1972–73 with a triumphant tour of the Caribbean, which he won, despite losing the services of Lillee, his main attacking bowler, through injury, and his second, Massie, who suffered a complete, and inexplicable, loss of form. This was probably his greatest feat as captain. From then on Australia under Ian Chappell reigned supreme, assisted by another piece of luck, the emergence of the perfect partner for the now recovered Lillee, Jeff Thomson, and the ideal third seamer, Max Walker.

What were the reasons for Ian Chappell's great success, other than leading a strong side for most of his career, and being a world-class player himself? In addition to being intelligent, decisive and having a shrewd cricket brain, Ian was a product of the unsettled sixties, which rejected much of the past without producing any lasting solutions: only dreams, like flower power, and nightmares, like the Red Brigade. Ian deliberately set out to be anti-establishment, which appealed to those under his command. As he was achieving the long-awaited success on the field, the establishment was prepared to accept standards of behaviour which they would never have condoned in the past, and with more money available he launched an overdue and successful campaign for increased financial rewards, which naturally increased his popularity with his players. An ideal anti-hero of the 1960s, Ian took Australia into the 1970s to the accompaniment of non-stop 'sledging', raucously backed up by colourful, though painfully limited language. Deliberately sloppy dress for formal functions was encouraged by Ian and approved by his players, so that jeans became the norm. An exception occurred at the Australian Centenary Dinner, one of the most prestigious events in their cricket history. I found myself in the same lift as the Australian captain, who was wearing what resembled more closely than anything else the uniform of a hotel bell boy and, though I am not a sartorial expert, it did seem distinctly, and quite deliberately, out of place.

The dress revolution by itself was unimportant, merely a sign of the times, but unacceptable were some of the incidents which occurred both on and off the field. I recall a respected tennis official who loved cricket coming up to me and asking if Australian cricketers usually behaved as badly as they had done in the hospitality tent during the Tennis Championship at Adelaide. I had to tell him that I was not surprised. Many Test matches were also conducted in an atmosphere of open hostility, which appealed to a considerable section of the Australian public who demanded winning at any price; but it dismayed many others.

Ian Chappell's team became a tight-knit, aggressive group, who were both far more successful and better financially rewarded than any of their immediate predecessors thanks to Ian's skill as captain and his frequent battles with the establishment. The players knew he would never let them down and they liked the way in which he managed to break through some of the petty officialdom which still existed in Australian cricket administration, a throw-back to the days when it had been an essentially amateur sport. Tactically, indeed, I would rate Ian Chappell as the best captain of the 1970s, while in addition he was a world-class performer as batsman, slip fielder and a useful change slow bowler. In these circumstances, it is easy to understand why those under his command were prepared to accept behaviour which, at times, was unacceptable, and certainly unnecessary. His record as captain speaks for itself, 30 matches, 15 wins, 10 draws, 5 losses.

He also twice led South Australia to victory in the Sheffield Shield and predictably, he was a prime mover in the World

Series Cricket breakaway. Probably no cricketer, apart from Don Bradman himself, has exerted more influence as a player in Australia than Ian, but on too many occasions he abused it, thus harming both the game and himself. It is sad to think, though all too predictable, that in his last first-class season he should have been suspended for verbal abuse against an umpire in Tasmania. He was seldom out of the headlines during his career, but too many of them had nothing to do with his ability as a player, or as a brilliant leader of men. I fancy that, providing he was not killed, he would have returned from any war loaded with decorations for bravery under fire, the macho man of cricket.

With the exception of Sir Donald Bradman, I would also rate Ian as Australia's best post-war captain in terms of player motivation, making the most of the talent under his command, and in his personal contribution as a player. He lacked Don's brilliant analytical brain, maturity and tact, while though he was an outstanding batsman, Don was a genius. However, Ian was such a fine leader, that it is hard to understand why he should have handed over the captaincy to his brother Greg so early and when he was still at the top himself. The answer surely lies on the opening page of his autobiography, *Cricket in our Blood*, where he wrote:

> The night I was appointed captain of Australia, I said to my wife Kay, 'They'll never get me like that'. I was referring, of course, to the sacking of Bill Lawry as Australian captain by the Test selectors. It was probably the most insensitive thing I had seen in more than fifteen years of first-class cricket. Not one cricket official, not the selectors or any member of the Australian Cricket Board, had informed Bill that he had been replaced as captain of Australia and dropped from the team to play England in the Seventh Test of the 1970–71 series. It was left to one of his Victorian teammates, Keith Stackpole, who had heard about it on the radio in his motel room in Adelaide, to break the news to Bill Lawry.

This unhappy episode, yet another example of insensitivity by the game's administrators, clearly influenced Ian's attitude towards the establishment when he became captain of Australia. He fought them over many issues, including pay, conditions, discipline, behaviour and dress. They soon discovered that they were up against an opponent who was just as tough, and far more astute than any trade union leader. Ian used the big increase in player power, and the success and the popularity he acquired from his successes on the field, to extract the concessions he demanded. During his reign he made no attempt to disguise his distaste for the Australian cricket authorities and so he was absolutely determined to retire before the selectors had the opportunity to sack him. It would certainly have appealed to some of them. He had been appointed initially under sufferance and his subsequent behaviour had done little to make them change their minds. As a result he followed the example of the best after-dinner speakers, but forgotten by most, to stop when ahead, and with the audience wanting more.

7

THE MAJOR CHANGES IN THE GAME

THE MAJOR CHANGES IN THE GAME

Batting

Pads were originally introduced to protect the batsman's legs, but players quickly learned how they could also be used to protect their stumps from any ball pitching outside the line between wicket and wicket. Batsmen became, in fact, so adept at ignoring anything which pitched fractionally outside the off stump that the great opening batsmen, like Sir Jack Hobbs and Herbert Sutcliffe, would regularly pad up to any good-length delivery outside their off stump, having first moved back and across their wicket. To counter this excessive pad play, it was decided in the 1930s to introduce a new Law – lbw (n) – which enabled the bowler to gain a leg-before-wicket decision from a ball which had pitched outside the off stump, providing that it hit the batsman while he was standing between wicket and wicket (and, of course, that it would have hit the stumps). The intention, to reduce pad play and increase off-side strokes was, like all changes to the Laws, admirable, but the effect was to increase the power of the off-break and the in-swing bowler, thus reducing the off-side play which it had hoped to encourage. It decreased the effectiveness of the away-swinger and leg-spinner, and changed the emphasis of pad play from the back to the front leg.

The pads themselves have also changed; instead of the standard heavy, well padded buckskin style, many batsmen now favour synthetic lightweight ones, which not only provide excellent protection, but make running between the wickets faster, though because the ball bounces further off them, they must increase the chances of giving a catch. Wicket-keepers once wore the same pair for both keeping and batting. Now an increasing number of keepers uses a much smaller and lighter pair when behind the stumps, while some prefer taping their pads, rather than using straps, in order to reduce pressure on their leg muscles.

Batting gloves have changed less, though a plastic splint over the sausage protector is favoured by some players. What has increased dramatically is the number of times they now change their gloves during an innings, which makes me wonder whether batsmen are sweating more profusely these days.

The heavy dependable boot has been replaced by the boot-slipper or shoe-slipper, which are considerably lighter but certainly do not provide the same ankle support or protection. Covered pitches have also led to an increase of rubber-soled shoes for batting and fielding, rather than spikes. This has resulted in many disasters through batsmen and fielders slipping at crucial moments, especially in England when the grass may look perfectly dry, but still contain some moisture.

In 1970 another change was made to the lbw Law, again in an effort to curb pad play by allowing a batsman to be given out to a ball which had pitched and struck him outside the off-stump providing he had attempted no stroke. Again, the intention was admirable, but the effect has been rather less so. It has certainly caused all bowlers to switch their line of attack further to the off. These days an in-swing bowler can afford to pitch well outside the off stump and rely on his slips for his catches, whereas formerly he had to pitch on and just outside off stump and rely on his leg-slips, because batsmen could afford to ignore anything outside the off stump. This new Law has made batting more difficult, as a fast good-length ball pitching outside the off stump and likely to move away now has to be played at, just in case it nips back off the seam. However, I have a suspicion that it has led to even more pad play, though of a different type. Nowadays, an ever-increasing number of batsmen push forward with their bat behind their front pad. The outcome is that the two 'bat-pad' or in some cases several 'bat-pad' fieldsmen, standing very close to the batsman on either side of the wicket, have become almost standard fixtures for spinners and seamers alike. In the past, the key catching position for an off-spinner on a pitch taking spin were leg-slip or leg-gulley, and the chances off the bat via the pad were remote, because the forward defensive stroke was played in front of the pad. The slow left-hand spinner sometimes used a silly mid-off for the mis-drive, or half-push, but never two 'bat-pad' fieldsmen for exactly the same reason, because the edged shot from the full forward defensive stroke goes to slip, or to square, very close gulley.

There is nothing new about the technique of playing the forward defensive with the bat behind the front pad. Colin Cowdrey used it to good effect on several occasions against Ramadhin, but it has become increasingly popular as a counter against seam, swing and spin bowling to the ball which pitches outside the off stump and might come back sufficiently to hit the stumps, and which, prior to 1970, batsmen would have dismissed with their front pad. It also provides a way, although a most unattractive one, of playing Abdul Qadir, if the batsman is unable to 'pick' his googly. It takes a brave umpire to give a batsman out lbw for having played no stroke, when he thrusts forward his left leg with his bat tucked in by the side of his knee.

Has the shift of line to outside the off stump led to a marked increase in off-side play? It probably has, as it has resulted in more off-side fieldsmen, and it has also encouraged the front-foot player; conversely, however, it has increased the rewards of hitting the ball off the stumps into the less populated legside, as any innings by Vivian Richards, Javed Miandad and Graham Gooch will illustrate. It has also helped the away-swing bowler, because he no longer needs to start his swing from around leg-and-middle or middle stump, as on or outside the off stump, which is much easier to do, will suffice. The majority of the slip catches that used to be taken off Lindwall and Trueman were from balls which pitched on the stumps; the majority now pitch outside, often a long way.

In addition, the off-spinner from over the wicket tends to attack the off stump, pitching outside. This noticeable shift in line means that his first requirement is a bat-pad catcher on the leg side, whereas in the past, when he had to pitch between wicket and wicket to obtain a lbw decision, a backward short-leg was essential. Since the batsman nowadays tends to play all spinners, not just off-break bowlers, with his bat behind his front pad rather than a foot in front of it, this increases the chances of being caught 'bat-pad' on either side of the wicket.

The new lbw Law makes an umpire's job more difficult. The batsman who cannot spot Qadir's googly may solve, or partially solve, his problem by thrusting his left leg firmly forwards down the line. If it is the 'wrong-un' it simply misses the bat, and if it is a leg-break which turns, the chances are that it misses everything.

Good players will make runs in all forms of the game, but there can be no doubt that the surfeit of limited-overs cricket, combined with batting bonus points in county cricket, has harmed batting in England. The young player coming into the game, ideally in his late teens, and batting in the middle order, frequently finds himself going to the crease with quick runs the main consideration. In contrast Keith Fletcher, at seventeen and eighteen, was batting for Essex at no. 6, and all that was wanted, or expected, was for him to play his normal game, which was essentially positive. Time, and the advice of Gordon Barker, would eventually convince him that driving seamers off his back foot over extra-cover, although both spectacular and exciting, would over the years prove unproductive in terms of percentage rewards!

Nowadays, in their formative years, young batsmen will often find that incorrectly executed attacking strokes will prove more productive than those that have been played correctly. The drive off the front foot to a ball outside the off stump, without the front foot being moved into the line, will often produce that flashy square drive, as David Gower has demonstrated on numerous occasions. It has been most noticeable that, over the last decade, the footwork of the majority of the best batsmen in England has been technically incorrect, with many runs coming from shots made from the half-cock position, neither forward nor back, but straddling the crease. Anyone who doubts this should watch England batsmen in the nets practising alongside the Indians.

Kim Barnett, the Derbyshire captain, also provides an interesting example, as he thrusts firmly forward and across his stumps before the ball is bowled. If it is over-pitched he will move further forward; if it is of good length he will remain in the half-cock position relying largely on his right hand to provide the power when seeking runs; and to the short ball he plays back from over the crease. His method may not be text-book, but it has provided him with plenty of runs and is especially effective on the many rather suspect pitches on which county games have been played in recent years.

The Indians, and not just their best batsmen, use the crease by playing right back or moving right forward on to their front foot and hitting the ball with a straight bat which may be angled from time to time to beat the field. As yet they have not become experts in the steer or run-down through the gulley and the dab all executed with minimal foot movement.

There is a fundamental principle in batting which transcends all others. It is a principle observed by every good batsman in every era wherever the game has been played, and is – *Keep the head still.* The one time this is easy is in the stance, which should be comfortable and relaxed. *The MCC Coaching Manual* expresses it this way:

> The Feet.
> (1) The heels should be some three inches apart, with the right foot parallel with or pointing just behind the crease and the left foot pointing to cover. The popping crease should run between them, and both toes should be just

clear of the line of the leg stump, assuming leg stump, or middle-and-leg, is taken as guard.
(2) The knees should be equally balanced between, and very slightly on the front part of, the feet.
(3) The knees should be very slightly relaxed, making for easy and quick movement.
The body should face squarely to point.
The head must be kept upright and turned towards the bowler with the eyes as level as possible.
Most players find it natural and comfortable to ground the bat about two inches behind the toes of the right foot, but just to the off side of them with the blade facing the left leg and the hands at ease just away from or even touching the left thigh.

Although there were variations (and one could recognise a batsman by his stance), this was how the majority of first-class batsmen have stood for more than fifty years, but now an ever-increasing number is standing with bat aloft, rather like a striker in baseball. This is worrying because it has been adopted by Graham Gooch, currently England's finest batsman, and there are a host of imitators – including Tim Robinson, John Carr and Chris Broad – so that youngsters are copying them and learning to bat without having a smooth, flowing backlift and down-swing. Obviously this does not apply to the Graham Gooches of this world, as they have the ability to make runs whatever stance they employ, but less talented players need to be aware of the dangers.

The 'bat aloft' style, which was popular in the Golden Age, was re-introduced by Tony Greig who, like most excessively tall men, found himself vulnerable against the fast yorker because he struggled to get his bat up and down again in time. Having the bat already lifted gave him a moment longer when confronted by exceptional pace; and others, including Mike Brearley, followed his lead. Incidentally, Tony's problem could also have been solved by simply reducing his backlift against pace.

The increased popularity of heavy bats, which make the backlift more difficult to execute for a small person, has also encouraged the 'bat aloft' style in this country, although it has had much less impact on the batsmen of the West Indies, India and Pakistan. In Australia there has recently been a move away from the heavy bat, and the talented Dean Jones has done well with one weighing 2lb.4oz., which used to be the standard weight for first-class batsmen. There is nothing wrong in big, tall men like Graeme Pollock and Clive Lloyd using much heavier bats, but one wonders about the wisdom of a small man arming himself with one of over 3lb. weight.

When I walked around the Gunn and Moore factory recently, I was fascinated not only by the weight of so many of their bats, but also by the thickness of the handles and the edges. What are the attractions? They certainly do not provide a further carry, as a bat weighing 2lb.4oz. is lifted faster and brought down faster than a club of 3lb.4oz. As a result, a ball which is middled with a light bat should produce a bigger six than one with a heavy club, in the same way that the longest drivers in golf do not use the heaviest clubs. The great attractions of a heavy bat lie in it being ideal for pushing fours, while it will achieve boundaries, sometimes sixes, even when the ball has not been 'middled', and it is admirably suited to the nudge and nick, so valuable in the limited-overs game.

The danger of the heavy bat and the 'bat aloft' stance is that it so often leads to the bat being brought down across the line, which is surely why Gooch has so often been out lbw. The heavy bat also makes the execution of delicate strokes, like the late-cut, more difficult, and this may account for why it is so seldom seen in county cricket these days. It could also be responsible for increasing the number of batsmen who, with their feet straddling the crease, and their weight on their front foot, simply clump the ball away, mainly square of the wicket on the off side – hence the popularity of the deep cover, or 'sweeper'.

It could well be the case also that the increase in the number of batsmen caught behind the wicket on the off side has been due not only to the bowlers shifting their line to just outside the off stump and the batsman having to play the ball, but also to the heavier bats. The weight, combined with the thick handles, has tended to decrease the importance of the part played by the left hand in the control of the bat, and increase the importance of the bottom hand which now provides the extra impetus for the straight push, as distinct from the full swing used in the straight drive. A correct off-drive is derived from a straight down-swing from a backlift in which the back of the bat will be facing square leg. When the bottom hand becomes lord and master, the down-swing will tend to have an on-side bias, thus increasing the chances of providing the slips with a catch.

The new stance with the bat held aloft, à la Graham Gooch, is, however, more likely to induce a false backlift and might help to explain why the footwork of so many English batsmen employing this method is faulty and limited. The backlift, down-swing and movement of the feet should all blend together. It might be said that there is no such thing as the top of a backlift, as part of the body has already commenced the down-swing.

The introduction of the helmet as standard equipment for batsmen has coincided with an increase of fast, short-pitched bowling, and a decline in the number of batsmen who are able to sway out of the line of a bouncer, and watch it fly harmlessly past. Admittedly there now are more bumpers bowled, especially at the tailenders, but since the wearing of helmets became common practice far more batsmen have been hit on the head, and not infrequently injured. Could it be that the helmet has provided a false sense of security? Are too many indifferent batsmen trying to hook, who, without a helmet, would never have considered the stroke? I also suspect that many of the helmets have been poorly designed and fail to provide the expected protection. In Barbados club cricket, where there is plenty of bowling as quick as on the English county circuit, helmets are seldom worn as they are too expensive, but nobody has been seriously hurt for a long time. Could it be that the helmetless make absolutely sure that they are not hit on the head?

Helmets, many complete with a visor and ear protectors, are impersonal, and have lessened the appeal of the game as a spectacle. There was a time when one could tell instantly who was batting: by the rakish angle of his cap, Cyril Washbrook; the blond wavy hair, upright stance and top of the handle grip, Joe Hardstaff; the small figure with the pugnacious face, Bill Edrich; and the dishevelled locks of the Brylcreem Boy, Denis Compton. Now all the batsmen tend to look the same, carbon-copy bikers. Some players do remove their helmets when the quicker bowlers have come off, while it is a joy to see Viv Richards wearing his West Indian cap and Ian Botham hatless. One of the game's more comic sights was that of Derek Pringle coming out to bat on a placid pitch at Lord's in 1982 against India. It was hard to imagine any of the Indian bowlers making the ball rise sufficiently to hit him on his head and, if they had, it would hardly have been fast enough to hurt. The players have, of course, become so helmet-conscious that they feel almost undressed without them, like jousting knights, and are prepared to accept the discomfort and the reduced vision.

Nobody wore a helmet in my time. Although I was a front-foot player, it never occurred to me that I might be hit on my head by a bouncer, and, although they were not as plentiful as they are today, there were a few flying around. I was often hit on the body though, and indeed Ray Lindwall once broke my thumb, as I foolishly used it instead of my bat to fend off a ball that rose sharply; but in over twenty years of first-class cricket I was only 'sweded' twice, once by Keith Miller and once by Fred Trueman. On both occasions, it was entirely my own fault, as I ducked and took my eye off the ball, which failed to rise to the height I expected. However I am sure that I would have been grateful for a helmet on a bad pitch where the ball was liable to lift off a length.

I have discussed the threat of head injury from bouncers with a number of famous and talented batsmen. The following are just a few who have never received a direct hit on the head from one: Weekes, Walcott, Sobers, Bill Edrich, Graveney, Harvey, and, of course, Bradman; though Denis Compton was once unlucky enough to hook a short *no-ball* from Lindwall into his face during his epic innings at Old Trafford in 1948.

Fielding

The most noticeable improvement in first-class cricket over the past two decades has been in the field. First, the throwing-in today is stronger (though a reduction in the size of outfields has made it easier) and more accurate. Anyone doubting this has only to count the number of times the stumps are hit by direct returns, not infrequently when there has been only one to aim at. It is true that Colin Bland, who played for South Africa, used to do this with impressive regularity but he was the exception. Now it is commonplace. Among the most impressive features are accuracy in the long, flat returns from the boundary, the pick-up and throw from the middle distances, and those attempted run-outs, using either the under-arm flick, or straightforward under-arm at pace and on the move.

Second, the ground fielding is generally better and certainly more spectacular. This has been assisted by most outfields now having thick carpets of grass, which slow down the pace of the ball and greatly reduce the chances of a bad bounce or a sudden change of direction. The Trent Bridge outfield is so soft and spongy that a fieldsman can fall, or dive, without danger of grazing or hurting himself, which helps to explain why fielders seem to spend so much more time in the horizontal position. It should, perhaps, be mentioned that though a chase round the boundary and a full-length dive are dramatic, there are occasions when the discreet use of a boot can be more effective and even turn three runs into two.

Third, the standard of catching, especially in the deep, has improved and I reckon to see more brilliant out-catches in one season than I used to see in five. It is not just the holding of catches which is better, but the fielders have become more athletic. This has enabled them to bring off some catches which probably would never have been attempted.

Limited-overs cricket – with its emphasis on the prevention of runs, the need to lift the ball, the slog, and the increased tempo of play – has done much, of course, to raise the standard of out-fielding. In the less frenetic first-class match, a county used to be able to hide a few players, non-benders and slow movers with poor arms, but in the one-day game they are a big liability. However, the main reason why the catching, throwing, and ground fielding have improved so much is the amount of time spent practising. You cannot create a good batsman or bowler, but you can, with sufficient practice, turn an indifferent fielder into a very competent performer and a natural athlete into a brilliant one. This was demonstrated back in the mid-1950s by Jack Cheetham, and the outcome of his efforts was that South Africa became a formidable international team, which emphasised in its turn the importance of good fielding. This is now generally recognised and the standard of fielding of most Test teams would be equal, and some better, than that of Jack Cheetham's 1955 side. The more time spent on throwing, fielding and catching, the more expert one becomes and it is sometimes possible to see the improvement in a comparatively short time. Many years ago that flamboyant opening batsman for Essex, Dickie Dodds, experienced an unhappy spell in the outfield, when he was putting down catches with such depressing regularity that inevitably he lost confidence. Several hours devoted to catching skiers provided the cure. Once he began holding on to them, his old confidence returned and he did not drop another that summer.

Although most aspects of fielding have steadily improved, I am not so convinced about the close catching, apart from in the 'bat-pad' position, which is an innovation. I have seen nothing in the past few years as good as the overall standard reached by the Australian slips and gulleys of the Lillee–Thomson–Walker era, and though the West Indian close fielders have brought off many wonderful catches, they have also dropped a number. England have also grassed more chances in the past three years than when Brearley, Hendrick and Botham were in the slips.

This poses a question: If constant practice has raised the general standard of fielding dramatically, why does it not appear to have had the same impact on the catching in the slips and short-legs? The reason may be that it is far more difficult to provide a form of practice whch approximates to the actual event. Catches at slip and leg-slip are frequently made instinctively, especially when the wicket-keeper is standing up and obscuring the fielder's view. The best way to practise slip catching is for a batsman to cut and snick full tosses which have been thrown at him. England regularly employs this method in pre-play practice sessions but, though it is useful, it cannot entirely recreate the genuine slip catch, which is so often an unexpected, as well as an unintentional edge, made even more difficult if it occurs when nothing has been happening for a couple of hours, and concentration has wavered. The batsman providing the imitation slip catches should aim to snick more than he cuts, as the snick, except for those aimed at gulley, is what slip fielders will mainly have to hold.

Because slip catching depends so much on concentration, which hardly fits into a pre-play warm-up, and quick reactions, there is probably a case for the re-introduction of the slip cradle. This, when used by pairs, or individually, provides excellent practice for instinctive close catches of all varieties. I am convinced that the time spent on the slip cradle at school, often as much as half-an-hour per day, assisted my fielding in the slips despite the considerable disadvantage of having ridiculously small and fragile hands.

The helmet has now become standard equipment for those fielding close in the bat-pad position on either side of the pitch.

The fielder is, of course, in considerably more danger of being hit than the batsman. Even the most agile, like Gus Logie, from a suicidal position almost on top of the bat, does not have sufficient time to avoid a powerful strike, especially if it has been mis-hit. A blow to the head is very painful, and can prove lethal, hence the helmet. However, as close fielders are liable to be struck even more frequently on other parts of the body, most bat-pad specialists now don a box and shin guards for additional protection. It could well be that we are fast approaching an era when fieldsmen will come out cocooned and encased like Michelin Men or American footballers. This makes a case for the introduction of the ruling, already operating in school cricket, which prevents fieldsmen standing too close to a batsman in front of the wicket. It is, after all, only another form of intimidation, the essential intention being to pressurise the batsman.

Bowling

Although the standard of fielding has improved considerably at first-class level in the last twenty years, the overall standard of bowling has surely declined. This applies especially to county cricket in England, but the Australian attacks since the Lillee and Thomson era have been lacking in penetration, while none of the other Test teams, apart from the West Indies and Pakistan, can currently field more than two top-calibre bowlers. The army of seamers capped by England during the past decade has – apart from Bob Willis and Ian Botham, and, in between injuries, Graham Dilley, Gladstone Small and Neil Foster – not been of international quality; and Willis is the only member of that quintet who falls into the genuinely fast category.

The 1988 season saw the introduction of a certain amount of four-day cricket in the hope that it will improve the standard of batting and also encourage younger batsmen by giving them more chance to play major innings in the middle order.

Personally, I have reservations about the value of the four-day game, but its supporters can point out that, on those occasions when a good pitch has been provided, several substantial totals were made. These look impressive until one examines the quality of the bowling. In Franklin Stephenson and Kevin Cooper Nottinghamshire had a good, but hardly exceptional, new-ball pair, yet both Stephenson, a competent fast-medium bowler with a big heart and a gem of a slower ball who might make the Barbados Second XI, and Cooper, an accurate away-swing bowler of just above medium pace, claimed a remarkable number of victims. The West Indian captured a hundred wickets quicker than anyone else, and went on to achieve the 'double', while Kevin Cooper finished with 101 wickets at 21.57 runs apiece. In terms of economy and size of haul they were the most effective of county opening bowlers. This helps to explain how Neil Radford, Philip Newport, Philip DeFreitas, David Capel and Derek Pringle, who fall into the good county bowler category, were all selected for England, as was David Lawrence, who relied almost entirely on speed through the air but was short on accuracy.

Except on indifferent, over-grassed pitches (of which there were too many) a good batsman should have fancied his chances of making runs against the majority of the counties. Apart from a handful of fine fast bowlers from overseas, fewer than usual in 1988 because of the West Indies tour, eighty per cent of the bowling was done by seamers, ranging from sharp to medium, who were in the main tidy, but, apart from a handful, unlikely to make much impression at international level.

The present cricket ball retains its seam and shine far longer than used to be the case, although, judging by the number which are changed, they do not maintain their shape as well. This is partially due to the lush outfields, as when a new ball is taken after 100 overs, the bowlers are still able to move the old one, both in the air and off the pitch, something which could seldom have occurred in the 1950s, as the ball after 100 overs would have been severely scuffed, while the seam, also less pronounced at the commencement of the game, would have been very flat. In other words, its condition, unlike today, would have been more suitable for spin than seam.

It is also noticeable that slow bowlers polish the ball to help retain the shine for the seamers, whereas there was a time when they would deliberately rub it on bare ground in order to rough up the cover and obtain a better grip. This latter practice is no longer permitted, although the polishing is – another example of how the dice have become loaded in favour of the seamer.

The county scene has never been so infested by seam. Some clubs are not bothering to include any slow bowlers, while the majority are prepared to settle for one. What is making the shortage of spinners even more worrying is the fact that most of them have been around for a very long time. There is only a trickle of new ones coming into the game, and they are then stifled by pitches on which a mundane medium-pacer is liable to move the ball as much as they can turn it. One hopes that the four-day match, in conjunction with good wickets and teams batting on into the second day, will eventually lead to the slow bowler once again becoming indispensable; but then one remembers what the West Indies have achieved, and are achieving, with pace in five-day matches!

It should not be thought that the spinner shortage is just an English disease, as, outside of Pakistan and India, it is difficult to think of many who would seriously trouble class players on a bad pitch, let alone on a plumb one, which explains why they are Mike Gatting's favourite breakfast.

The majority of Test matches is decided by an attack capable of dismissing the opposition twice. This accounts for England's sad record in recent years, because we have not had one. We have been unable to find another strike bowler as fast and as hostile as Bob Willis, while the irrepressible Ian Botham has not only been absent, but has lost some of his original bite. The situation has been made worse because the three best replacements, Dilley, Foster and Small have all been hampered by injuries, so that inevitably the attack has lacked punch. In addition none of the spinners available was likely to produce the figures to win a Test.

If one excludes the overseas imports, a glance at the current county attacks reveals that the selectors have not had many alternatives. Some of the bowling averages for 1988 were very impressive, but the final figures of, for example, Cooper, Newport, Sidebottom, Mallender, Topley, have owed much to those 'result pitches'. It is worth noting the considerable number of competent county as distinct from Test batsmen who, despite the number of bad pitches, still scored heavily. One reason was that once the two main bowlers had been seen off, runs could be plundered without much difficulty. There were certainly not many bowlers on the circuit likely to dismiss an international XI cheaply on a good wicket. This explains how England came to field this bowling line-up at Old Trafford in 1988: Dilley, DeFreitas, Capel, Emburey and Childs, which did not look too menacing, while the attack at Headingley consisted of a seam quartet of Dilley, Foster, Pringle and Cowdrey, which by Test standards could only be termed anaemic.

Nevertheless, the general outlook in the seam section is not too gloomy. Pace bowlers can improve dramatically and Fletcher, Fraser, Igglesden, Bicknell, and Robinson are just some of the young quickies who might have the ability to cross the gap dividing the competent county bowler from the international new-ball bowler. They would all benefit from having to operate on more good batting wickets, when their success will depend on themselves, not the pitch. They have not been helped by the quantity of one-day games, where control is more vital than pace. But limited-overs cricket has been responsible for one marked improvement. When a quick bowler has been slogged to the boundary, there is the obvious temptation to try and send down the next ball even quicker, but with a well-set field the best answer is a well-disguised slower ball. Although Stephenson possesses the best slower ball in the business at present, there are a number of bowlers, including Dilley, who now include this useful weapon in their armoury.

Most of the best fast bowlers in Test and in county cricket come from the West Indies. The extent of their domination is so great that one must seek reasons.

First, the club pitches in the Caribbean are usually fairly fast, and reasonably true, and the grounds small, which does not assist the slow bowler. There is also little future for an English-style seamer there, unless he can swing the ball in the air, because it comes sweetly on to the bat, and the bounce is fairly even. It is the natural habitat for fast, and lively fast-medium bowlers, who also quickly learn in two-innings club matches, which last over three Saturdays, that accuracy pays.

Second, given the natural ability to propel a ball straight and very quickly through the air, it does not take long to become an effective bowler, much, much quicker than becoming a good batsman, or, for that matter, a spinner. In a year Curtley Ambrose went from an unknown to a Test star, and he did not even play much club cricket. Third, a fast bowler, like a heavyweight boxer, has enormous crowd appeal. Everyone, apart from opposing players, wants to see him in action. Only a truly great batsman commands more adoration. Fourth, in the Caribbean, cricket provides an escape route to another world, one in which the rewards are far higher than can be expected at home. In the case of the genuine fast bowler, it is also a very quick route. The fact that Roberts, Garner, Holding and at least another ten pacemen from the Caribbean have done so well has encouraged youngsters to emulate them.

Finally, and most important of all, the black West Indian is born with the natural aptitude, physique and stamina needed to become a fast bowler. A semi-tropical climate throughout the year, and adequate food, has helped to produce a population with long, powerful arms and legs, plus the broad backs which are ideally suited to hurling down cricket balls at great speed for long spells, and plenty of time to practise since unemployment is high.

There can be no doubt that too many bouncers have been bowled during the past twenty years and umpires have been much too tolerant. I enjoy a bowler unleashing from time to time a delivery which has a batsman in trouble, as it threatens to decapitate him; but watching a bumper barrage over a period of time is very boring indeed, a spectators' nightmare. Does that matter? Well, they have paid to watch.

There is nothing remotely new, of course, about the bouncer, or bumper, a fast ball pitched deliberately short in order to make it bounce high in the air between chest and chin. Kortright is said to have singed the great W.G.'s beard; Gregory and Macdonald 'dropped' a number of English batsmen, and frightened many more, in the 1920s; Larwood and Voce returned the compliment with interest in the 1930s; Lindwall and Miller enlivened the post-war scene with some delicious bouncers and it was, quite rightly, considered to be a weapon in every fast bowler's armoury. A well directed one would hit the batsman at the receiving end if he failed to take evasive action, or used his bat. Its objectives might be summed up as follows: first, to obtain a catch as a result of the batsman either attempting to hook, or fending the ball off. Second, to make sure that batsmen did not thrust forward early and to force him on to his back foot. Third, to frighten the apprehensive, and a great many, including several fine batsmen, fall into that category. Fast bowlers smell fear as avidly as a shark scents blood. You could read Fred Trueman's mind ticking over: 'Absolutely terrified, one to tickle him up, followed by a leg-stump yorker as he retreats towards the square-leg umpire'. Fourth, it provided the quick bowler, especially on an easy batting wicket, with a chance to release his frustration. Fifth, to obtain a direct hit, as part of the softening-up process, not necessarily of that batsman at the receiving end but as a reminder of what might happen to those who followed.

Although these objectives still apply, there are two differences. First, the bouncer has almost become a stock, rather than shock, ball. In my opinion, the umpires have permitted far too many to be bowled during the last decade, and I believe that more than one per over constitutes deliberate intimidation. However, it could also be argued that, since the bowling of too many bouncers, apart from the danger, is boring, it is the responsibility of the administrators and the players. When in the late 1950s the great throwing purge took place, the umpires were blamed for not having been more decisive, but I have always felt that the real culprits were the clubs and the officials who picked bowlers with suspect actions!

Second, the non-batsmen are now regarded as prime targets for the bouncer whereas in the past it was only employed against recognised batsmen, who should possess the ability required to cope. This was especially noticeable between members of the pace bowling union. Fred Trueman could afford quite safely to push forward against Wes Hall! Yet it would be wrong to think that in the 1950s we were more concerned with the welfare of players, as the 'beamer', the head-high full toss, which is infinitely more dangerous, was used and this is now, quite correctly, outlawed. We just felt that the genuine 'rabbit' was too likely to be hurt by a bouncer and could be bowled out anyway without too much trouble.

Pitches and the shortage of spinners

The shortage, often the complete absence of slow bowling, has been one of the saddest features of Test cricket since I wrote *The Greatest of my time* (1968). For more than a decade the West Indies have based their strategy on a quartet of very good, and contrasting, fast bowlers who, apart from the odd occasion when they were confronted by a slow, turning pitch, have carried nearly all before them.

Why have four-man pace-quartets proved so successful in recent years, because they are not an innovation? In the second Test of the 'Bodyline' tour in 1932–33, Douglas Jardine included Harold Larwood, Bill Voce, 'Gubby' Allen and Bill Bowes in his team, while Wally Hammond, who could be decidedly hasty, was also available. But Jardine lost that match. On two post-war tours, England decided to go in with four seamers, with even more disastrous results: at Sabina Park, Jamaica, in 1954, Fred Trueman, Brian Statham, Alan Moss and myself; and, on the next tour, against Australia in Brisbane, Frank Tyson, Brian Statham, Alec Bedser and myself. I also had the opportunity of batting against Australian sides top-heavy with pace. At The Oval in 1953, when we regained the Ashes, we faced Ray Lindwall, Keith Miller, Bill Johnston, Alan Davidson and Ron Archer, though I have always believed that if Sir Len Hutton had won the toss in 1953, or we had been put into bat, we would have lost the match, but in those days the wickets were not covered after the start. Five years later Ian Meckiff, Gordon Rorke, Alan Davidson and Ray Lindwall demonstrated that four quickies could be effective.

The main reason why international cricket has witnessed the great increase in fast bowling and, sadly, a depressing drop in the amount of slow bowling, has been the pitches, which have made the spinner a luxury rather than the necessity he once was.

It is impossible to over-emphasise the importance of the pitch, especially in a Test match, as it can not only decide the result, and sometimes the outcome of a series, but it can also exert more influence on the composition of the team and how it performs than can either captain. The big increase in seam, and the decrease in spin, therefore, has stemmed from the wickets on which international cricket has been played in recent years. This especially applies in England when the first blow to slow bowling was the partially covered pitch, and the knock-out punch, the completely covered pitches for both county and Test matches.

In the normal English summer rain is always a distinct possibility, especially at night, so that every well-balanced county used to include a couple of spinners as insurance. After heavy rain followed by hot sun, they were the potential match winners, while on a sodden pitch they were usually the most effective type of bowler. In addition, on a worn or damaged third-day wicket, they often were the key figures, while they always provided variety and could be gainfully employed on really good wickets as stock bowlers. In the same way as a batsman needs to have the opportunity to make runs, a slow bowler needs plenty of practice if he is to master his difficult trade. Since the 1960s few spinners have been allowed to do enough bowling in county cricket, so that these days, on the rare occasions when the conditions are in the spinners' favour, they are seldom able to exploit them to the full. The shortage has become so acute that England had to call on John Childs, who was in his middle thirties and never, in his long career with Gloucestershire and Essex, was more than a good county slow left-hand bowler. He did not even claim a permanent place in the Essex team when he was selected for England as the best spinner in the land. However, the lack of young finger-spinners has been apparent for many years, as all the leading performers had been on the county circuit for at least a decade, and several – Derek Underwood, Jack Simmons and Norman Gifford – for more than two decades.

As county attacks have become increasingly dependent upon seam, this has predictably led to the preparation of pitches which have been designed to suit pace bowlers, so that the bowling averages are dominated by the seamers.

Other reasons for the slow bowler shortage, which I discuss in more detail in other sections, are: the batting equipment now used, limited-overs cricket, smaller grounds, commercial sponsorship and over rates. It might also be added that we live in a world where instant success is regarded as important, and the fast bowler can achieve this quicker than batsmen and slow bowlers, as Curtley Ambrose has illustrated. In 1988 he was given plenty of work to do, which helped his development. Paradoxically, though, the spin bowler needs even more work than the quick bowler if he is to refine his skill and technique.

The importance of slow bowlers still applies in India, Pakistan and Sri Lanka, as was underlined by England selecting three – Emburey, Childs and Hemmings – to go on the aborted

1988–89 tour to India, but note that none of this trio is in the first flush of youth.

Slow Over Rates

In 1948 the Australians were bowled out by Essex in a day which started at 11.30am and finished with the fall of their tenth wicket at 6.28pm, after they had scored a little matter of 721 runs. Despite the number of runs scored, together with the fall of the wickets using up some time, the intriguing fact, in the light of present-day teams struggling to bowl more than 13 overs per hour, is that Essex in that day's play bowled 128 overs. This was not considered unusual then because around twenty overs per hour was the normal expectation. Over rates did not become a tactical weapon until the 1950s, when it became standard practice either to speed over rates up when the wickets were falling, or slow them down when the batting side was on top: but this was never taken to the extent that West Indies sides have taken it in recent years; or, for that matter, and with far less excuse, England and India who used slow bowlers.

The importance of over rates and its effect on the game is enormous. This is a subject which the West Indies Board of Control has been unable to understand, claiming that new regulations were directed solely at them, because they had most to gain from a slow over rate. How did the West Indies benefit when they were averaging about 12 overs an hour, or 72 overs in a full day's play? First, in the composition of their attack, i.e. four fast bowlers, which was so good that it regularly could dismiss England within that time – on the last tour of the Caribbean they seldom even required the second new ball! Second, there was never any danger of any of their four fast bowlers being over-bowled, when an hour's spell only consisted of six overs. Third, if the opposition remained at the crease, they would probably only score just over 200 runs, even if they averaged three runs per over. This was likely to be less if the

West Indies felt it desirable to set run-saving fields. Fourth, the West Indies bowlers remained fresh even if they were still in the field on the second day, because the number of overs sent down on the first was relatively so small.

In 1988 the West Indies reluctantly agreed to play in England being extended past 6pm if 90 overs had not been bowled, a not altogether satisfactory compromise because it is a help to the paying public to know exactly when a performance is due to end, while there are occasions when the non-offender's batsmen will find themselves batting long after 6pm as a result of their opponents' sluggish over rate.

The only ultimately effective way of ensuring a healthy over rate is by heavy financial or playing penalties such as loss of runs or points. It is noticeable how the West Indies were able to increase their tempo in limited-overs tournaments, when failure to do so would have cost them a great deal of money.

Anyone who doubts the importance of over rates has only to turn to Law 17/6, which states that there will be a minimum of 20 overs in the last hour of the match. This Law was introduced to stop deliberate time-wasting by the fielding side when it suited them. It has proved very satisfactory, and avoided much unpleasantness. It might be asked, 'Why should 20 overs only apply to the final hour of a match?' The importance of over rates is also emphasised in those one-day games governed by overs, not time, to avoid one side sending down fewer overs, and by so doing reducing their opponents' chances of scoring as many runs.

Once the players began regularly using over rates as a tactical weapon in the 1950s I found that I could adjust the length of one over from three and a half minutes to five minutes without too much trouble. It was soon apparent that steps would have to be taken to counter an approach which was hardly in the spirit of the game, and was certainly unfair on spectators, who were being robbed of possible entertainment. However, the International Cricket Conference, hardly famed for its speed of action or its effectiveness, is still seeking the best solution.

I am inclined to favour an agreed number of overs per session, rather than per day, with the umpires reducing the number for interruptions, such as time lost through injury, time lost deliberately by the batsmen, time lost changing the ball or by the fall of wickets. It should also be feasible to carry on into the intervals, if the fielding side drops behind the legislated level – I have noticed there is a strong dislike of overtime without extra payment! – though this would necessitate having a third umpire available, but it is already required in Tests. This method would also be useful in those countries where the light fades more quickly at the end of the day than in England.

Physically fitter, yet more injuries

In the 1950s a county season and an overseas tour (which in many respects was the easier) rather resembled a marathon which lasted several months and included several sprints and the occasional steeplechase, so that the main requirement was stamina. A county cricketer was expected to play six days per week with a Benefit match about every other Sunday, plus travelling long distances by car before the motorways had cut journey times by half. He seldom had more than a week off during the summer, and professional footballers used to find it more exhausting than the football season, when one trained to a peak. Conversely I discovered that, although I was fit to play cricket, I was unable to adapt immediately to the demands of soccer without more intensive training.

There is no doubt that modern cricketers are fitter than those of my time, yet, strangely, they appear to be more susceptible to injury. Considering that they do not have the opportunity to play as many innings, or send down as many overs, I find this difficult to understand. Could it be that some of our cricketers are over-trained, and that bowlers might be better employed spending more time practising their chosen craft and less on weight training and exercises? Strong legs remain the number one essential, and it could be that in the past we were assisted by a childhood in which one walked, ran and cycled far more than is now the case?

Another explanation for the increase in injuries could be that a cricket season marathon these days contains more pressure, mental and physical. There are certainly a greater number of crunch matches. It used to be easy to raise one's game for a specific match like a Test, but it must be difficult having to do this frequently, as now is the case.

In 1988 Graham Gooch, to take a prominent example, had to try to lift his game for six Test matches, three one-day internationals and, say, ten County Championship matches, as well as a number of Essex limited-overs games. This represents a daunting challenge to which he responded well. But it could easily have been more demanding if his county had gone further in either of the knock-out cups. It was not so much the number of innings he had to play, but the number of games in which additional pressure was present.

In a summer with Essex my par for the course was to play about 45 innings, score over 1000 runs with an average in the mid-thirties, and bowl around 800 overs, take over 100 wickets for under 25 runs apiece. This demanded a reasonable standard of fitness, but I did not require as much physical training as the modern player, and in the case of my county, I had far fewer nets, for the very good reason that Essex did not have any.

Assuming the weather was fine, we would spend two weeks in the nets at the Old Blues ground at Fairlop. When it was wet, we used the Ilford Indoor Cricket School, but there were no facilities for practice on any of our eight home grounds, although we used to take full advantage of the nets available at venues like Lord's, Fenner's, Worcester and Old Trafford. I always enjoyed net practice, and regretted that there were not more opportunities, as they were very useful when one encountered a bad spell, or wanted to iron out a weakness, or experiment at either batting or bowling. However, I regarded nets as a handy extra rather than as an essential. Essex always opened their season with a match against Cambridge University at Fenner's, which provided the ideal start, for we reckoned that an hour or so spent in the middle was worth more than ten nets. In general, so far as Essex was concerned, the only practice at home games – once the first-class season had started – was a fifteen-minute fielding session each day shortly before the start, which definitely raised the standard of the catching which is even more vital in a three-day match than a one-day game. This did not mean that we under-rated the value of ground fielding, but rough outfields on an unfenced ground with plenty of spectators wandering about and young children playing cricket was not the ideal venue.

I have always been a 'breakfast-man', and believe it should be an unhurried occasion when one devours both the meal and the newspapers, sitting quietly whether at home or in a hotel. For me it constituted the ideal preparation for a day to be spent at a cricket ground. As a player, I normally started my breakfast around 8.30am and finished by 9.30am, which, assuming the ground was close, gave me plenty of time to reach it at 10.15am, fifteen minutes before the time that the team was due to report in the dressing-room.

Over the last decade I have frequently found myself staying at the same hotel, both at home and abroad, as the England team, or their opponents, and have noticed that breakfast for them has become an earlier and more hurried affair, because they are required at the ground two hours before the 11am start. They then spend the best part of an hour doing physical exercises, plus a certain amount of batting, bowling and fielding. I do not envy them this routine. I used to find that six hours in the field and bowling, say, 25 overs was sufficient and I would not have welcomed an additional work-out of more than one hour. Nor do I believe that it would have improved my performance, especially if the match was played at Melbourne with the temperature in the high nineties, and eight-ball overs the order of the day.

It was understandable and perhaps inevitable that the increased employment of ultra-close fieldsmen in suicidal positions in front of the bat would, despite protective clothing, lead to more casualties in the field. In fact, the surprise is that not more people have been seriously injured, while those frantic dives at pace to stop boundaries have also taken their toll.

By the nature of their profession, there is nothing new about fast or fast-medium bowlers breaking down – they have always had more than their share of torn muscles, bruised heels, swollen knees and bad backs. However, and although I reckon I spent more than my quota of time on the massage table, I missed very few matches. Fibrositis yielded quickly to treatment, a manipulative operation and a girdle cured a bad back in two weeks, and the occasional torn muscle usually took about a week to recover. Seam bowlers are bound to suffer some injuries, but surely not on today's scale? Despite far more physical training and fewer overs to bowl in matches, quick bowlers are not only breaking down more frequently than in the past, but are requiring serious operations to various portions of their anatomy which keep them out of the game for considerable periods. Graham Dilley, Neil Foster, Gladstone Small, Paul Jarvis, Ian Botham and Neil Williams are just a few of the bowlers who missed a number of matches in the 1988 season. It has been rather unkindly said, though with some truth, that Chris Old never completed a tour without breaking down. Is there a reason why more county quickies require medical treatment than was the case twenty yars ago?

One solution, strongly supported by Alec Bedser, who not infrequently bowled more overs before the first Test than many fast-medium bowlers now send down in an entire season, is that they do not spend enough time simply bowling, not merely when they are on the staff, but at school. Alec's prescription would be less weight training, fewer exercises, less running and more bowling; but Dennis Lillee, a fitness fanatic, would probably not agree. Admittedly the extra tours do put on additional strain, but it is not just the star quick bowlers who are continually breaking down; this also happens to reliable county seamers, like Kevin Cooper, who took 101 wickets in 1988, but was absent for most of the previous season.

In ten years I went on five major overseas tours, yet I only missed one of the 25 Tests through injury, and that was after Ray Lindwall had broken my thumb while I was batting. It is also noticeable that the West Indian pacemen, who have the additional strain of being genuinely fast rather than fast-medium, have usually been able to stand up to a county season plus tours and cricket in the Caribbean in the winter without too many injury problems, to judge by the wickets taken for their respective counties by Garner, Roberts, Boyce and Marshall. This also applied to the New Zealander, Richard Hadlee, who, in addition to his wickets for Nottinghamshire, also scored some runs. Richard, of course, benefited enormously from a run-up which was both economical and effective and, even more important, from his smooth, easy and completely grooved action. This helped to reduce the stress, whereas that long delivery stride of Graham Dilley has placed additional strain on his body, while the extremely fast arm action of Paul Jarvis, combined with the straightness of his back in a 'rocker's' action, has almost certainly been responsible for the problems he has experienced. Fast bowlers need to be well built or wiry, but above everything else they ought to have a smooth, comfortable and grooved body action which does not put a strain upon their particular build.

In the final analysis it comes back to what Alan Knott in his autobiography, *It's Knott Cricket* aptly terms 'cricket fitness'. He chooses Derek Underwood as an ideal example. Derek was not a highly trained athlete, but there was no doubt as to his 'supreme cricket fitness', as he never seemed to break down and was an ever-present member for both Kent and England. His recipe was bowling, not commando courses.

Behaviour

The saddest change to have taken place in cricket during the past twenty years has been, in my opinion, a decline in attitudes and standards of behaviour by both players and spectators. In the past Test cricket did on occasions become too fierce and ruthless, as was demonstrated by the Bodyline tour; although it is interesting to note that not nearly as many batsmen were hit and felled in that series, as in the Third Test at Melbourne in late 1988.

There has been an increase in what might be termed a meanness of spirit, which makes a mockery of that time-honoured phrase, that anything which was unfair was 'not cricket'. It is exemplified by 'sledging' in which the fielding side pressurises the umpires by incessant appealing; the bat-pad specialist fielder who now combines agility with considerable acting ability; deliberate intimidation by fast bowlers who are more concerned in hitting batsmen than stumps; and the animosity, almost hatred, which sometimes exists between two teams. As a result a sporting arena has been transformed into an ugly battlefield. This occurred during England's unhappy visit to Pakistan in 1988 and on several other recent international tours too.

The Pakistan flare-up was really ignited back in the summer of 1987 when the tourists requested that the umpire David Constant should not stand in a Test in England, because they had no confidence in him. This stemmed from their previous visit and shows how visiting sides do remember umpiring decisions which have gone against them. If the TCCB had only said that, in their opinion, David Constant was a top-class umpire, paid him the match fee, and appointed a replacement, the unpleasantness which followed might have been avoided, or at least reduced. After all England sides have often asked for umpires to be replaced on tour and the Board's refusal was bound to cause problems in Pakistan, where the standard of umpiring has always been, and judging by Australia's brief 1988 tour there, still is suspect. Thus it proved.

An absurdly tiring and complicated touring winter schedule – which included the Reliance World Cup, the Pakistan tour, playing in Australia, and a trip to New Zealand where the standard of the cricket and the attendances were both low – did little to enhance England's reputation for sportsmanship. The icing on this indigestible cake was the award made by the Chairman of the TCCB, Raman Subba Row, of an extra £1000 bonus for their efforts in Pakistan, a bonus which had the approval of the England Manager, Peter Lush. It is inconceivable that these events could have occurred in the 1950s or, if they had done, several players would have been fined and some probably sent home.

It would however be absurd to imagine that today's Test cricketer is any better, or worse, a person than one from those of the past. The difference lies in the fact that so many aspects of life, as well as cricket, have changed and what is now acceptable was unacceptable then. Take, for an example, dress. Blazers used automatically to be worn at lunch on the ground and a tie was considered essential at breakfast and dinner in any hotel. Now it is all much more informal. Nevertheless the ragged shorts and thongs worn by two New Zealand players to watch a one-day international in India did seem rather more suitable for the beach. That simply lacked style, like wearing jeans at a function when dinner jackets had been stipulated.

There is nothing remotely new about players losing their temper or giving vent to bad language. Bowlers have always cursed, lamented and cried out for justice, or vengeance, but this was, unlike today, seldom personalised, because by and large players abided by an unwritten code which forbad swearing at individual members of the opposition, or, worse still, at the umpires. I still believe that primitive oral abuse is not acceptable behaviour on the field, and there can be no doubt that its use has reduced the humour and the back-chat which used to contribute so much to the enjoyment of cricket. It cannot be easy to socialise at close of play with an opponent who has deliberately insulted your wife, while incidents like charging into a member of the other side, or into an umpire, are totally unacceptable in what is intended to be a civilised game, however keenly fought.

Overseas Players

After the fourth Test at Headingley in 1988, which followed the West Indian massacre of England at Old Trafford, Micky Stewart, the England manager, gave as one of the main reasons why England had failed to win one of the last sixteen Tests since he took charge, was that too many overseas cricketers were on the county circuit, while for many of them, like Viv Richards and Malcolm Marshall, that same circuit has provided a valuable training ground. Equally predictable were the counter-arguments of both Vivian Richards and Imran Khan. Imran wrote as follows in the *Daily Telegraph*:

> The standard argument given is that the crucial bowling and batting positions are taken up by these imports, thus retarding the progress of local talent. And because of this reasoning, overseas cricketers were reduced from two to one per county in 1979.
>
> Since this move has made no difference in improving English cricket, Mr Stewart has suggested that English cricket should have no overseas players at all. To me it is common sense that the better the competition, the better quality of players will be produced by the system. Players with talent improve quicker while the marginal ones are weeded out. The greatest improvement in my career took place when I played World Series Cricket. I was playing for a World XI against Australia and the West Indies, then the two top teams in the world. It was the toughest cricket I had ever played, and I learnt so much in such a short space of time playing with and against so many great cricketers.
>
> So it seems bizarre to me when I hear these strange stories that English players are suffering, because they have such a golden opportunity to learn in county cricket provided they have the talent and the desire to do so.

There is truth in both these points of view. The serious damage to English cricket really occurred in the 1970s when, for example, half the Worcestershire side had learned their cricket overseas, and the Warwickshire XI contained four players imported from the Caribbean.

The danger was obvious but the counties, with their limited and parochial outlook, chose to ignore the obvious. The threat was certainly recognised by Alec Bedser, then Chairman of the Selectors, but his voice went unheeded, just another crying in the wilderness. Eventually the TCCB opened their eyes and decided to limit each club to one overseas import, which I believe is entirely reasonable, but what I do not like to see is the way the clubs are contracting several overseas players, despite being only allowed to include one in their side. This is wasting money which could be better spent on developing home-grown talent. Rather sadly, it can also be said that Stewart's England XIs would have been even weaker without the presence of three players who learned their cricket in South Africa.

Allan Border, the Australian captain, reckons that county cricket provides a marvellous training ground for overseas cricketers, and in this sense it certainly has assisted our opponents; but if this is correct, as I believe it to be, why have we failed to produce more talented English-born players?

It is also intriguing to note that the pressure of county cricket does not appear to have had an adverse effect on the likes of Vivian Richards, Malcolm Marshall, Gordon Greenidge, Glenn Turner, Richard Hadlee and Sir Gary Sobers, to name but a few. Perhaps even more significant is why has Yorkshire, which has never included any overseas players, not produced a single world-class cricketer since Geoffrey Boycott? It makes me think that our present predicament is due more to our system than to the presence of players from abroad. We are asking some of our players to take part in eight varieties of cricket, all with slightly different rules – Test cricket, three-day and four-day county championship matches, first-class friendlies, and four versions of limited-overs cricket – the Texaco Cup, the Refuge Assurance League, the Benson & Hedges Trophy and the NatWest Trophy.

Although the counties have done much to assist in the development of overseas players, the Leagues have played a far more important role. They have provided a host of young cricketers from abroad with the opportunity to adapt to our conditions, so that when they have returned as tourists they were able to avoid the mistakes they might well have made if it had been their first visit. The pace bowlers discovered the difference between English and Australian length, while the batsmen learned that the ball was liable to move more off the seam and therefore it often paid to spend more time on the front foot to counter the threat of the 'nip-backer'.

In addition to the overseas professionals with the major Leagues, an ever-increasing number of young cricketers is being brought over here with money provided by patrons, and sometimes commercial sponsors, to take part in club, and even village cricket.

There is nothing new about cricketers from abroad participating in county cricket, it has been occurring for over a hundred years. W. L. Murdoch, usually reckoned to be the first great Australian batsman, made five tours to this country between 1878 and 1890 and, after being dropped from the Australian team on the basis of increasing age, captained Sussex with considerable flair for seven years and also kept wicket for England against South Africa in Cape Town. Ted McDonald was reckoned to be among the greatest fast bowlers of all time, yet he only played in eleven Test matches; he went into the Lancashire League while he qualified for that county. Between 1924–31 he played a major role in their four Championship successes. He captured over 1000 wickets at under 21 runs apiece for his adopted county using a fifteen-pace approach and a beautiful action, combined with an expression even more taciturn than that of Andy Roberts. Three great Indian batsmen, Ranjitsinhji, Duleepsinhji, and the Nawab of Pataudi played for Sussex and England before India had a Test side. After the last war several Australians, including Jack Walsh, George Tribe, Vic Jackson, Jock Livingston and Bill Alley all contributed much to the county scene. The worrying feature in the last twenty years, however, has been the size of the invasion. In the past the majority of overseas players were nearing the end of their international careers, failed to hold, or obtain, a regular place in their Test team, or came from a country which did not play Test cricket. England was also the only country where they could earn a reasonable wage doing the job they most enjoyed, playing cricket.

The four main categories of overseas player to be found on the county circuit during the last twenty years have been: the established stars, like Alvin Kallicharran, Allan Border and Richard Hadlee; the young player, who was able to use the county system to help him become a Test player in his own country, like Viv Richards, Glenn Turner and Keith Boyce; those who wanted a pleasant and financially rewarding finish near the end of their international career, like Lance Gibbs and Mike Holding; and South Africans who, barred from international cricket in their own country, have used it as an avenue towards it, via a place in the England team, like the Greig brothers, the Smith brothers and Allan Lamb.

The two main problems are, first, the volume of the traffic, which has been made financially possible by commercial sponsorship, money which could have been spent on the development of home talent, and is now going out of the country into the pockets of overseas players; and, second, the extent that such players have dominated the county circuit. The limitation to one player per county has helped, despite the way clubs have deliberately flouted the intention of the TCCB by bringing in cricketers who have learned their skill abroad but do have a vague British connection. The extent of the domination by 'mercenaries', however, is best illustrated by the leading first-class averages over the past decade. These show the very high number of imports occupying the top places in both the batting and the bowling averages.

Although the presence of overseas cricketers has naturally raised the standard of play, which should assist home talent, it also has assisted Test opposition by providing them with a splendid nursery.

Sponsorship

Without commercial sponsorship no professional sport, and most amateur sport, could not exist in its present form; and cricket, with its comparatively low gates and very heavy expenditure (as a team game which can last for five days), is especially dependent. Fortunately, the game does provide the two main requirements of most sponsors: first, wide publicity on TV, radio and in the press; and second, as a cost-effective way of entertaining important customers, because it provides an ever-increasing number of civilised venues. A cricket ground in fine weather is usually an ideal place for both enjoyment and business. The customer cannot escape easily and, providing both the cricket and the hospitality are good, will not wish to do so.

The success of cricket as a marketing vehicle is underlined by the length of its sponsorships and by the fact that, so far, it has never had problems in finding more commercial firms keen to participate, with Cornhill Insurance providing the perfect example of how increased name identification can pay very big dividends, by helping them to gain a big increase of the market. It was the Cornhill decision to sponsor the Tests which has made our leading cricketers, comparatively speaking, rich men, certainly far richer than any of their predecessors. Although the newfound funds provided by sponsorship for Tests and overseas tours do not apply so directly to run-of-the-mill county cricketers, they too have benefited from a massive cash injection from both national and local firms at county level.

Their salaries have increased, though not nearly so dramatically as those of the international stars. The size of county staffs, both playing and administrative, has become much bigger. Numerous extra perks are now available to the county players – free, emblazoned cars, larger benefits, considerable extra financial inducements to be collected from the numerous tournaments, the seemingly endless 'Man of the Match' awards, and for providing different forms of profitable publicity for local and national businesses, such as players attending various commercial events and functions.

The new wealth enjoyed by the stars has inevitably increased player power. They are able to change counties more quickly and easily than once was the case. They can afford to turn down tours worth over £12,000 and can make even more money from a wide range of not too demanding extraneous activities, not to the same extent as golf or tennis players, perhaps – which are both individual as distinct from team sports – but still well paid. They can now afford Annabel's, rather than the local palais de danse, champagne rather than beer, and French cuisine rather than fish and French fries.

In an age when television can transform weathermen, chat show hosts, newscasters, pop performers, and even commentators into personalities, those cricketers who appear for long periods on television fall into the same category. They are much in commercial demand, particularly as television provides a perfect setting for advertising unofficially a product like sports equipment through the wearing or using of it.

The additional fame and fortune now enjoyed by the few star cricketers does have its price, however. They are news *both on and off the field*. Mike Gatting, sadly, earned far more coverage for his off-the-field conduct than for his many outstanding performances with the bat. The finest cricketers of the 1950s and 1960s did not have to worry about revelations in the media and, although in general I consider they were rather more discreet than the present-day players, they were never confronted by the ruthless investigative journalist who is quite prepared to set up his victim when he thinks it necessary, or by unscrupulous girls prepared to reveal all for the price of a substantial cheque from a newspaper.

Another major form of income for counties and at Test

matches has been the growth of corporate entertainment. In addition to the main sponsors, an ever-increasing number of firms has bought or rented boxes at cricket grounds in which they will entertain customers and staff. Tented cities are erected at all the major Test grounds as well as permanent boxes, and they are used in quite a lavish style. It is noticeable, though rather a sad sight, that these days a large number of seats remains empty for most of the afternoon while the port and brandy are consumed, as a high percentage of the guests is not interested in cricket, but in enjoying a day out at somebody else's expense. Also weekdays are far more popular than the weekend, as most of the guests only accept invitations during the working week.

Corporate entertaining certainly produces much needed revenue for the clubs, for the TCCB, and for the players, as it also does at most of the premier sporting occasions. In contrast, the normal cricket fan has discovered that taking his wife and two children to a Test match, always assuming that he can obtain the tickets, is expensive. Commercial firms who are wining and dining customers can easily afford the prices which many cricket lovers cannot. This can hardly be in the long-term interest of the game, but the money received unquestionably is to the short-term advantage of the Boards.

Cricket sponsorship, in fact, has brought problems as well as benefits, because the five parties involved in what may be termed the 'greed syndrome' will always be wanting a little more. These are the players, the middle men, the controlling bodies or boards, television, and the sponsoring companies.

There is always a danger that the players, without whom there would be no sponsorship, will regard it merely as an additional source of income for themselves without giving sufficient consideration to the needs of the sport, the future, or the sponsor. This shows itself when they fail to co-operate sufficiently with the sponsor, or constantly demand an increased share. In cricket this has been largely avoided, because it is a team game with a complex schedule, rather than, shall we say, an athletics meeting, where a few individuals can virtually ruin the event by their non-appearance and then go to another venue which is prepared to pay their price. Cricketers also are fully aware of how assisting the sponsors can work to their advantage, as beneficiaries have recently discovered when playing in Tests, with Cornhill running close-of-play Benefit raffles.

The middle men have become an important link in most major sponsorships. Without their expertise the sport and the sponsor would often lack the necessary resources for either the sport or the sponsor to maximise on the event, though this applies less in cricket than in other sports. The middle men should possess a detailed knowledge of the game, of the administrators, and of marketing, which enables them to provide the best presentation of the sport to the public and the media. The danger to sport is if the middle men start to dictate to the administrators by also controlling the top performers, again much easier in individual sports than in team games, though it should be remembered how easily Kerry Packer achieved a virtual coup with his World Series Cricket. However, the middle men are aware that, over a period of time, they will benefit as much by a successful sponsorship as anyone else. Less trustworthy are some individual agents whose sole interest is to exploit the ability of their client.

Although there is a danger of sporting bodies being tempted to accept the highest bidder without reference to other criteria, or become over-demanding of a sponsor who has served the sport well, the TCCB has largely avoided this, which is why most major cricket sponsorships have been so successful. The TCCB has appreciated the value of the company which has been prepared to sponsor over a long period, and has been able to keep them happy with what is essentially a business arrangement. However, like all sporting bodies, the TCCB always wants more revenue and believes that television does not pay them enough. In commercial terms they may be correct, but it is all part of what is a circle of greed as, without television, there would not be commercial sponsorship on the present scale. While television could exist without cricket,

cricket in its present form could certainly not exist without television, something which the BBC obviously takes into account when making its bids for rights. These, though not over-generous, have been reasonable and the coverage extensive, much to the delight of the sponsors, especially those who use perimeter advertising.

Television and, to a lesser degree, radio find sport a comparatively inexpensive form of family entertainment. Costume drama currently costs approximately £500,000 an hour and ordinary drama around the £400,000 mark, whereas sport works out around £27,000 per hour. It was, of course, the relative cheapness of TV time which sparked Kerry Packer's incursion into the game. The temptation for television is to exploit its power to increase the value of the sponsorship as a weapon to drive a bargain which is basically unfair on the sport, and this has occurred with certain minor sports.

Some sponsoring companies, for their part, have become avaricious for extra publicity. In their search for column inches in the press they are inclined to forget that in some respects sport sponsorship is a cheap substitute for buying advertising space on the box and in the newspapers. The danger of such over-kill was the televised snooker match in which the advertising banners nearly out-numbered the 22 snooker balls!

Although cricket has avoided this particular danger, there have been occasions when television and sponsors have insisted on changes to the basic formula which are clearly not in the best interest of either the game and its players, or the followers. In this connection it would be hard to justify the additional Refuge Sunday Cup Matches, apart from the money they provide. The sponsor has also to make sure that its employees and shareholders are satisfied with the promotion, which can be difficult because its value is harder to quantify than advertising. I still smile when I recall the Cornhill workers who picketed blindly, and chanted mindlessly, outside The Oval at the commencement of the Test sponsorship to complain that the money invested in cricket should have been used to increase their salaries. How wrong they were!

Without the introduction and the popularity of limited-overs cricket, many of the existing first-class clubs would have long since gone bankrupt. It began in 1963 with the Gillette Cup which, in the later stages, proved an instant success, but what really made this form of the game popular with the general public were the Rothman Cavaliers matches against the counties on Sundays. These had been specifically designed to suit the requirements of television. The games not only produced large crowds, but attracted big viewing figures. The surprising feature was the length of time it took the TCCB to realise the potential of Sunday cricket on the box, for it was not until 1969 that the John Player League started; less surprising was that they should ditch the original sponsor, but pinch the golden formula.

What made the Gillette Cup and the John Player League so popular with the counties, though often not with their more conservative members, was that they not only attracted far bigger crowds than most three-day matches, but, more vital, they appealed to commercial sponsors because they were neat, compact and produced a definite result. Although any administrator who knew anything about the game realised that two competitions were sufficient, the prospect of even more one-day cricket, cash for the clubs and their players, led to yet another – the Benson & Hedges Cup – which proved yet another financial winner.

Once limited-overs cricket had become an essential part of the county programme, it was only a question of time before it spread to other parts of the world, first with the Prudential World Cup. In Australia, with sponsors and plenty of TV the concept really caught on with World Series Cricket and finally all the members of the International Cricket Conference have followed.

Personally, I like limited-overs cricket, and as one of that small MCC Committee which drew up the rules for the Gillette Cup, feel proud that, apart from some minor amendments and improvements, our regulations have formed the basis of subsequent one-day cricket. It has much to offer, the opportunity of seeing both sides bat and bowl, the elimination of the dull draw, the excitement of the frequent close finishes and fast scoring on good pitches. Over the years I have seen numerous entertaining one-day games all over the world, and at times I find it hard to believe what happened before my first Gillette Cup match at Old Trafford against Lancashire. I had arranged with the Lancashire Secretary, Geoffrey Howard, that he and his captain, Ken Grieves, plus a couple of their players would meet my side at Altrincham Police Station on the day before the match as soon after midnight as possible, as they were putting us up for the night. It may not have been the ideal preparation for cricket, but Essex could not afford an hotel!

Limited-overs cricket is fun to play, has appealed to many who did not find first-class cricket entertaining because it took too long, and it has brought a new and much needed prosperity to the game; but it would be foolish to imagine that this form of cricket is either invariably exciting, or that it has no adverse side-effects. When the side batting first either scores too many, or insufficient, runs, the one-day game can be extremely dull, and there have been several finals at Lord's which I would willingly have left at lunchtime.

One of the damaging side-effects of the limited-overs game has to do with the shortage of slow bowlers in county cricket. It is not that slow bowlers are ineffective in this type of game, but because the average county captain is unwilling to risk a young spinner, while it is also liable to have an adverse effect on an experienced bowler. John Emburey would surely have taken more wickets in Test match cricket if he had not spent so much of his time bowling defensively in the one-day game. However, it is the young slow bowler who, unless he can also bat, really suffers, because if he cannot gain a place in the glamour games before the big crowds, there is an obvious temptation for him to turn to seam bowling and try to become one of that army of 'bits and pieces' cricketers who is unlikely to become of much use at Test level, where the prime objective is to take wickets.

Limited-overs cricket is also another reason why there are so many English seamers and so few *fast* bowlers. It has spawned a breed of medium-paced seamers, steady, accurate and inexpensive, unlikely to bowl many batsmen out on a good pitch, unless they were seeking quick runs. They usually combine their role of support bowler with that of a middle-order attacking batsman and a good all-round fielder. They are invaluable to their club in all of the three one-day competitions, which is why most counties have at least two such men on their books.

In addition to the limited-overs game having an adverse effect on slow bowling and making potential pacemen think more in terms of accuracy than extra speed, it has influenced club and, rather more important, school cricket. At schools it has now become the main format. Of course, it has several positive advantages in a wet, abbreviated summer term, when time is in short supply. In a school match, when it was usually necessary to dismiss the opposition to win the match, the two most effective bowlers used to be the 'quickie' and the wrist-spinner, who sent down more overs than anybody else; but the potential slow bowler is now tempted to abandon his style because he does not possess sufficient control for a game in which the denial of runs can be more vital than the taking of wickets. As a result, the schoolboy taken on to a county staff at sixteen or seventeen will not only have done less bowling than once would have been the case, but he will also have spent less time bowling when the essential aim was to capture wickets.

It may be coincidence, but I believe that the alarming decline, not in the basic ability but in the technique of so many England batsmen – especially compared with those of the West Indies, India, Pakistan and Sri Lanka – is directly related to the vast amount of limited-overs cricket now being played in the country. It has encouraged young batsmen to improvise before they have acquired a sound technique, and this may well account for those hybrid shots in their repertoire which they would be better off without. Forcing strokes played from the half-cock position rely largely on the bottom hand. If one was to make a general criticism of England batsmen, it is that they do not use their top hand enough when playing their strokes. In the West Indies v. Essex match at Chelmsford in 1988, Atherton, a young and not very experienced left-hander, played one straight drive of great force on the rise along the ground, despite having, at the moment of contact, removed his left (bottom) hand, something which few home-grown county players could possibly have done.

This form of cricket also breeds a defensive attitude among young bowlers of 'keep it tight' at all costs, or the 'dot-ball' mentality, instead of the desire, or need, to take wickets.

Further to these playing or technical dangers in limited-overs cricket, there is now clear evidence, in India and Pakistan as well as in Australia and New Zealand, that the one-day internationals have become so popular that they are having a bad effect on the receipts from Test matches. Clearly this could have a far-reaching effect on the future of the first-glass game.

The Future

Over the years cricket has become more than a game, almost a way of life – with its own Laws, culture, and a considerable literature – which brings pleasure not only to the players but also to the wide variety of its followers. Its appeal is virtually ageless, timeless, and classless. At Test level the game has sufficient subtlety to fascinate a Mike Brearley, yet it also provides fun for young children, as can be seen by the success of the Wrigley Softball Cricket Tournament for Primary Schools involving over 2000 schools from England, Scotland and Wales. The fascination of this team game with its eternal battle between bat and ball is also illustrated by the way indoor cricket has, against the odds, caught on in Australasia. It proved such a big financial success there that it has now spread to this country. As long as people enjoy playing it, cricket will prosper. That is the key.

Changes will still be made – some good, some bad, as has always been the case – but the fundamentals will remain. Good batsmen will make runs, and the very good will make a great many. Good bowlers will take wickets and the very good will take a great many. I predict that there will be a big increase in artificial pitches for school, village, and club cricket, at least until somebody discovers how to provide a cheap way of producing a grass pitch which plays well, lasts, and requires little maintenance. This may seem improbable, but so did sending men into space or landing them on the moon even thirty years ago.

The future of the first-class game, and especially Test cricket, on the other hand, looks less certain and assured. This is worrying because it provides an important stimulus, especially for the young, who are the future. When England won the World Cup it gave a great boost to the players and soccer clubs in this country, while the success of the Great Britain hockey team at the 1988 Olympics is having a similar effect on hockey. England needs a powerful cricket team which is realistically capable of challenging for the unofficial championship of the world, something we have lacked for more than two decades. Unfortunately there are not too many signs of a renaissance on that scale, and at that level, taking place, but, as has been said for centuries, 'Cricket is a funny old game'; indeed it is its unpredictability which is one of its greatest charms.

There are five main dangers that currently threaten the Test match scene. First, and this applies to all the major sports, the game has become too dependent for survival on sponsorship, marketing and television, and nobody knows on what scale this will be available in the future, though with the advent of cable television there will probably be more cricket on the 'box'. However, does this also mean that there will be more cricket played? The main consideration of the governing body must be the welfare of the game and there are signs among the first-class counties and in the TCCB that the marketing men are taking over. This is worrying, because they are liable to be more concerned about money issues than about the quality of the cricket.

Second, there is a surfeit of Test cricket, much of which is sub-standard. This stems from the increase in the number of Test playing countries and also because the governing bodies are anxious to keep their star players contented, wealthy, and unable to take part in too many matches outside ICC jurisdiction. When England's tour to India was cancelled, because the Indian government would not give visas to some of the selected players, the TCCB was well aware that many of them would benefit from a winter's rest, but they frantically sought, eventually and fairly predictably without success, to find an alternative venue. They were, of course, trying to recoup some of the money they had committed to pay the players and to make sure that nobody under contract would be lured to take part in the South African centenary celebrations. What is especially disturbing about the present situation, in addition to a possible split between the white and the black cricket-playing countries, is the present low standard of Test cricket in Australia and England, where the financial returns are the highest. This must inevitably reduce the appeal of the fight for the Ashes.

Third, there has been a noticeable drop in attendance at Test matches throughout the world, but this has been especially evident in India and Pakistan, where capacity attendances were not unknown on all five days. In contrast, the one-day internationals have become increasingly popular. This was recognised by Kerry Packer whose World Series Cricket included a large number of limited-overs games and also pioneered floodlight cricket, the white ball, coloured clothing, and American-style 'razzamatazz'. When Australian cricket returned to the established fold, the drawing-power of the one-day international was realised and exploited to such an extent that much of the enjoyment of players touring Australia has since been dissipated by their having to spend so much of their time flying to take part in a seemingly endless series of instant matches, increasing numbers of which are concluded late in the evening. The justification is provided by the large attendances at the one-day games, far larger than for the Tests.

Many Australians who come to this form of cricket would not have been attracted by the traditional Test match, which usually requires some knowledge of the finer points of cricket, rather in the same way as the audience for an opera or a ballet is different to that for a pop concert. Some of the 'new Australians', despite their European background, have found limited-overs cricket to their taste, but one cannot help feeling that the Australian Board of Control has allowed its Test heritage to be devalued and harmed by staging too much pop cricket. England, on the other hand, has so far avoided the danger of playing too many one-day internationals; but the counties, unable to resist the attraction of easy money, have devalued the County Championship through taking part in too much limited-overs cricket.

Fourth, the biggest threat to all sport lies in direct interference by governments for political reasons. They have discovered the publicity which can be acquired at minimal cost, except to the sport concerned. In February 1981, in Guyana, Robin Jackman's entry permit was withdrawn. This, together with the resulting cancellation of a Test match, earned the Guyanese government larger media coverage world-wide than it had received in the previous decade, or is likely to receive in the next.

Two Olympic Games were partially ruined by politics, which caused the withdrawal of so many nations, while cricket, more than most games or sports, is vulnerable and easy to interrupt.

What is especially sad is that the game which, over the years, has done so much to bring together people of different races, colours, and creeds, is now finding itself being used by various human rights groups who exploit the publicity for their own causes. At the moment this concerns apartheid in South Africa, but there is no reason to suppose that other groups with equally laudable moral aims will not use cricket to achieve greater coverage for their objectives. It is possible that, in the future, campaigns will be aimed at gaining greater support for the Tamils in Sri Lanka, Indians in Guyana, Sikhs in India, democracy in Pakistan, the aborigines in Australia, or the Maoris in New Zealand. But in any such battles cricket itself will inevitably be the loser.

Finally, there is the International Cricket Conference, which ostensibly controls Test cricket but is so much more reminiscent of the old League of Nations, though even less effective. It took the ICC twenty years to realise that the problem of over rates was a serious one and a decade would represent a conservative estimate of the time required for it to reach a decision. Its ineffectuality since the war makes one worried about the future of international cricket, especially since the introduction of politics and moral crusades. The great advantage enjoyed by MCC when it virtually controlled cricket throughout the world was that its prime concern was for the welfare of the game. Although it was gloriously undemocratic, old-fashioned, and blinkered, it was not influenced by government pressure, something which cannot be said about the present ICC, or indeed most of the current sporting organisations such as FIFA or the Olympic Committee. To make matters worse Boards of Control have increased in size and decreased in efficiency, with the TCCB a prime example.

When a governing body fails to satisfy those who participate in a sport – especially if the sport is an individual one which is both easier to organise and more rewarding for its participants than a team sport – the players are liable to seize control, as is happening at the present time in tennis. Although this will produce more money for the top professionals, in the long term it will probably harm the game because the LTA spends at present a great deal of money encouraging tennis at 'grass roots' level and subsidising tennis clubs. However, more dangerous than a game or a sport being managed by its star performers, is when it is controlled by individuals, or companies, who in turn own or control the leading exponents, as for example in boxing and snooker. The vast majority of players have a deep love for their particular sport, whereas agents and company promoters may well not have the same affection. A high financial return for a limited period is more liable to be their principal concern.

Kerry Packer clearly demonstrated how easy and comparatively cheap it was to organise international cricket which was not under the auspices of the ICC and it could occur again. What happens if, for example, an organisation like the International Management Group, probably the most effective and expensive agency in the sporting world and which controls the West Indies, the best team in the world, were to become dissatisfied with the terms for a particular tour? However, the major concern of the ICC now is to come up in 1989 with a compromise solution which will satisfy all the countries involved. The future of Test cricket is threatened by the South African connection which is due to the considerable number of professional cricketers from England who earn a living in South Africa during the off season. This coincides with the cricket season for all the other Test-playing countries, and is, of course, what our professional cricketers have been doing for over a hundred years.

Despite the threats and the dangers confronting first-class cricket, it will survive providing that it offers fun for the players and entertainment for the spectators and followers. So long as it does this – for cricket without laughter is as depressing as a cricket ground under water – the game will continue buoyantly into the twenty-first century.